Creative Beading, Vol. 2

The best projects from a year of *Bead&Button* magazine

Printed in Singapore.

11 10 09 08 07   1 2 3 4 5

Publisher's Cataloging-In-Publication Data (Prepared by The Donohue Group, Inc.)

Creative beading. Vol. 2 : the best projects from a year of *Bead&Button* magazine.

    p. : col. ill. ; cm.

  Includes index.
  "The material in this book has previously appeared in Bead&Button magazine."
  ISBN: 978-0-87116-244-1

1. Beadwork--Handbooks, manuals, etc. 2. Beads--Handbooks, manuals, etc. 3. Jewelry making--Handbooks, manuals, etc. I. Title: Bead&Button magazine.

TT860 .C743 2007
745.594/2

Cont

ents

Stitching

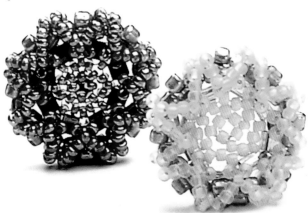

Introduction

One thing that's true about creating beautiful jewelry and objects with beads is that the variety of materials, colors, and styles from which to choose is infinite. Imagination is the bridge between all of the possibilities open to you as a beading enthusiast – and, of course, your imagination knows no bounds.

Whether you choose to work with crystals, pearls, or glass beads, or gemstones, buttons, or seed beads, you'll find inspiring projects presented in *Creative Beading, Vol. 2.* We offer more than 80 projects from the past year of *Bead&Button* magazine, giving you a chance to learn, grow, and excel at dozens of stringing, stitching, and wirework techniques. Make beaded beads, spiral rope necklaces, chain mail bracelets, and bead-crocheted pieces at your own level of enterprise. Whether you have a night here and there to string a saucy bracelet or a weekend to stitch a sophisticated necklace, you'll find a full compendium of techniques and projects here.

The staff of *Bead&Button* magazine is always at your service. The projects we publish have been fully tested. We simplify techniques as needed and supplement written directions with precise how-to photos and illustrations so that you can accurately reproduce each piece.

While accuracy is essential, we never forget what leads us to creating new works in the first place. We are drawn to the satisfaction of working with pleasing objects to produce wearable works of art. We may be enamored with the materials, whether that includes all of their attributes – color, texture, finish, dimension – or one in particular, such as hue alone. Or, we are driven to solve the structural and aesthetic puzzles involved in creative, complex projects. We are also inspired to engage our individual kinetic energy in a relaxing process that is calming and pleasing to us. And, for many of us, shopping for beads, clasps, pendants, tools, and other resources offers a singular sense of excitement.

Regardless of your own motivation for making jewelry and beaded objects, the experimentation involved in creating a piece of beadwork and the feeling of accomplishment you earn by completing a treasured project are alluring. As our fast-paced world becomes more demanding, beauty and creativity become even more important. The process of making jewelry stimulates your intellect as well as your emotions and your visual and tactile responses. At *Bead&Button*, we encourage you to use your imagination to adapt the ideas presented in *Creative Beading, Vol. 2.* Your satisfaction will be your own, well-deserved reward.

Ann Dee Allen
Editor
Bead&Button magazine

Tools and materials

Excellent tools and materials for making jewelry are available in bead and craft stores, through catalogs, and on the Internet. Here are the essential supplies you'll need for the projects in this book.

TOOLS

Chainnose pliers have smooth, flat inner jaws, and the tips taper to a point. Use them for gripping and for opening and closing loops and rings.

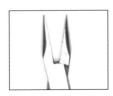

Roundnose pliers have smooth, tapered, conical jaws and are used to make loops. The closer to the tip you work, the smaller the loop will be.

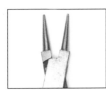

On **diagonal wire cutters**, use the inside of the blades to make a pointed cut and the outside (back) of the blades to make a flat cut. Do not use your jewelry-grade wire cutters on memory wire, which is extremely hard; use heavy-duty cutters or bend it back and forth until it breaks.

Crimping pliers have two grooves in their jaws that are used to fold or roll a crimp into a compact shape.

Split-ring pliers simplify opening split rings by inserting a curved jaw between the rings.

Beading needles are coded according to size. The higher the number, the finer the beading needle. Unlike sewing needles, the eye of a beading needle is almost as narrow as its shaft. In addition to the size of the bead, the number of times you will pass through the bead also affects the needle size that you will use – if you pass through a bead multiple times, you need to use a smaller needle.

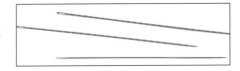

FINDINGS

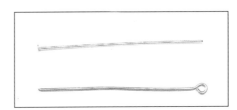

A **head pin** looks like a blunt, long, thick sewing pin. It has a flat or decorative head on one end to keep the beads from falling off. Head pins come in different diameters, or gauges, and lengths.

Eye pins are just like head pins except they have a round loop on one end, instead of a head. You can make eye pins from wire or head pins.

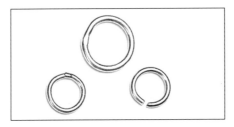

A **jump ring** is used to connect two loops. It is a small wire circle or oval that is either soldered or comes with a split that you can twist open and closed.

Split rings are used like jump rings but are much more secure. They look like tiny key rings and are made of springy wire.

Crimp beads are small, large-holed, thin-walled metal beads designed to be flattened or crimped into a tight roll. Use them when stringing jewelry on flexible beading wire.

Clasps come in many sizes and shapes. Some of the most common are the toggle, consisting of a ring and a bar; the lobster claw, which opens when you push on a tiny lever; the S-hook, which links two soldered rings or split rings; the box, with a tab and a slot; and the slide, consisting of one tube that slides inside another.

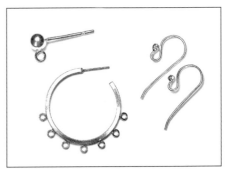

Earring wires come in a huge variety of metals and styles, including post, lever-back, French hook, and hoop. You will almost always want a loop (or loops) on earring findings so you can attach beads.

WIRE

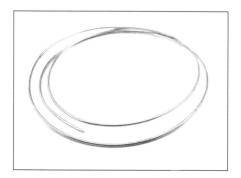

Wire is available in a number of materials and finishes, including brass, gold, gold-filled, gold-plated, fine silver, sterling silver, anodized niobium (chemically colored wire), and copper. Brass, copper, and craft wire are packaged in 10–40-yd. spools, while gold, silver, and niobium are sold by the foot or ounce. Wire thickness is measured by gauge – the higher the gauge, the thinner the wire – and is available in varying hardnesses and shapes, including round, half-round, and square.

STRINGING MATERIALS

Selecting beading thread and cord is the single most important decision you'll make when planning a project. Review the descriptions below to evaluate which material is best for your design.

Threads come in many sizes and strengths. Size (diameter or thickness) is designated by a letter or number. OO and A/O are the thinnest; B, D, E, F, and FF are subsequently thicker. Cord is measured on a number scale; 0 corresponds in thickness to D, 1 equals E, 2 equals F, and 3 equals FF.

Parallel filament nylon, such as Nymo or C-Lon, is made from many thin nylon fibers that are extruded and heat set to form a single-ply thread.

Parallel filament nylon is durable and easy to thread, but it can be prone to fraying and stretching. It is best used in beadweaving and bead embroidery.

Plied nylon thread, such as Silamide, is made from two or more nylon threads that are extruded, twisted together, and coated or bonded for further security. It is strong and durable and some brands have had the stretch removed. It is more resistant to fraying than parallel filament nylon. It's a good material for twisted fringe, bead crochet, and beadwork that needs a lot of body.

Plied gel-spun polyethylene (GSP), such as Power Pro or DandyLine, is made from polyethylene fibers that have been spun into two or more threads that are braided together. It is almost unbreakable, it doesn't stretch, and it resists fraying. The thickness can make it difficult to make multiple passes through a bead. It is ideal for stitching with larger beads, such as pressed glass and crystals.

Parallel filament GSP, such as Fireline, is a single-ply thread made from spun and bonded polyethylene fibers. It's extremely strong, it doesn't stretch, and it resists fraying. However, crystals will cut through parallel filament GSP, and it can leave a black residue on your hands and your beads. It's most appropriate for bead stitching.

Polyester thread, such as Gutterman, is made from polyester fibers that are spun into single yarns and then twisted into plied thread. It doesn't stretch and comes in many colors, but it can become linty with use. It is best for bead crochet or bead embroidery when the thread must match the fabric.

Flexible beading wire is composed of wires twisted together and covered with nylon. This wire is stronger than thread and does not stretch; the higher the number of inner strands (between 3 and 49), the more flexible and kink-resistant the wire. It is available in a variety of sizes. Use .014 and .015 for most gemstones, crystals, and glass beads. Use thicker varieties, .018, .019, and .024, for heavy beads or nuggets. Use thinner wire, .010 and .012, for lightweight pieces and beads with very small holes, such as pearls.

Basics

CRIMPS

Flattened crimp

1 Hold the crimp using the tip of your chainnose pliers. Squeeze the pliers firmly to flatten the crimp.
2 Tug the wire to make sure the crimp has a solid grip. If the wire slides, repeat the steps with a new crimp.

Folded crimp

1 Position the crimp bead in the notch closest to the crimping pliers' handle.
2 Separate the wires and firmly squeeze the crimp.

3 Move the crimp into the notch at the pliers' tip and hold the crimp as shown. Squeeze the crimp bead, folding it in half at the indentation.
4 Test that the folded crimp is secure.

LOOPS AND JUMP RINGS

Opening and closing loops or jump rings

1 Hold the loop or jump ring with two pairs of chainnose pliers or chainnose and roundnose pliers, as shown.
2 To open the loop or jump ring, bring one pair of pliers toward you and push the other pair away. String materials on the open loop or jump ring. Reverse the steps to close the open loop or jump ring.

Plain loop

1 Trim the wire or head pin ³⁄₈ in. (1cm) above the top bead. Make a right-angle bend close to the bead.
2 Grab the wire's tip with roundnose pliers. The tip of the wire should be flush with the pliers. Roll the wire to form a half circle. Release the wire.

3 Reposition the pliers in the loop and continue rolling.
4 The finished loop should form a centered circle above the bead.

Wrapped loop

1 Make sure you have at least 1¼ in. (3.2cm) of wire above the bead. With the tip of your chainnose pliers, grasp the wire directly above the bead. Bend the wire (above the pliers) into a right angle.
2 Using roundnose pliers, position the jaws in the bend.

3 Bring the wire over the top jaw of the roundnose pliers.
4 Reposition the pliers' lower jaw snugly into the loop. Curve the wire downward around the bottom of the roundnose pliers. This is the first half of a wrapped loop.

5 Position the chainnose pliers' jaws across the loop.
6 Wrap the wire around the wire stem, covering the stem between the loop and the top bead. Trim the excess wire and press the cut end close to the wraps with chainnose pliers.

KNOTS

Overhand knot

Make a loop and pass the working end through it. Pull the ends to tighten the knot.

Square knot

Cross the right-hand cord over the left-hand cord, and then bring it under the left-hand cord from back to front. Pull it up in front so both ends are facing upward. Cross right over left, forming a loop, and go through the loop, again from back to front. Pull the ends to tighten the knot.

Surgeon's knot

Cross the left end over the right end and go through the loop. Go through again. Pull the ends to tighten. Cross the right end over the left end and go through once. Pull the ends to tighten.

Lark's head knot

Fold a cord in half and lay it behind a ring, loop, bar, etc. with the fold pointing down. Bring the ends through the ring from back to front, then through the fold, and tighten.

Half-hitch knot

Come out a bead and form a loop perpendicular to the thread between beads. Bring the needle under the thread and away from the loop. Then go back over the thread and through the loop. Pull gently so the knot doesn't tighten prematurely.

CONDITIONING THREAD

Conditioning straightens and strengthens your thread and also helps it resist fraying, separating, and tangling. Pull unwaxed nylon threads like Nymo or C-Lon through either beeswax (not candle wax or paraffin) or Thread Heaven to condition. Beeswax adds tackiness that is useful if you want your beadwork to fit tightly. Thread Heaven adds a static charge that causes the thread to repel itself, so it can't be used with doubled thread. All nylon threads stretch, so maintain tension on the thread as you condition it.

STITCHES

Stop bead

Use a stop bead to secure beads temporarily when you begin stitching. Choose a bead that is distinct from the beads in your project. String the stop bead about 6 in. (15cm) from the end of your thread, and go back through it in the same direction. Go through it one more time for added security.

Adding and ending thread

To add, thread the needle on the tail end of the thread (where you cut it from the spool). Insert the needle in the bead where the old thread exits, and go down four beads (**a–b** in the figure below). Go up three beads in the adjacent stack (**b–c**). Go down two beads in the first stack (**c–d**). Go up three beads in the second (**d–e**). Go down four to six beads in the third (**e–f**). Trim the short tail off and thread the needle on the long end. To end, follow a similar path to the way you added the new thread, working in the opposite direction.

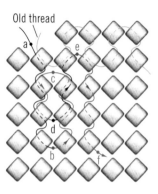

Old thread

Ladder

1 Pick up two beads. Leave a 4-in. (10cm) tail. Go through both beads again in the same direction. Pull the top bead down so the beads are side by side. The thread exits the bottom of the second bead (**a–b**). Pick up a third bead, and go back through the second bead from top to bottom. Come back up the third bead (**b–c**).

String a fourth bead. Go through the third bead from bottom to top and the fourth bead from top to bottom (**c–d**). Continue adding beads until you reach the desired length.

2 To stabilize the ladder, zigzag back through all the beads.

Basics

Brick stitch

Begin brick stitch with a ladder of seed or bugle beads (see "Ladder").

1 String two beads. Go under the thread between the second and third beads on the ladder from back to front. Pull tight. Go up the second bead added, then down the first. Come back up the second bead again.

2 For the row's remaining stitches, pick up one bead. Pass the needle under the next loop on the row below from back to front. Go back through the new bead.

Herringbone (Ndebele)

1 Stitch an even number of beads into a bead ladder (see "Ladder"). Turn the ladder, if necessary, so your thread exits the end bead pointing up. Pick up two beads and go down through the next bead on the ladder (a–b). Come up through the third bead on the ladder, pick up two beads, and go down through the fourth bead (b–c). Repeat across the ladder.

2 To turn, come back up through the second-to-last bead and continue through the last bead added in the previous row (a–b). Pick up two beads, go down through the next bead in that row, and come up through the next bead (b–c). Repeat across the row.

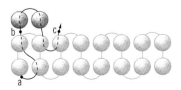

Tubular herringbone

Stitch an even number of beads into a bead ladder (see "Ladder"), and join it into a ring. Pick up two beads, and go down the next bead on the row below (the ladder). Come up the next bead, and repeat. There will be two stitches when you've gone down the fourth bead (a–b).

You need to work a step-up to be in position to start the next row. To do this, come up the bead next to the one your needle is exiting and the first bead of the first stitch (c–d). Continue adding two beads per stitch and stepping up at the end of each round.

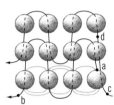

Peyote: flat even-count

1 Pick up an even number of beads. These beads become rows 1 and 2.

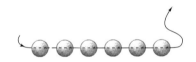

2 To begin row 3, pick up a bead, and stitch through the second bead from the end. Pick up a bead, and go through the fourth bead from the end. Continue across the row. End by going through the first bead picked up. To count rows, count the beads along the outer edges.

3 To start row 4 and all other rows, pick up a bead, and go through the last bead added on the previous row.

Peyote: flat odd-count

Work the first three rows as for flat, even peyote, but string an odd number of beads. Since the first two rows total an odd number of beads, you won't have a place to attach the last bead on odd-numbered rows.

Work a figure-8 turn at the end of row 3, which will position you to start row 4: Pick up bead #7, and go diagonally through #2, then #1 (a–b). Pick up #8, and go diagonally through #2, and #3. Turn, and go through #7, #2, and #1. Then turn, and go through #8 in the opposite direction (b–c).

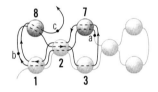

You can continue to work this turn at the end of each odd-numbered row, but this edge will be stiffer than the other. Use the following alternate method to turn on subsequent odd-numbered rows.

Pick up the last bead of the row, then go under the edge thread immediately below. Go through the last bead to begin the new row.

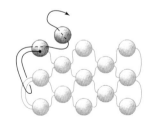

Peyote: tubular even-count

1 Pick up an even number of beads to equal the desired circumference. Tie the beads into a ring, leaving some slack. Put the ring over a form, if desired.

2 Even-numbered beads form round 1; odd-numbered beads form round 2. Go through the first bead to the left of the knot. Pick up a bead, skip a bead, and go through the next bead. Repeat until you're back at the start.

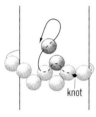

knot

3 Since you started with an even number of beads, you need to work a step-up to start the next round. Go through the first beads on rounds 2 and 3. Pick up a bead, and go through the second bead on row 3; continue.

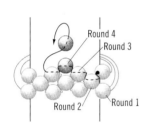

Round 4
Round 3
Round 2
Round 1

Peyote: tubular odd-count

Start as for circular even-count steps 1–2 above. However, when you begin with an odd number of beads, there won't be a step-up; you'll keep spiraling.

Peyote: two-drop

Work two-drop peyote stitch just like peyote stitch, but treat every pair of beads as a single bead. Start with an even number of beads divisible by four. Pick up two beads, skip the first two beads, and go through the next two beads. Repeat across, ending by going through the last two beads.

Peyote: zipping up (joining)

To join two sections of a flat peyote piece invisibly, fit the high beads on each side together, like the teeth of a zipper. "Zip up" the stitches by zigzagging through each high bead.

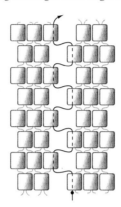

Square stitch

1 String the required number of beads for the first row. Then string the first bead of the second row, and go through the last bead of row 1 and the first bead of row 2 in the same direction. The new bead sits on top of the old bead and the holes are horizontal.

2 String the second bead of row 2, and go through the next-to-last bead of row 1. Continue through the new bead of row 2. Repeat this step for the entire row.

LOOMWORK

Set up the warp

Tie the end of the spool of thread to a screw or hook at the end of the loom.

Bring the thread over one spring and across to the spring at the other end of the loom. Wrap the thread around the back of the rod, behind the bottom spring, and back to the spring at the top of the loom.

Continue wrapping the thread between springs, keeping the threads a bead's width apart, until you have one more warp thread than the number of beads in the width of the pattern. Keep the tension even, but not too tight. Secure the last warp thread to a hook or screw on the loom, then cut the thread from the spool.

Weave the pattern

1 Tie the end of a 1-yd. (.9m) length of thread to the first warp thread just below the spring at the top of the loom. Bring the needle under the warp threads. String the first row of beads as shown on the pattern, and slide them to the knot.

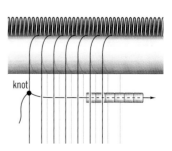

knot

Basics

2 Push the beads up between the warp threads with your finger.

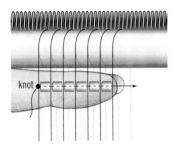

3 Sew back through the beads, keeping the needle above the warp threads. Repeat, following the pattern row by row.

Once you complete the last row, secure the working thread by weaving it into the beadwork.

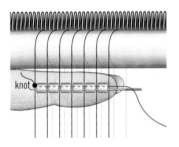

BEADED BACKSTITCH

To stitch a line of beads, come up through the fabric from the wrong side. String three beads. Stretch the bead thread along the line where the beads will go, and go through the fabric right after the third bead. Come up through the fabric between the second and third beads, and go through the third bead again. String three more beads, and repeat. For a tighter stitch, string only two beads at a time.

BEAD CROCHET

Chain stitch

1 Make a loop in the thread, crossing the ball end over the tail. Put the hook through the loop, pull the yarn over the hook, and draw it through the first loop.
2 Yarn over the hook again, and draw through the loop. Repeat for the desired number of chain stitches.

Beaded chain stitch

Slide a bead against the base of the loop on the hook. Work a chain stitch. The bead is between the chains.

Single crochet

1 Insert the hook through the front and back of the first or second stitch from the hook. Yarn over and draw through the chain (two loops remain on the hook).

2 Yarn over, and draw through both loops (one loop remains on the hook).

Beaded single crochet

Before starting a single crochet, slide a bead against the base of the loop on the hook. Work normally.

Slip stitch

Go into the next stitch as for a single crochet. Yarn over, and draw through the stitch and the loop.

Beaded slip stitch

Go into the next stitch. Slide a bead down to the hook, yarn over, and bring the yarn through both the stitch and the loop on the hook

Join a ring

When your chain is the desired length, use a slip stitch to join it into a ring. Insert the hook into the first stitch. Yarn over, and bring yarn through both the stitch and the loop on the hook.

KNITTING

Cast on

1 Pull the yarn end from the center of the skein and make a loop, leaving a 6-in. (15cm) tail. Insert the needle into the loop as shown. Tighten the loop around your needle. This counts as your first stitch.

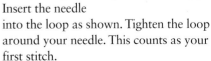

14

2 Hold the needle with the first stitch in your left hand, keeping the tail in front of the needle

and the yarn from the skein in back of the needle.

3 Hold the empty needle in your right hand and slide its tip through the stitch on the left needle from left to right (from the front of the

stitch to the back). The needles will form an X, with the right needle behind the left needle.

4 Hold the crossed needles between your left thumb and forefinger. Using your right hand, wrap the yarn from the skein counter-clockwise around

the tip of the right needle. Pull the tip of the right needle down and through the stitch, pulling the new loop through.

5 Gently stretch the loop on the right needle.

6 Working from left to right, slide the tip of the left needle through the loop on the right needle as shown.

7 Slide the right needle out of the loop, leaving two loops on the left needle. Pull gently to tighten the second stitch.

8 Repeat steps 3–7 until you have cast on the required number of stitches.

Knit stitch

1 Hold the needle with the cast-on stitches in your left hand, with the first stitch (the last cast-on stitch) about 1 in. (2.5cm) from

the needle tip. Slide the tip of the right needle into the first stitch, forming an X with the right needle in back. Wrap the yarn from the skein counterclockwise around the tip of the right needle.

2 Slide the right needle and its loop down through the middle of the first stitch.

3 Slide the loop off the left needle. The stitch is on the right needle. Repeat steps 1–2 until all of the stitches have been

knit off the left needle; this completes your first row. Switch the empty needle to your right hand and the full one to your left hand.

Bead knit

Position the right-hand needle into the next stitch, slide a bead on the yarn against the right-hand needle, and wrap the yarn around the needle as you did in "Knit stitch." Complete the stitch.

Bind-off

Place the full needle in your left hand and the empty needle in your right. Knit two stitches onto the right needle.

1 Slide the tip of the left needle into the outer stitch, pull it up and over the inner stitch, and drop it off the needle.

2 This leaves one loop on the right needle. To continue, knit another stitch onto the right needle, and repeat step 1.

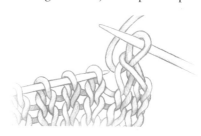

3 When you reach the last stitch on the left needle, knit it onto the right needle, and repeat step 1. One loop remains on the needle. Cut the yarn from the ball, remove the loop from the needle, pass the yarn through the loop, and tighten.

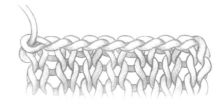

Yarn over

Before knitting a stitch, bring the yarn to the front and over the top of the right needle. This leaves an extra loop on the needle. Knit the next stitch. For a double yarn over, wrap the yarn around the needle twice. For a triple yarn over, wrap the yarn around the needle three times, as shown.

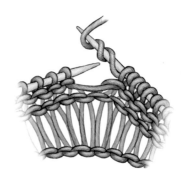

Drop the yarn

Slide the yarn over(s) off the left-hand needle to create a row of elongated stitches. Knit the next stitch.

Stringi

Leaf pendant necklace

String an ode to nature with a lovely vintage-reproduction leaf pendant

by **Julia Gerlach**

Hang a front-drilled pendant from a seed bead bail, and string it with a pretty assortment of glass and crystal beads. A single strand of beads expands to three strands in a simple yet intriguing design.

EDITOR'S NOTE:
If you use beading wire that is thicker than .010, you'll need to substitute a large-hole bead for the 2mm bead between the crimp and the clasp, as in the purple necklace.

MATERIALS

both projects
- Fireline 6 lb. test
- flexible beading wire, .010
- beading needles, #12
- crimping pliers
- wire cutters

maple leaf necklace
19 in. (48cm)
- 35mm vintage maple leaf pendant (Eclectica, 262-641-0910, eclecticabeads.com)
- **16** 12mm beads
- **2** 5–6mm round beads
- **2** 4mm large-hole beads
- **46** 3mm bicone crystals
- **2** 2mm round beads

- 10g size 11º seed beads, in **1** or **2** colors
- clasp
- **2** crimp beads

grape leaf necklace
19 in. (48cm)
- 30mm vintage grape leaf pendant (Eclectica)
- **24** 8mm oval beads
- **2** 8mm silver beads
- **29** 4mm bicone crystals
- **2** 4mm large-hole beads
- **23** 2mm round beads
- 10g size 11º seed beads, in **1** or **2** colors
- clasp
- **2** crimp beads

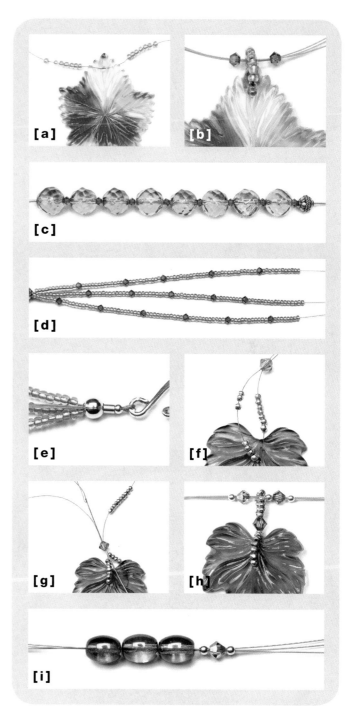

[a]

[b]

[c]

[d]

[e]

[f]

[g]

[h]

[i]

step*by*step

Maple leaf necklace

[1] On 10 in. (25cm) of Fireline, string seven 11º seed beads, the pendant, and seven 11ºs **(photo a)**. Tie the ends together with a surgeon's knot (see Basics, p. 10), then go through all the beads again. Secure both ends of the thread with a few half-hitch knots (Basics) between beads, and trim the tails.
[2] Determine the desired length of your necklace. (This one is 19 in./48cm.) Add 6 in. (15cm), and cut three pieces of beading wire to that length.
[3] Over all three wires, center a crystal, the seed bead loop, and a crystal **(photo b)**.
[4] On one end, string a 12mm bead and a crystal eight times. Then string a 5–6mm bead **(photo c)**. Repeat on the other end.
[5] Separate the three wires, and string each with a random or repeating pattern of 11ºs and crystals **(photo d)** for about 4¼ in. (10.8cm). Repeat on the other end.

[6] Test the fit, and add or remove beads as needed.
[7] Over all three wires, string a 4mm large-hole bead, a crimp bead, a 2mm round bead, and half the clasp. Go back through the beads just strung **(photo e)**, and crimp the crimp bead (Basics). Snug up the beads, and, leaving a little slack, repeat on the other end. Trim the excess wire.

Grape leaf necklace

[1] Thread a needle on each end of a 12-in. (30cm) piece of Fireline. On one needle, string six 11º seed beads, a 2mm bead, the pendant, a 2mm, and six 11ºs.
[2] With both needles, go through a crystal **(photo f)**.
[3] With one needle, pick up ten 11ºs, and go back through the crystal **(photo g)**. With the other needle, go through the 11ºs just picked up in the other direction. Retrace the thread path at least once, then tighten the thread to snug up the beads, and secure each tail in the beadwork with half-hitch knots. Trim.

[4] Determine the desired length of your necklace. (This one is 19 in./48cm.) Add 6 in. (15cm), and cut three pieces of beading wire to that length.
[5] Over all three wires, center a 2mm, a crystal, the seed bead loop, a 2mm, a crystal, and a 2mm **(photo h)**.
[6] On each end, string three 8mm oval beads, a 2mm, a crystal, and a 2mm **(photo i)**.

Repeat the pattern three more times.
[7] String an 8mm silver bead on each end.
[8] Separate the three wires, and string each with a random or repeating pattern of 11ºs and crystals for about 3¾ in. (9.5cm). Repeat on the other end.
[9] Follow steps 6 and 7 of the maple leaf necklace to finish this one.

Boho hoops

Suspend shimmering mother-of-pearl beads in generous double hoops

by **Zurina Ketola**

Make graceful earrings that are both stylish and retro. Best of all, these Bohemian hoops are a breeze to make.

step*by*step

[1] Cut the eye from a 2-in. (5cm) hoop earring (photo a), and make a plain loop (see Basics, p. 10) at one end.

[2] String cylinder beads on the hoop, leaving ¼ in. (6mm) of wire at the end. Make another loop (photo b).

[3] Repeat steps 1 and 2 with a 2½-in. (6.4cm) hoop.

[4] Cut a 4-in. (10cm) piece of wire, and string a mother-of-pearl bead, leaving 1½ in. (3.8cm) of wire on one side of the bead.

[5] Cross the wires above the bead (photo c).

[6] Use chainnose pliers to bend both wires straight up and parallel. Cut the shorter wire to ⅛ in. (3mm) above the bend (photo d).

[7] Make the first half of a wrapped loop (Basics) with the long wire, keeping the loop in the same plane as the bead (photo e). Make several wraps around both wires (photo f). Trim the excess wire.

[8] Open a 2mm jump ring (Basics), and string it through the wrapped loop. Close the jump ring.

[9] Open a 5mm jump ring and attach the 2mm jump ring and the hoop-earring loops (photo g). Close the jump ring

[10] Attach the 5mm jump ring to an earring finding.

[11] Make a second earring to match the first.

EDITOR'S NOTE:
To make your own earring hoops, shape 22-gauge sterling silver wire around a small bottle or jar.

MATERIALS
one pair of earrings
- 2 ¾ x 1-in. (1.9 x 2.5cm) top-drilled, fan-shaped mother-of-pearl beads (Fire Mountain Gems, firemountaingems.com)
- 4g Japanese cylinder beads
- 2 2½-in. (6.4cm) sterling silver endless hoop earrings (artbeads.com)
- 2 2-in. (5cm) sterling silver endless hoop earrings (artbeads.com)
- 8 in. (20cm) 22-gauge sterling silver wire
- 2 5mm jump rings
- 2 2mm jump rings
- pair of earring findings
- chainnose pliers
- roundnose pliers
- wire cutters

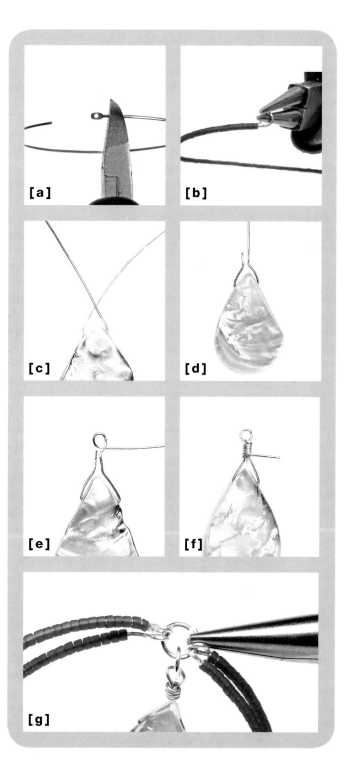

[a]   [b]   [c]   [d]   [e]   [f]   [g]

Three-strand garnet necklace

Use graduated bead sizes and strand lengths for an elegant silhouette

by **Helene Tsigistras**

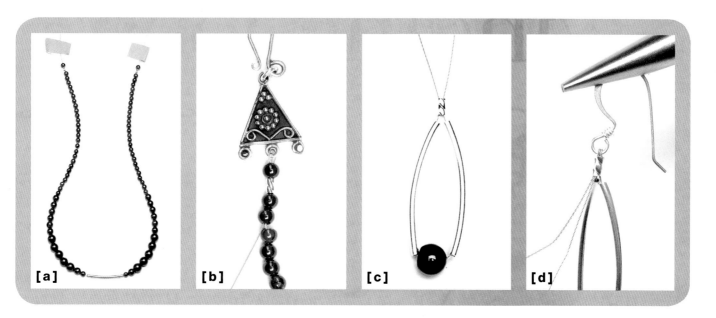

[a] [b] [c] [d]

Float slivers of silver between garnet beads for a classic three-strand necklace. Simple drop earrings complete this sophisticated ensemble.

step*by*step

Necklace

[1] Determine the length of the shortest strand of your necklace. (This one is 15 in./ 38cm.) Add 6 in. (15cm), and cut a piece of beading wire to this length. Cut a second piece 2 in. (5cm) longer than the first, and cut a third piece 2 in. longer than the second.

[2] On the shortest wire, center a silver tube bead. On each end, string a 4mm bead, a 5mm bead, five 6mm beads, and six 5mms. String 4mms until the strand is 1 in. (2.5cm) short of the desired length. On each end, string a crimp bead and a 4mm. Tape the ends (photo a).

[3] On the medium wire, center a silver tube bead. On each end, string a 4mm, a 5mm, seven 6mms, 17 5mms, and enough 4mms to yield a strand that is 1 in. longer than the first strand. On each

end, string a crimp bead and a 4mm. Tape the ends.

[4] On the longest wire, center the last silver tube bead. On each end, string a 4mm, a 5mm, 19 6mms, 15 5mms, and enough 4mms to yield a strand that is 1 in. longer than the second strand. On each end, string a crimp bead and a 4mm. Tape the ends.

[5] Untape one end of the medium strand, and go through the middle loop of the clasp. Go back through the last 4mm, the crimp bead, and the next two beads (photo b). Repeat on the other end.

[6] Repeat step 5 with the other two strands, going through the corresponding loops. Test the fit, and add or remove beads if necessary.

[7] Crimp the crimp beads (see Basics, p. 10), and trim the excess wire.

MATERIALS

both projects
- flexible beading wire, .012
- crimping pliers
- wire cutters

necklace 15–17 in. (38–43cm)
- 3 26 x 2mm sterling silver curved tube beads (Fire Mountain Gems, firemountaingems.com)

- 3 16-in. (41cm) strands of round garnet beads, 1 in each of 3 sizes: 6mm, 5mm, 4mm
- three-strand clasp
- 6 crimp beads

one pair of earrings
- 4 26 x 1mm sterling silver curved tube beads
- 2 6mm round garnet beads
- 2 crimp beads
- pair of earring findings

EDITOR'S NOTE:
The hole sizes in natural gemstone beads vary widely. Be certain that the last few beads at the end of each necklace strand will accommodate two passes with the beading wire so you can attach the clasp.

Earrings

[1] On 6 in. (15cm) of beading wire, string a silver tube bead, a 6mm bead, and a tube bead.

[2] String a crimp bead over both ends (photo c).

[3] String the ends through an earring finding and back through the crimp bead (photo d). Snug up the wires,

and crimp the crimp bead (Basics). Trim the tails.

[4] Make a second earring to match the first.

Swinging loops

by **Mel McCabe and Claudia Navarette**

EDITOR'S NOTE:
In these earrings, the beading wire is partially exposed. If you don't have wire with a gold or silver finish, as shown here, string a few more beads until the beading wire is completely covered.

Add some sparkle to your wardrobe with beautiful briolette earrings

Add a stylish accent to any outfit with easy, playful gemstone earrings. They're surprisingly simple to assemble using beading wire and crimps.

step*by*step

Red and yellow earrings

[1] Cut two 5-in. (13cm) pieces of beading wire.

[2] On each wire, string two rondelles, a spacer, a color B briolette, a spacer, two rondelles, a spacer, a color A briolette, a spacer, two rondelles, a spacer, a B, a spacer, and two rondelles **(photo a)**.

[3] Hold the ends of one wire together, and string a crimp bead over them. Slide the crimp down toward the beads until the wire loop is the desired size. Use a pen to mark the crimp's placement **(photo b)**. Remove the crimp, and mark the second wire to match the first.

[4] String the crimp bead again, then string the earring wire's loop **(photo c)**. Take the ends back through the crimp bead, making a small loop around the earring wire **(photo d)**. Crimp the crimp bead (see Basics, p. 10), and trim the excess wire close to the crimp.

[5] Hold the crimp cover in the round opening at the tip of your crimping pliers, with the opening facing away from the pliers.

[6] Place the cover over the crimp bead **(photo e)**. Gently squeeze the crimping pliers to close the cover over the crimp bead.

[7] Finish the second earring to match the first.

Purple and blue earrings

[1] Begin as in steps 1 and 2 of the red and yellow earrings. Tape one end of each wire.

[2] String a crimp bead on the untaped end of one wire. Go through the loop on the earring post and back through the crimp bead **(photo f)**. Crimp the crimp bead, and trim the excess wire.

[3] Remove the tape, string a crimp bead on the other end of the beading wire, and go through a loop on the earring back. Then go through the crimp bead again **(photo g)**. Adjust the beading wire until the earring is the desired length and crimp the crimp bead. Trim the excess wire.

[4] Cover the front crimp bead with a crimp cover as in steps 5 and 6 of the red and yellow earrings.

[5] Finish the second earring to match the first.

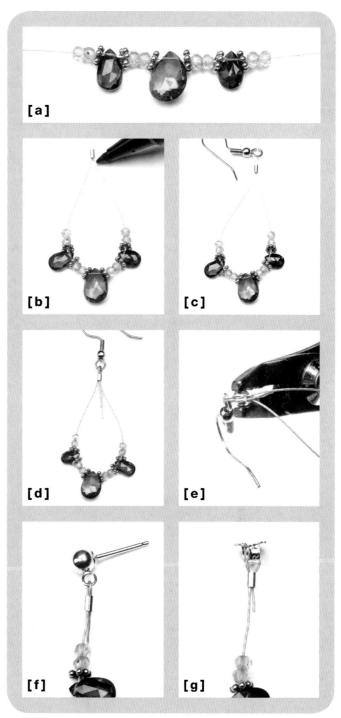

[a]

[b]

[c]

[d]

[e]

[f]

[g]

MATERIALS
both projects
- flexible beading wire, .012–.014, gold or sterling silver finish
- crimping pliers
- wire cutters

one pair of red and yellow earrings
- 6–8mm gemstone briolettes
  2 color A, red
  4 color B, yellow
- 16 3–4mm faceted gemstone rondelles
- 12 3–4mm daisy spacers
- 2 medium-size crimp beads

- 2 3mm crimp covers (The Bead Shop, 650-328-7925, beadshop.com)
- pair of earring wires

one pair of purple and blue earrings
- 2 8mm gemstone briolettes, color A, purple

- 4 6mm gemstone briolettes, color B, blue
- 16 3–4mm faceted gemstone rondelles
- 12 3–4mm daisy spacers
- 4 crimp beads
- 2 3mm crimp covers
- pair of post earring findings
- pair of earring backs

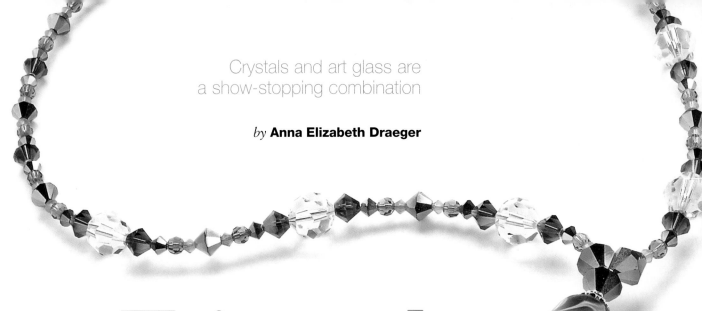

by **Anna Elizabeth Draeger**

Fringed focal bead necklace

The 2006 Bead&Button Show commemorative
bead by Stuart Abelman is beautiful all on
its own. Show it off as the focal point of a
sparkling fringed necklace.

step*by*step

[1] Cut four 24-in. (61cm)
pieces of flexible beading
wire. Fold a piece of tape
around each strand about
6 in. (15cm) from one end.
[2] On the 6-in. end of the
first strand, string the first
fringe: a seed bead, a 3mm
bicone crystal, a 4mm round
crystal, a 4mm bicone crystal,
a 6mm bicone crystal, a 4mm
bicone, a 4mm round, a 3mm,
and a seed bead. Skip the seed
bead, and take the tail back

through the rest of the beads
(**photo a**). On the remaining
strands, string the following
patterns, and secure the tails.
Strand 2: seed bead, 3mm,
4mm round, 4mm bicone,
6mm bicone, 4mm bicone,
4mm round, 3mm, 4mm
round, 4mm bicone, 6mm
bicone, 4mm bicone, 4mm
round, 3mm, seed bead.
Strand 3: seed bead, 3mm,
4mm round, 4mm bicone,
4mm round, 3mm, 6mm
bicone, 3mm, 4mm round,
6mm bicone, 4mm round,

3mm, seed bead.
Strand 4: seed bead,
3mm, 6mm
bicone, 3mm,
4mm round,
4mm bicone, 6mm
bicone, 4mm bicone,
4mm round, 3mm, seed
bead (**photo b**).
[3] Remove the tape. Put all
four strands and the tails
from the fringe through the
large opening of a bead cap,
an 8mm bicone, and the
small end of another bead
cap (**photo c**).

[4] String a 4mm
bicone and a crimp
bead over all four
strands and fringe tails
(**photo d**). Crimp the crimp
bead (see Basics, p. 10), and
trim the fringe tails next to
the crimp.
[5] On all four wires, string
the show bead, a 4mm
bicone, the large end of a
bead cap, and an 8mm bicone
(**photo e**).
[6] Split the strands into two
pairs, and string an 8mm
bicone on each pair (**photo f**).

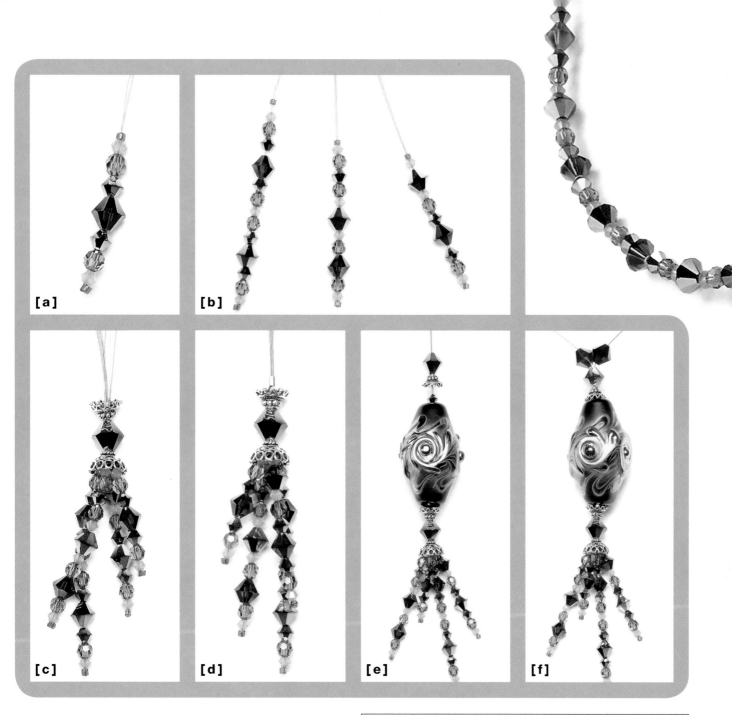

[a]

[b]

[c]

[d]

[e]

[f]

[7] String the following pattern on each pair: 3mm, 4mm round, 4mm bicone, 6mm bicone, 8mm round, 6mm bicone, 4mm bicone, 4mm round, 3mm, 6mm bicone. Repeat the pattern twice.

[8] String the following pattern on each pair: 3mm, 4mm round, 4mm bicone, 6mm bicone, 4mm bicone, 4mm round, 3mm, 6mm bicone. Repeat.

[9] String the following pattern on each pair: 3mm, 4mm round, 4mm bicone, 6mm bicone, 4mm bicone, 4mm round, 3mm.

[10] On one pair, string a crimp bead and half the clasp. Go back through the crimp bead, check the fit, and crimp the crimp bead. Trim the tail. Repeat with the other pair.

MATERIALS

necklace 19 in. (48cm)
- 2006 Bead&Button Show bead (800-554-0197, beadandbuttonshow.com, or abelmanartglass.com)
- Swarovskicrystals
  6 8mm round, light azore AB
  4 8mm bicone, jet AB 2X
  35 6mm bicone, jet AB 2X
  33 4mm bicone, jet AB 2X
  36 4mm round, indicolite
  36 3mm bicone, pacific blue
- **8** size 11º or smaller seed beads to match crystals
- clasp
- **3** 6mm bead caps
- **3** crimp beads
- flexible beading wire, .010
- crimping pliers
- wire cutters

Teardrop ensemble

by **Helene Tsigistras**

String small teardrop beads between large glass beads for an easy yet substantial two-strand necklace. The matching bracelet and earrings are a cinch.

step*by*step

Necklace

[1] Cut a 4-ft. (1.2m) piece of beading wire, and center the loop of one clasp half.

[2] Over both ends, string a rondelle and a crimp bead (**photo a**). Crimp the crimp bead (see Basics, p. 10).

[3] Over both ends, string a rondelle, a 10mm bead, and a rondelle (**photo b**).

[4] Separate the wires, and string ten teardrop beads on each wire (**photo c**).

[5] Repeat steps 3 and 4 nine times. Repeat step 3. You will have 11 10mm beads.

[6] Over both ends, string a crimp bead, a rondelle, and the other clasp half. Go back through the last three beads (**photo d**). Snug up the beads to remove any slack. Crimp the crimp bead, and trim the wire ends.

Bracelet

[1] Cut a 20-in. (51cm) piece of beading wire, and center the loop of one clasp half.

> **EDITOR'S NOTE:**
> Because the beading wire is somewhat visible in the earring design, consider using one of the new sterling- or gold-coated varieties for a more finished look.

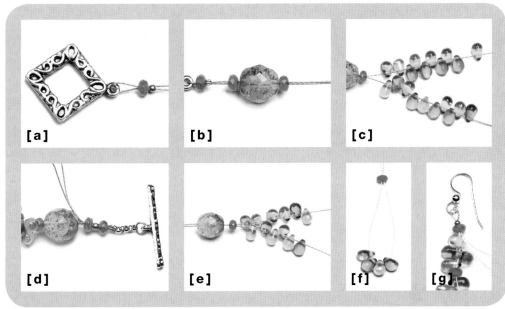

[a] [b] [c]

[d] [e] [f] [g]

Follow steps 2 and 3 of the necklace.

[2] Follow step 4 of the necklace, but string six teardrop beads on each end (**photo e**).

[3] Repeat the pattern (rondelle, 10mm, rondelle alternating with six teardrops) four times. You will have five 10mm beads and will end with teardrops.

[4] Finish as in step 6 of the necklace.

Earrings

[1] Cut a 6-in. (15cm) piece of beading wire, and center four teardrop beads on it. String a rondelle over both ends (**photo f**).

[2] String two teardrops on each end. Over both ends, string a rondelle, a crimp

bead, and an earring wire. Go back through the crimp bead and the top rondelle (**photo g**). Snug up the beads, and crimp the crimp bead (Basics). Trim the excess wire.

[3] Make a second earring to match the first.

MATERIALS

all projects
- flexible beading wire, .014
- crimping pliers
- wire cutters

necklace 20 in. (51cm)
- **11** 10mm round beads
- **200** 4 x 6mm teardrop beads
- **24** 4 x 6mm rondelles
- toggle clasp
- **2** crimp beads

bracelet 7 in. (18cm)
- **5** 10mm round beads
- **60** 4 x 6mm teardrop beads
- **12** 4 x 6mm rondelles
- toggle clasp
- **2** crimp beads

one pair of earrings
- **16** 4 x 6mm teardrop beads
- **4** 4 x 6mm rondelles
- **2** crimp beads
- pair of earring wires

Pair silver with glass
beads for a necklace
and bracelet with
unusual centerpieces

by **Cheryl Phelan**

FLORAL
centerpiece set

Think outside the box, and use components in unexpected ways. Here, a cluster of silver bead caps becomes the focal point in an elegant necklace. The matching bracelet is a perfect mate.

[a]

step*by*step

Necklace

[1] String a 6mm fire-polished bead and a silver flower on a head pin **(photo a)**.
[2] Make the first half of a wrapped loop (see Basics, p. 10) close to the flower **(photo b)**. Finish the wraps, filling in the space between the loop and the bead. Trim the excess wire. Make a total of three flower components.

[3] Determine the finished length of your necklace. (This one is 16 in./41cm.) Add 6 in. (15cm), and cut a piece of beading wire to that length.
[4] Center the three flower components on the wire **(photo c)**. Take one end of the wire back through the loops on the flower components **(photo d)**. Repeat with the other end of the wire.
[5] Pull both ends of the wire to gather the flower

components together. String a 4mm rondelle on each side of the flowers **(photo e)**.
[6] One each side, string a repeating pattern of five 6mm rondelles, a flat silver spacer, three 6mm rondelles, and a flat silver spacer **(photo f)** until you reach the desired length minus the length of the clasp.
[7] On each end, string a 4mm rondelle, a crimp bead, a 3mm round silver bead, and

MATERIALS

both projects
- chainnose pliers
- crimping pliers
- roundnose pliers
- wire cutters

necklace 16 in. (41cm)
- **3** 16mm Hill Tribe silver flower bead caps (Kamo1, 206-465-0492, kamo1beads@hotmail.com)
- Czech glass beads
  80 6mm faceted rondelles
  4 4mm faceted rondelles
  3 6mm fire-polished beads
- **20** 5–6mm flat silver spacers
- **2** 3mm round silver beads
- toggle clasp
- **3** 2-in. (5cm) head pins

- **2** crimp beads
- flexible beading wire, .014–.015

bracelet 7 in. (18cm)
- 16mm silver flower bead cap
- 6mm Czech fire-polished bead
- **166** 4mm faceted Czech glass rondelles
- **6** 3mm round silver beads
- **34** 3mm flat silver spacers
- **6** three-hole spacer bars
- three-strand slide clasp
- 2-in. (5cm) head pin
- **6** crimp beads
- flexible beading wire, .014–.015

[b] [c] [d] [e] [f] [g] [h] [i] [j] [k]

a clasp half. Go back through the beads just strung, the last large spacer, and the 6mm rondelle **(photo g)**. Tighten the wire, and check the fit. Add or remove beads from each end if necessary. Crimp the crimp beads (Basics), and trim the wire.

Bracelet

[1] Follow steps 1–2 of the necklace to make one flower component.
[2] Determine the finished length of your bracelet, add 5 in. (13cm), and cut three pieces of beading wire to that length. String three 4mm rondelles on the top and bottom wires. On the middle wire, string a rondelle, a flat spacer, the flower component, a flat spacer, and a rondelle **(photo h)**.
[3] On each end, string a spacer bar on all three wires.

Center the beads on the wires **(photo i)**.
[4] Working one end at a time, string the following pattern on the top and bottom wires: three rondelles, a flat spacer, four rondelles, a flat spacer, and three rondelles. On the center wire, string five rondelles, a flat spacer, and five rondelles. Then string a spacer bar on all three wires **(photo j)**. Repeat on the other end.
[5] Continue this pattern on both ends until you reach the desired length minus the length of the clasp.
[6] Working one strand at a time, string a flat spacer, a crimp bead, a flat spacer, a 3mm round silver bead, and the corresponding loop on the clasp half. Go back through the beads just strung and the last rondelle **(photo k)**. Repeat with the other wire ends.

[7] Check the fit. Add or remove an equal number of beads from each end of each strand, if necessary. Adjust the tension of each strand, and crimp the crimp beads. Trim the excess wire.

Enamel

An easy two-strand technique
holds buttons in the balance

by **Gita Maria Sturm**

Enamel buttons adorn an easy-to-
make necklace. Crystals and pearls
accent the delicate color scheme.

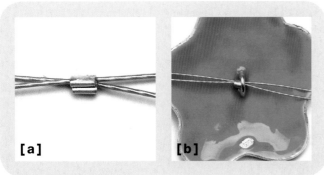

[a]

[b]

step*by*step

[1] Determine the finished
length of your necklace. This
one is 15½ in. (39.4cm). Add
8 in. (20cm), and cut two
pieces of beading wire to that
length.
[2] Center a crimp bead over
both wires, and crimp it (see
Basics, p. 10 and **photo a**).

String the large button over
both wires (**photo b**).
[3] On one end, separate
the wires, and string a 6mm
crystal, a 5mm crystal, a
button pearl, a 4mm crystal,
and a 5mm on each. Over
both wires, string a 6mm
(**photo c**).
[4] String a crimp bead over
both wires, pull the wires

button necklace

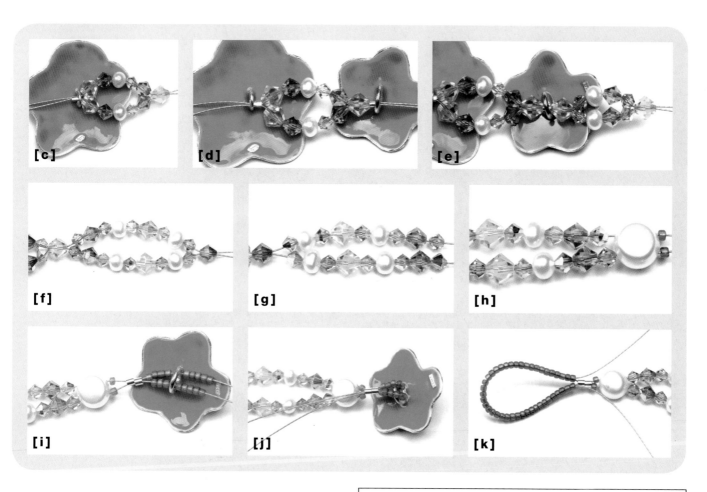

[c] [d] [e]

[f] [g] [h]

[i] [j] [k]

snug, and crimp the crimp bead. String a small button (photo d).

[5] String a 6mm over both wires. Separate the wires, then string a 4mm, a button pearl, a 5mm, and a 4mm on each. String a 6mm over both (photo e).

[6] Repeat steps 4 and 5.

[7] Separate the wires, and string a 4mm, a 5mm, a 4mm, a button pearl, a 4mm, a 6mm, a 4mm, a button pearl, and a 4mm on each. Over both, string a 5mm (photo f).

[8] Separate the wires, and string a 4mm, a button pearl, a 4mm, a 6mm, a 4mm, a button pearl, a

4mm, a 5mm, and a 4mm on each (photo g).

[9] Repeat steps 3–8 on the other end. Test for fit. The necklace should be about 2 in. (5cm) short of the desired length. If it's not, add or remove beads as necessary.

[10] String each wire on one end through a two-hole pearl. Then string an 11º seed bead on each (photo h).

[11] String two crimp beads over both wires, then string nine or ten 11ºs on each. String a small button over the 11ºs (photo i). Take the wires back through the crimp beads (photo j). Crimp, and trim the excess wire.

[12] Repeat step 10 on the other end, then string two crimp beads over both wires. Separate the wires, and, on one wire, string enough 11ºs to fit comfortably around the button. Go through these beads in the other direction

with the other wire (photo k). Go through the crimp beads with both wires. Crimp the crimp beads, and trim the excess wire.

MATERIALS

necklace 15½ in. (39.4cm)
- 1⅜-in. (3.5cm) floral button (all buttons at gitamaria.com)
- 5 1-in. (2.5cm) floral buttons
- bicone crystals
  25 6mm, light rose AB
  26 5mm, topaz AB
  62 4mm, light amethyst AB
- pearls
  2 8mm two-hole
  26 4 x 6mm button
- 1g size 11º seed beads
- 9 crimp beads
- flexible beading wire, .018
- crimping pliers
- wire cutters

Crossover cuff

Use an easy technique to produce a stunning and sophisticated bracelet

by **Anna Elizabeth Draeger**

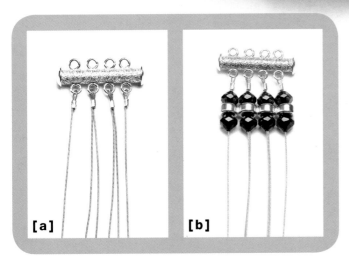

[a]   **[b]**

The crisscrossing strands of this bracelet create a complex look that belies the simplicity of the technique. Crimp beads hidden within the spacer bars are the key to success.

step*by*step

Make sure the holes in the spacer bars are big enough to accommodate the crimp beads. Otherwise you may have to use micro crimps.

[1] Cut six 12-in. (30cm) pieces of beading wire. String a crimp bead on the end of one piece, and go through the first loop of the clasp. Go back through the crimp bead, and crimp it (see Basics, p. 10). Trim the tails close to the crimp bead. Repeat on the fourth loop of the clasp.

[2] Repeat on each of the middle two loops, using two wires for each loop instead of one (photo a).

[3] String a 6mm bicone or rondelle over the first wire, a 6mm over the first pair of wires, a 6mm over the second pair of wires, and a 6mm over the last wire.

[4] String a spacer bar over the wires, then string 6mms over the wires as before (photo b).

[5] String five color A 4mm bicone crystals on the first, third, and fifth wires. String five color B 4mm bicone crystals on the second, fourth, and sixth wires (photo c).

[6] Group the first and fourth wires, and string a 6mm over both. Repeat with the third and sixth wires. String a 6mm on the second wire and one on the fifth (photo d). Make sure the Bs cross over the As.

[7] String one crimp bead next to each 6mm. Tighten any slack in the strands, and crimp the crimp beads (photo e).

[8] String a spacer bar over the wires (photo f).

[9] Repeat steps 5–8 four times. Alternate crossing As over Bs and Bs over As with

each repetition. String 6mms on the wires as before after each repetition.

[10] String a crimp bead after each 6mm, go through the corresponding loops on the clasp, and go back through the crimp beads. Crimp the crimp beads. Cover the crimp beads with crimp covers (photo g).

MATERIALS

bracelet 7½ in. (19.1cm)
- Swarovski crystals
  48 6mm bicones or rondelles
  75 4mm bicones, colors A and B
- **6** four-hole spacer bars (Rio Grande, riogrande.com)
- four-strand clasp (Rio Grande)
- **32** crimp beads or **8** crimp beads and **20** micro crimp beads
- **8** crimp covers
- flexible beading wire, .014
- chainnose pliers
- crimping pliers
- micro crimping pliers (optional)
- wire cutters

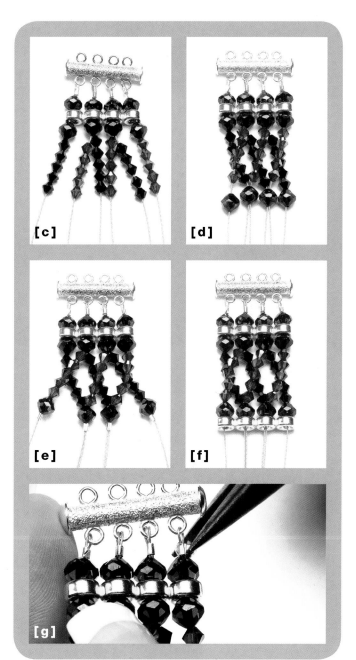

[c]

[d]

[e]

[f]

[g]

Carmen Miranda
necklace & earrings

Playful shapes and colors unite in a festive necklace-and-earring set

by **Christine Strube**

It's time to party when you wear the exciting tropical colors favored by the queen of Brazilian samba. Notice how the soothing influence of blue and rose balances the sizzle of mango, fuchsia, and lime. Use the bead colors and patterns shown here, or design a color palette of your own. Making substitutions is half the fun!

step*by*step

Necklace

Dangles

The more dangles you make, the fuller the piece will be. This necklace uses 36 dangles.
[1] To make the necklace dangles, string each of the following combinations on head pins.
• a 6mm teal pearl and five 11º seed beads **(photo a)** (make 24)
• a 10mm mango pearl **(photo b)** (make six)
• a paddle bead **(photo c)** (make six)

[2] Make a wrapped loop (see Basics, p. 10) above each dangle. Trim the excess wire.

Focal piece
[1] Make the first half of a wrapped loop at one end of the 4-in. (10cm) wire.

[a]   [b]

37

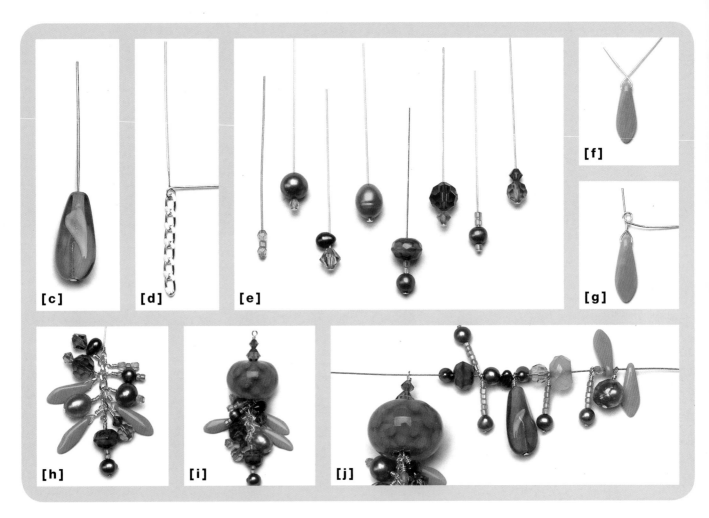

[c] [d] [e] [f] [g]

[h] [i] [j]

[2] Cut a six-link piece of 3mm chain. Slide the end link into the wrapped loop (photo d). Finish the wraps, and trim the excess wire.

[3] String the following combinations on a sterling silver head pin (photo e):

• a 3mm orange fire-polished bead, an 11º, and a 3mm orange bead

• a 3mm orange bead and an 8mm rose pearl

• a 6mm olivine bicone crystal and a 5mm fuchsia pearl

• a 10mm mango pearl

• a 6mm teal pearl, two 11ºs, and an 8mm blue rondelle

• a 4mm sun bicone and an 8mm fuchsia round crystal

• an 11º, a 6mm teal pearl, and two 11ºs

• a 6mm fire-opal round crystal and a 4mm fuchsia bicone

[4] Make the first half of a wrapped loop above each dangle.

[5] To make a dagger bead dangle, cut the head off a head pin. Slide a dagger one-third of the way onto the wire. Cross the wire ends above the bead (photo f). Bend both ends straight up where they cross, then make the first half of a wrapped loop with the longer wire (photo g) (make three). When you finish the loops, wrap over both wires.

[6] Attach one dangle to the bottom chain link, and finish the wrapped loop.

[7] Attach a dangle to each side of the remaining five links. Finish the wrapped loops, and trim any excess wire (photo h).

[8] Use chainnose pliers to gently squeeze the top chain

link and the wrapped loop above it into a narrow oval.

[9] String the focal bead over the wire and the squeezed chain link. String a 6mm olivine bicone and a 4mm fuchsia bicone, and make a wrapped loop (photo i).

Necklace assembly

[1] Cut a 22-in. (56cm) piece of beading wire, and center the focal piece on it.

[2] On one side, string a 5mm fuchsia pearl, an 8mm blue rondelle, two teal dangles, a 6mm teal pearl, a 5mm fuchsia pearl, a paddle dangle, a 5mm fuchsia pearl, a 6mm fire-opal round crystal, a teal dangle, a 10mm chalcedony rondelle, a teal dangle, a 3mm orange bead, a dagger, a mango dangle, and a dagger (photo j).

[3] String a 3mm orange bead, a teal dangle, an 8mm blue rondelle, a teal dangle, a 6mm teal pearl, a 5mm fuchsia pearl, a paddle dangle, a 5mm fuchsia pearl, a 6mm fire-opal round crystal, a teal dangle, a 10mm chalcedony rondelle, a teal dangle, a 3mm orange bead, a dagger, a mango dangle, and a dagger (photo k). Repeat.

[4] String a 3mm orange bead, an 8mm blue rondelle, a 6mm teal pearl, two daggers, a 10mm mango pearl, a 4mm turquoise bead, a 10mm chalcedony rondelle, a 4mm olivine bicone, an 8mm blue rondelle, two 5mm fuchsia pearls, and a 4mm olivine bicone (photo l).

[5] String a crimp bead, a 4mm turquoise bead, and one end link of the 5mm chain. Go back

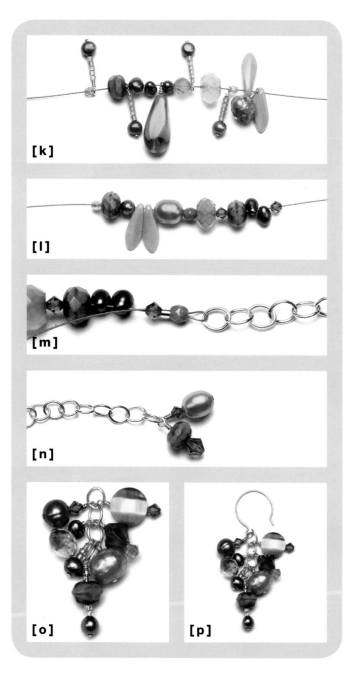

[k]

[l]

[m]

[n]

[o]

[p]

MATERIALS

both projects

- chainnose pliers
- roundnose pliers
- wire cutters

necklace 16 in. (41cm) with
2-in. (5cm) extension

- 22mm focal bead
  (Libby Leuchtman,
  sorellabeads.com)
- **8** 10mm chalcedony
  rondelles, pink
- **6** 10 x 20mm glass paddle
  beads, green
- pearls
  9–10 10mm faceted round,
  mango
  8mm round, rose
  34 6mm round, teal
  19 5mm top-drilled drops,
  fuchsia
- Swarovski crystals
  8mm round, fuchsia
  7 6mm round, fire-opal
  2–3 6mm bicone, olivine
  4 4mm bicone, olivine
  3–4 4mm bicone, fuchsia
  4mm bicone, sun
- **11–12** 8mm glass rondelles,
  blue
- **19** 6 x 15mm glass dagger
  beads, lime green
- **4** 4mm glass beads,
  turquoise
- **15** 3mm fire-polished
  beads, orange
- 5g size 11º seed beads, lime

- lobster claw clasp
- 4 in. (10cm) 22-gauge
  sterling silver wire
- 2 in. (5cm) sterling silver
  chain, 5mm links
- 1 in. (2.5cm) sterling silver
  chain, 3mm links
- **36** 2-in. stainless steel
  head pins
- **13** 2-in. 24-gauge sterling
  silver head pins
- **2** crimp beads
- flexible beading wire, .019
- crimping pliers

one pair of earrings

- **2** 10mm faceted fiber-optic
  coin beads, lime green
- pearls
  2 10mm faceted round,
  mango
  2 8mm round, rose
  6 6mm round, teal
- Swarovski crystals
  2 8mm bicone, fuchsia
  2 4mm bicone, fuchsia
  2 4mm bicone, olivine
  2 4mm bicone, sun
- **2** 8mm glass rondelles, blue
- **2** 8mm glass rondelles,
  green
- **12** size 11º seed beads,
  lime
- 2 in. (5cm) sterling silver
  chain, 5mm links
- **14** 2-in. (5cm) 24-gauge
  sterling silver head pins
- pair of earring wires

through the last three beads
(**photo m**).
[6] Repeat steps 2–5 on the
other end, substituting the
clasp for the 5mm chain in
step 5.
[7] Test the fit, and add or
remove beads as necessary.
[8] To make the optional
dangles for the chain extender,
string a 10mm mango pearl
and a 4mm fuchsia bicone on
a sterling silver head pin.
String a 6mm olivine bicone
and an 8mm blue rondelle on
another sterling silver head

pin. Attach the dangles to the
last chain link with wrapped
loops (**photo n**).

Earrings
[1] Cut a four-link piece of
5mm chain.
[2] To make the seven
dangles, string each of the
following combinations on
a sterling silver head pin:
- a 6mm teal pearl, two 11º
seed beads, an 8mm blue
rondelle, and two 11ºs
- a 6mm teal pearl and
two 11ºs

- a 10mm mango pearl
- an 8mm green rondelle
and a 6mm teal pearl
- a 4mm sun bicone crystal
and an 8mm fuchsia bicone
- an 8mm rose pearl and
a 4mm olivine bicone
- a 4mm fuchsia bicone
and a 10mm faceted fiber-
optic coin
[3] Make the first half of a
wrapped loop (Basics) above
each dangle.
[4] Slide the loop of the blue
rondelle unit into the end
chain link. Finish the wraps.

[5] Attach a dangle to each
side of the remaining three
chain links with wrapped
loops (**photo o**).
[6] Open the loop of an
earring wire (Basics), and
attach the chain (**photo p**).
Close the loop.
[7] Make a second earring
to match the first.

*The author offers kits for this
necklace. See page 255 for
more information.*

Multistrand
shell donut necklace

Lightweight yet substantial, shell donuts make
a wonderful summertime accessory

by **Julia Gerlach**

Paua shell and other natural materials have recently
enjoyed a renewed popularity and are featured
prominently in contemporary jewelry designs.
Create this fashionable necklace with a handful
of shell donuts, seed beads, pearls, and silver beads.

step*by*step

Getting started
[1] Cut six pieces of .010
beading wire, two in each
of the following lengths:
28 in. (71cm), 20 in. (51cm),
and 16 in. (41cm).
[2] Cut two 3-in. (7.6cm)
pieces of 24-gauge wire. At
one end of one piece, make

a wrapped loop (see Basics,
p. 10). String an 8mm pearl,
and make a wrapped loop at
the other end **(photo a)**.
Repeat to make a second
pearl unit.

Longest strand
[1] Over both 28-in. pieces
of beading wire, center about
2 in. (5cm) of 11° seed beads.

Loosely fold the wires in half,
and string the 50mm donut
over the loop **(photo b)**.
[2] Bring the four wire ends
through the loop **(photo c)**.
Add or remove beads if
necessary so that no wire
is exposed and no beads
extend past the loop. String
an 8mm pearl over all four
wires **(photo d)**. Separate

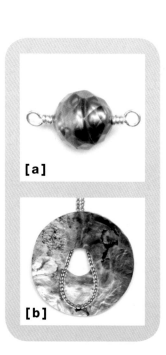

[a]

[b]

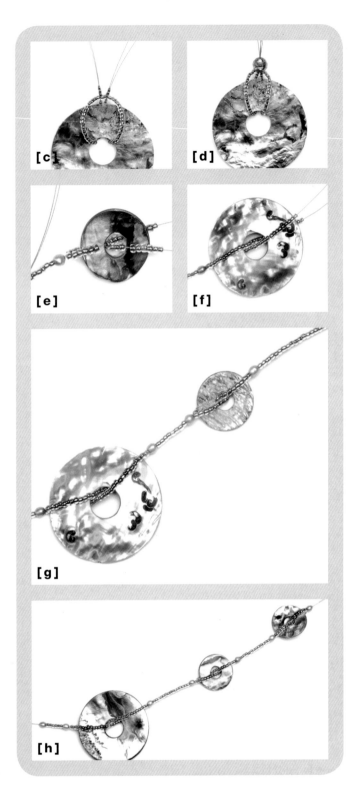

[c]

[d]

[e]

[f]

[g]

[h]

the wires into two pairs of two wires each.

[3] On one pair of wires, string six 11ºs and a 4mm pearl. Separate the wires.

[4] String approximately 18 11ºs on each wire. String a 20mm donut, crossing the wires through the center (photo e). Add or remove beads as needed.

[5] Over both wires, string a 4mm, eight 11ºs, and a 4mm.

[6] Separate the wires, and string approximately 30 11ºs on each. String a 40mm donut as in step 4 (photo f).

[7] Repeat step 5. Repeat step 4.

[8] Over both wires, string a 4mm and 18 11ºs (photo g). Tape the ends.

[9] Repeat steps 3–8 with the other pair of wires.

Middle strand

[1] Over both 20-in. pieces of beading wire, center a 4mm, six 11ºs, and a 4mm.

[2] On one end, string a 40mm donut as in step 6 of the longest strand.

[3] Over both wires, string a 4mm, 15 11ºs, and a 4mm.

[4] String a 20mm donut as in step 4 of the longest strand.

[5] Over both wires, string a 4mm, 12 11ºs, and a 4mm.

[6] String a 20mm donut as above, and string a 4mm over both wires (photo h). Tape the ends.

[7] Repeat steps 2–6 on the other end of the necklace.

Shortest strand

[1] On one 16-in. piece of beading wire, center 26 11ºs.

[2] Go through a 40mm donut. Over both ends, string a 4mm, six 11ºs, and a 4mm (photo i).

[3] String a 20mm donut as in step 4 of the longest strand.

[4] Over both ends, string a 4mm, six 11ºs, and a 4mm.

[5] String a 20mm donut as above.

[6] Over both ends, string a 4mm and 20 11ºs (photo j). Tape the ends.

[7] Repeat steps 1–6 with the remaining 16-in. wire, stringing it through the other side of the 40mm donut used in step 2.

Assembly

[1] Gather the three strands, and untape the wires on one end.

[2] Over all six wires, string an 8mm silver bead, a crimp bead, and an 8mm silver bead. Go through the loop of a pearl unit, and go back through the last three beads (photo k). Crimp the crimp bead (Basics), and trim the excess wire.

[3] Repeat on the other end, making sure to snug up the beads all along the strands before crimping.

[4] Cut two 8-in. (20cm) pieces of .014 beading wire.

[5] On one wire, string an 8mm silver bead, a crimp bead, an 8mm silver bead, and the remaining loop of a pearl unit. Go back through the beads just strung (photo l). Crimp the crimp bead, and trim the excess wire.

[6] String five 8mm pearls, a 3mm spacer, a crimp bead, a 3mm, and one clasp half. Go back through the last three beads (photo m), and crimp the crimp bead.

[7] Repeat steps 5 and 6 with the other 8-in. piece of beading wire.

[8] If desired, cover the crimp beads with crimp covers (photo n).

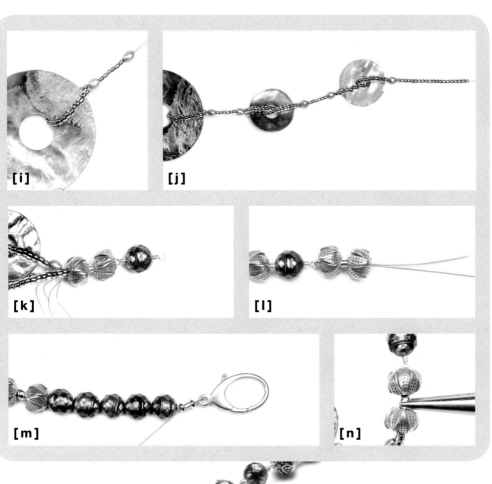

[i]

[j]

[k]

[l]

[m]

[n]

MATERIALS
necklace 27 in. (69cm)

- Paua shell donuts
  (Fire Mountain Gems,
  800-355-2137,
  firemountain.com)
  50mm
  5 40mm
  12 20mm
- **8** 8mm round silver beads
- pearls
  13 8mm
  34 4mm
- 10g size 11º seed beads
- **4** 3mm spacers
- clasp
- 6 in. (15cm) 24-gauge
  wire
- **6** crimp beads
- **6** crimp covers (optional)
- flexible beading wire,
  .010 and .014
- chainnose pliers
- crimping pliers
- roundnose pliers
- wire cutters

Enchanting
enamel
sensation

Enhance the rich
colors of enamel beads
with a simple design

by **Cheryl Phelan**

Fabulous enamel beads
show off a glorious array
of color. They're wonderful
combined with crystals in
this lavish necklace, bracelet,
and earring ensemble.

stepbystep

Necklace
[1] On 8 in. (20cm) of
beading cord, pick up an
11º seed bead and a 3mm
bicone crystal four times.

Sew through the hole on the
pendant, and pick up an 11º
and a 3mm crystal four times.
[2] Tie the tail and working
thread together with a square
knot (see Basics, p. 10) to
form the beads into a ring

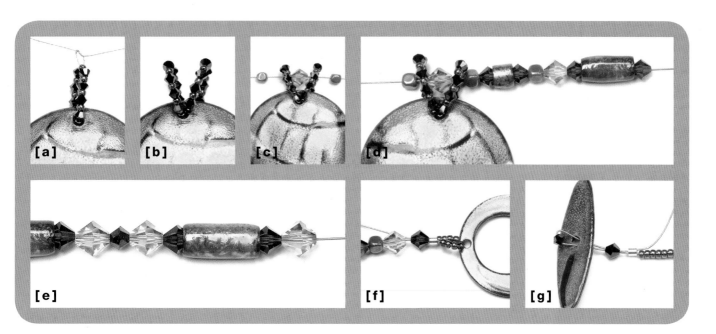

[a] [b] [c] [d]

[e] [f] [g]

(photo a). Sew through the ring of beads again. Secure the tails with a few half-hitch knots (Basics) between beads, dot the knots with glue, and trim the tails.

[3] Repeat steps 1–2 to make a second ring (photo b).

[4] Determine the finished length of your necklace. (This one is 17½ in./ 44.5cm.) Add 6 in. (15cm), and cut a piece of beading wire to that length.

[5] Center a 4mm square Czech glass bead, the pendant, a 6mm bicone crystal, and a 4mm square bead on the wire, positioning the crystal between the loops on the pendant (photo c).

[6] On one side of the necklace, string the following pattern: a 5mm bicone crystal, a 5mm enamel bead, a 5mm crystal, a 4mm square bead, a 6mm crystal, a 5mm crystal, a 12mm enamel bead, and a 5mm crystal (photo d). Then string a 6mm crystal, a 4mm crystal, a 6mm crystal, a 5mm crystal, a 12mm enamel bead, a 5mm crystal, and a 6mm crystal (photo e).

Repeat on the other side of the necklace.

[7] Continue stringing the patterns from step 6 on both sides of the pendant until your necklace is the desired length minus the length of the clasp.

[8] String a crimp bead and four 11ºs on one end of the necklace. Bring the wire through the hole on the toggle's ring, pick up four 11ºs, and go back through the crimp bead and the next bead or two (photo f). Adjust the wire's tension as needed, crimp the crimp bead (Basics), and trim the tail.

[9] On the other end of the necklace, pick up seven 11ºs, a crimp bead, and a 4mm crystal. Bring the wire through the hole on the toggle bar, pick up a 3mm crystal, and go back through the toggle bar, the 4mm crystal, and the crimp bead (photo g). Adjust the tension (see Editor's Note on p. 46), crimp the crimp bead, and trim the tail.

MATERIALS
necklace 17½ in. (44.5cm)
- 38mm domed-circle pendant*
- enamel beads*
  8 12mm regular tubes
  6 5mm shorties
- Swarovski bicone crystals
  19 6mm, light Colorado topaz champagne
  30 5mm, tourmaline
  5 4mm, jet nut 2x
  17 3mm, jet nut 2x
- 12 4mm square Czech glass beads, lavender
- 1g size 11º Japanese seed beads, dark green
- toggle clasp, enamel*
- 2 crimp beads
- Dandyline beading cord, .006
- flexible beading wire, .012–.014
- beading needles, #12
- G-S Hypo Cement
- crimping pliers
- wire cutters

bracelet 7½ in. (19.1cm)
- 5 5mm enamel beads, shorties*
- Swarovski bicone crystals
  12 6mm, light Colorado

topaz champagne
  10 5mm, tourmaline
  6 4mm, jet nut 2x
- 6 4mm square Czech glass beads, lavender
- toggle clasp
- 2 crimp beads
- flexible beading wire, .012–.014
- crimping pliers
- wire cutters

one pair of earrings
- 2 15mm domed-circle enamel beads*
- 2 6mm Swarovski bicone crystals, light Colorado topaz champagne
- 4 in. (10cm) 22-gauge silver wire
- pair of earring findings
- chainnose pliers
- roundnose pliers
- wire cutters

*enamel beads and components by Sara Lukkonen of C-Koop Beads, Duluth, Minnesota, (218) 525-7333, or innovativebeadsupply.com

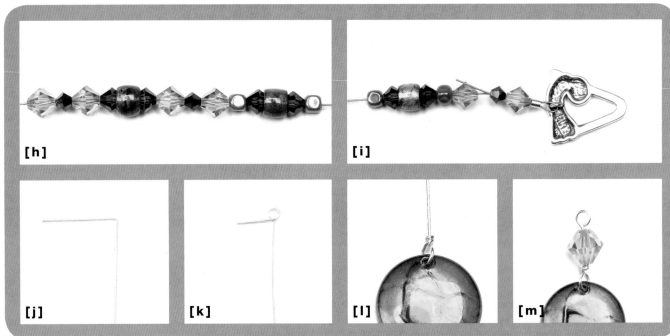

[h]

[i]

[j]

[k]

[l]

[m]

Bracelet

[1] Determine the finished length of your bracelet. Add 5 in. (13cm), and cut a piece of beading wire to that length. Tape one end.

[2] String the following pattern: a 6mm crystal, a 4mm crystal, a 6mm crystal, a 5mm crystal, a 5mm enamel bead, a 5mm crystal, a 6mm crystal, a 4mm crystal, a 6mm crystal, a 4mm square bead, a 5mm crystal, a 5mm enamel bead, a 5mm crystal, and a 4mm square bead **(photo h)**.

[3] Continue stringing the pattern until your bracelet is the desired length minus the length of the clasp.

[4] String a crimp bead, go through the loop on one of the toggle components, and back through the crimp bead and the last two beads strung **(photo i)**.

[5] Adjust the wire's tension, crimp the crimp bead (Basics), and trim the tail.

[6] Remove the tape and repeat steps 4–5 on the other end of the bracelet.

Earrings

[1] Cut a 2-in. (5cm) piece of 22-gauge wire. Make a right-angle bend in the wire ¾ in. (1.9cm) from the end **(photo j)**.

[2] Make the first half of a wrapped loop (Basics and **photo k**). Slide a domed-circle bead onto the loop, and finish the loop with two wraps (Basics) **(photo l)**.

[3] Pick up a 6mm bicone crystal, and make a plain loop (Basics) perpendicular to the wrapped loop **(photo m)**.

[4] Open the plain loop (Basics), attach it to the loop on an earring finding, and close the loop.

[5] Make a second earring to match the first.

EDITOR'S NOTE: Before you crimp the crimp beads on the necklace and bracelet, leave about 4mm of slack in the wire. Without the slack, the 5mm crystals that tuck inside the enamel beads won't be able to flex, leaving your pieces stiff and uncomfortable to wear.

Tips & Techniques

Earrings in a flash

If you've been searching for fast, easy earring ideas, try this great-looking pair. On a 4-in. (10cm) piece of .012 or .014 flexible beading wire, center your choice of beads and two four-loop components, as shown. Cross the wire's ends through the loop on an earring finding, then bring each wire through the corresponding loop on the top silver component. Slide a crimp bead over both wire ends. Adjust the tension of the wires, flatten the crimp bead with chainnose pliers (see Basics, p. 10), and trim the excess wire. Make a second earring to match the first.
– Helene Tsigistras, Brookfield, Wis.

Beads to go

I use 2-oz. sauce cups – the kind your favorite take-out comes in – to store and transport my beads. They conveniently stack into each other for compact storage. If I want to take them with me, I place the stacks in Tupperware-style containers, cover the top layer only, and off we go. Purchased at restaurant-supply stores, the cups are inexpensive and available in sizes ranging from 2–5 oz.
– Mindy Gang, Fort Lauderdale, Fla.

Modified toggles

If you want clasps to match your outfit, here's a great solution – customized toggle clasps. Keep several interchangeable toggles on hand to suit your mood, outfit, or occasion. First, finish both ends of your necklace with the circle end of a toggle clasp. Thread a needle on a 1-yd. (.9m) length of

Fireline 8 lb. test, and string a stop bead (Basics) and the bar end of the clasp. String 1–2 in. (2.5–5cm) of beads and the other bar end. Go back through all the beads and the first bar end. Retrace the thread path, tie a few half-hitch knots (Basics), and trim.

Another option is to make a bead-and-gemstone dangle to hang from one bar end of a clasp. Begin as above, but string about 3 in. (7.6cm) of beads, and omit the second bar end. Finish as above. Add fringe and dangles as desired. Wear this design as a Y-necklace with the clasp in front.
– Barbara Schwartz, East Meadow, N.Y.

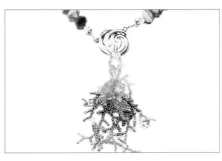

Making inexpensive bead boards

Like most beaders, I often have more than one project going at a time. Since I only have one bead design board, but still want to see my designs as I lay them out, I have found a way to make my own disposable boards. These are

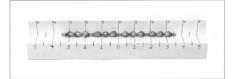

portable, inexpensive, and great to have on hand for a jewelry-making party.

To make one, cut an 8½ x 11-in. (21.6 x 28cm) piece of cardstock in half so you have two pieces that are 4¼ x 11 in. (10.8 x 28cm). Fold one piece in half lengthwise. Then fold the edges back toward the center fold, making an M shape. Mark the center with a 0, and, using a ruler, mark inches in the channel, using 0 as the center as on a commercial design board. Make another board with the other piece of cardstock.
– Tracey Kirk, Clarksville, Tenn.

Beads make everything better

I use beading and scrapbooking techniques to transform inexpensive spiral notebooks into custom keepsakes. Select a book with a colorful cover design or adhere decorative paper to the front using double-sided tape. Add a layer of stamps or stickers. Sew beads and sequins onto the cover using an embroidery needle and conditioned Nymo. Cover exposed threads by taping decorative paper to the inside cover. Remove the wire spiral. Wind the spiral back into the book, adding a few beads to the wire each time it exits one of the binding's holes.
– Althea Church, Oxford, Miss.

Wir

ework

Chained crystals

Beads take this
design beyond chain

by **Anne Mitchell**

Combine two classic chain mail techniques – Japanese Overlay and Corduroy Weave – to make an unusual chain with layers and a flat base. Add color to the chain with crystals, as shown here, or substitute glass beads, semiprecious stones, or freshwater pearls.

step*by*step

Bracelet
Connect the jump rings
Always open and close jump rings using two pairs of pliers. Hold the jump ring with one pair, and open or close it with the second pair (see Basics, p. 10).

[1] Close 44 and open 11 5.5mm jump rings.

[2] Slide four closed 5.5mm rings on an open 5.5mm ring (photo a). Close the jump ring. Repeat with the remaining rings from step 1 to make 11 four-in-one sets.

[3] Open 12 10mm rings.

[4] Separate the four rings in a four-in-one set into two pairs. Flip one pair of rings so they are side by side on your work surface (photo b). Slide a 10mm ring through the two side-by-side 5.5mm rings (photo c).

[5] Close the 10mm ring, and tape it to your work surface so the rings are easier to position. Flip the other pair of 5.5mm rings toward each other. The inside edge of the rings will touch, and the rings will not lie flat (photo d).

[6] Repeat step 4 with another four-in-one set. Connect the new 10mm ring

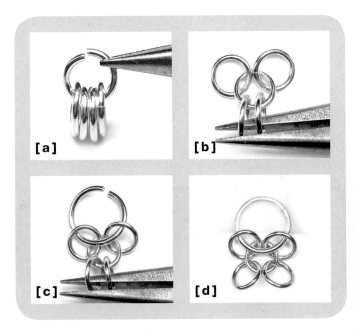

[a]

[b]

[c]

[d]

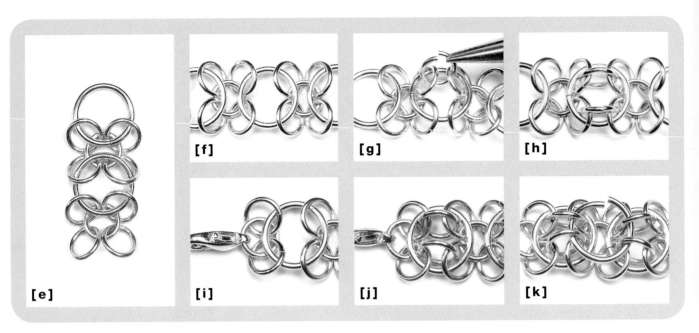

[e] [f] [g] [h]

[i] [j] [k]

MATERIALS

both projects

- bentnose pliers
- chainnose pliers
- crimping pliers
- wire cutters

bracelet 8 in. (20cm)

- **11** 6mm round crystals
- ½ troy oz. (16g) sterling silver jump rings, 10mm inside diameter, 15-gauge wire (annemitchell.net, code WW)
- ¾ troy oz. (24g) sterling silver jump rings, 5.5mm inside diameter, 17-gauge wire (annemitchell.net, code QQ)
- lobster claw clasp
- **2** crimp beads
- flexible beading wire, .014

choker 14 in. (36cm)

- **22** 6mm round crystals
- 1 troy oz. (32g) sterling silver jump rings, 10mm inside diameter, 15-gauge wire (annemitchell.net, code WW)
- 1½ troy oz. (48g) sterling silver jump rings, 5.5mm inside diameter, 17-gauge wire (annemitchell.net, code QQ)
- lobster claw clasp
- **2** crimp beads
- flexible beading wire, .014

to the available pair of 5.5mm rings on the previous four-in-one set. Remove the tape, close the 10mm ring, and flip the next pair of 5.5mm rings as in step 5 **(photo e)**.

[7] Continue connecting four-in-one sets with the remaining 10mm rings from step 3 **(photo f)**. You won't need to secure the chain to your work surface. Connect the last 10mm ring to the end pair of 5.5mm rings.

[8] Open 20 5.5mm rings.

[9] Starting at the second 10mm ring on the chain, slide a 5.5mm ring through the top two 5.5mm rings within the 10mm ring **(photo g)**. Close the 5.5mm ring, and repeat with the bottom two 5.5mm rings **(photo h)**. Continue along the length of the chain.

[10] Close one 5.5mm ring, and open ten 5.5mm rings.

[11] Working on one end of the chain, connect two 5.5mm rings to the end 10mm ring. Flip the rings as shown, and connect the lobster claw clasp to the two 5.5mm rings using a third ring **(photo i)**. Connect two rings to the 5.5mm rings within the end 10mm ring, as in step 9 **(photo j)**.

[12] Repeat step 11 at the other end of the chain, substituting the closed 5.5mm ring for the lobster claw clasp.

[13] Open 11 10mm rings.

[14] Starting at one end, slide a 10mm ring through the vertical 5.5mm rings in the centers of the first two 10mm rings **(photo k)**. Close

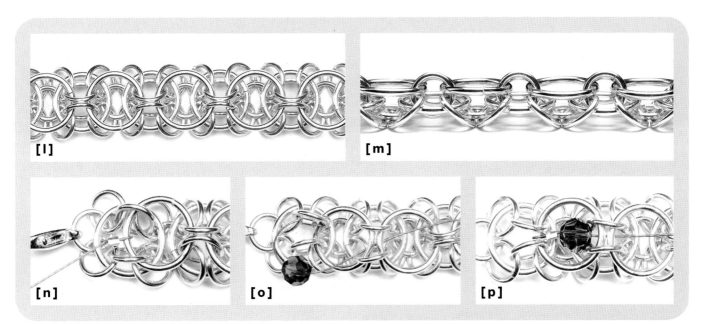

[l]

[m]

[n]

[o]

[p]

the ring. Repeat along the chain (photo l). Photo m shows the side view of the finished chain.

String the crystals

[1] Cut a 1-ft. (30cm) length of flexible beading wire, and string a crimp bead. Starting at one end of the chain, slide the end of the wire between the two vertical 5.5mm rings and up through the center of the 10mm ring. Bring the wire back through the crimp bead. Position the crimp bead next to the 10mm ring, crimp the crimp bead (Basics), and trim the tail as close to the crimp bead as possible (photo n).

[2] String a crystal, and bring the end of the wire under the other side of the 10mm ring, between the next two vertical 5.5mm rings, and out through the center of the next 10mm ring (photo o).

[3] Pull on the wire, popping the crystal into the center of the first 10mm ring (photo p).

[4] Repeat steps 2 and 3 along the chain. String a crimp bead after the last crystal, and crimp the wire to the other end as in step 1.

Choker

Follow the directions for the bracelet, using the number of jump rings necessary to reach your desired length. When stringing the crystals, use a length of flexible beading wire 4 in. (10cm) longer than the chain length.

EDITOR'S NOTE:

To keep the crystals from sliding inside the chain and to hide the beading wire between the crystals, adapt the instructions as follows: Work steps 1–3 of "String the crystals." String a 2mm round silver bead, a 4mm crystal, and a 2mm bead. Position the crystal under the two 5.5mm jump rings. Repeat this pattern, ending with a crimp bead instead of a 2mm bead. The photos below show the crystals' placement on the top, side, and bottom of the chain.

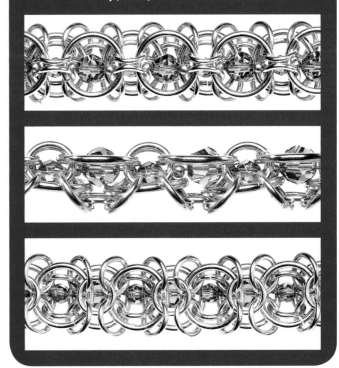

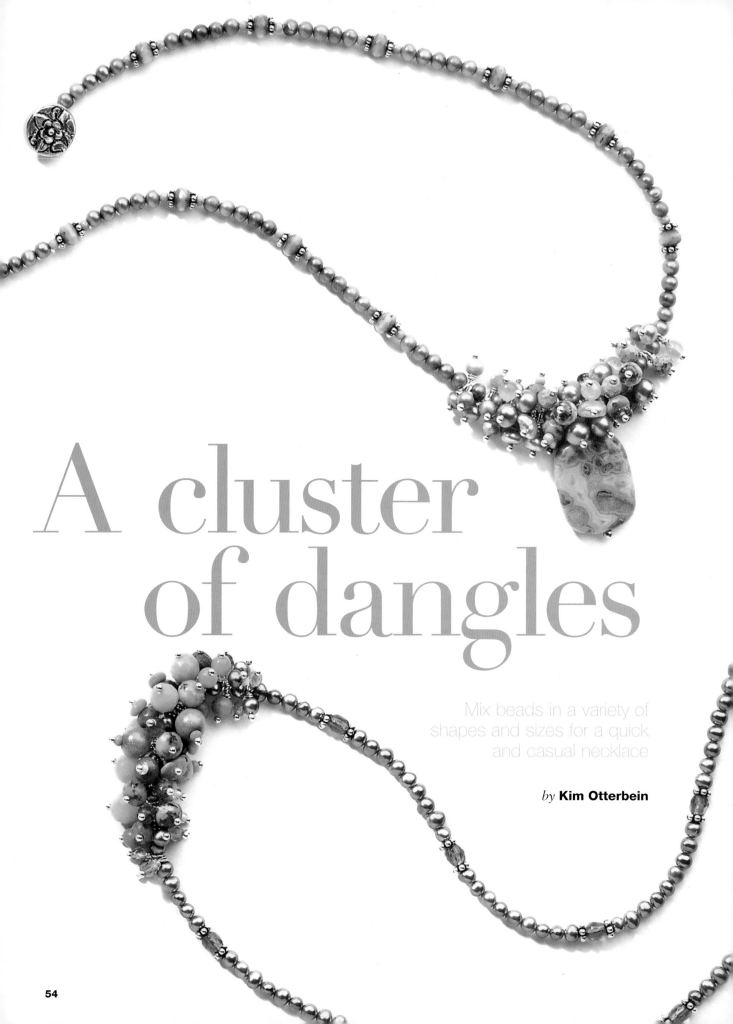

A cluster
of dangles

Mix beads in a variety of
shapes and sizes for a quick
and casual necklace

by **Kim Otterbein**

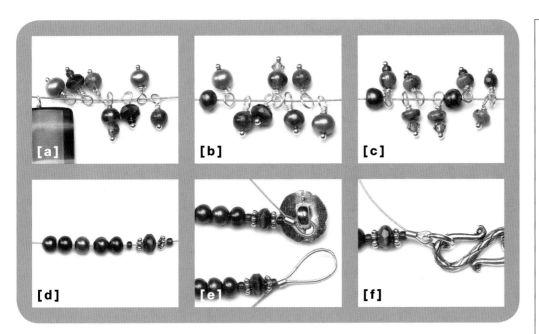

[a]

[b]

[c]

[d]

[e]

[f]

MATERIALS

necklace 17 in. (43cm)

- 15 x 20mm gemstone (tan necklace only)
- **56–68** 3–6mm beads, assorted shapes and materials
- 16-in. (41cm) strand 4mm potato-shaped pearls
- **10–14** 3–4mm accent beads
- **20–28** 4mm flat spacers
- 1g seed beads, size 11º (tan necklace only)
- button with shank, or S-hook clasp and **2** soldered jump rings
- French (bullion) wire
- **56–68** 1½-in. (3.8cm) decorative head pins
- 2-in. (5cm) decorative head pin (tan necklace only)
- **2** crimp beads
- flexible beading wire, .014–.015
- chainnose pliers
- crimping pliers
- roundnose pliers
- wire cutters

Make this fabulous necklace with or without a pendant – either way you'll be thrilled with the results. Plus, it's a great way to use up complementary beads left over from other projects.

step*by*step

Tan necklace

[1] String the 15 x 20mm gemstone on the 2-in. (5cm) head pin, and make a wrapped loop (see Basics, p. 10) above the bead.
[2] String one or two 3–6mm beads on each decorative head pin. Make a wrapped loop above each bead.
[3] Determine the finished length of your necklace. (This one is 17 in./43cm.) Add 6 in. (15cm), and cut a piece of beading wire to that length.
[4] Center the gemstone on the beading wire. Using the longest dangles first, string seven on one side of the gemstone (photo a). Repeat on the other side.
[5] String a pearl and seven dangles on each end (photo b). Repeat.

[6] String a pearl, four dangles, a pearl, and three dangles on each end (photo c).
[7] String five pearls, an 11º seed bead, a spacer, an accent bead, a spacer, and an 11º on each end (photo d). Repeat until the necklace is about 1 in. (2.5cm) short of the finished length. Check the fit, and add or remove beads if necessary.
[8] Cut one piece of French wire long enough to loop through the button's shank. Cut a second piece long enough to loop over the button for a closure.
[9] On one end of the beading wire, string a crimp bead, the French wire for the shank, and the button. Go back through the crimp bead and tighten it until the French wire forms a loop around the shank. On the

other end, string a crimp bead and the French wire for the loop. Go back through the crimp bead (photo e), tighten the wires, and crimp the crimp beads (Basics). Trim the excess wire.

Teal necklace

[1] Follow steps 2 and 3 of the tan necklace. Center 14 dangles on the beading wire.
[2] Center a pearl on the wire, and string seven dangles on each end. Follow step 6 of the tan necklace.
[3] String five pearls, a spacer, an accent bead, and a spacer on each end.
[4] String nine pearls, a spacer, an accent bead, and a spacer on each end. Repeat until the necklace is about 1 in. short of the desired length.
[5] Cut a ⅜-in. (1cm) length of French wire. On one end

of the necklace, string a crimp bead, the French wire, and a soldered jump ring with an S-hook clasp. Go back through the crimp bead (photo f), and tighten the wire loop. Repeat on the other end with the remaining jump ring. Crimp the crimp beads, and trim the excess wire.

Fringed chandelier earrings

Get ready for a night on the town with glitzy earrings

by **Rachel Nelson-Smith**

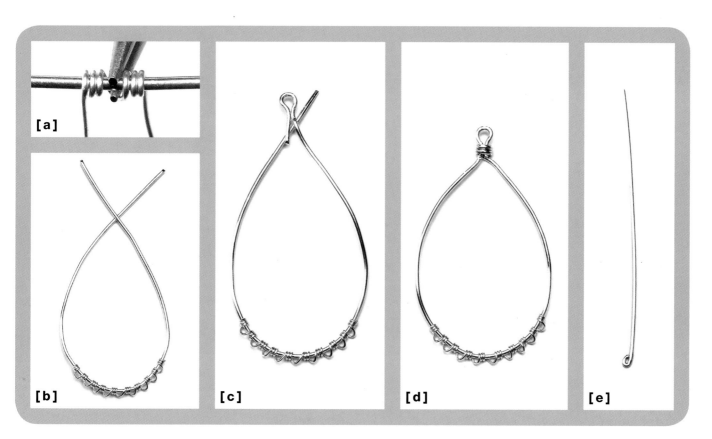

[a]

[b]

[c]

[d]

[e]

Dangle a variety of beads from wire loops to make a pair of fun, fringy earrings. Combine crystals, fire-polished beads, pearls, and gemstones for maximum impact.

step*by*step

Getting started

[1] Cut a 6-in. (15cm) piece of 18-gauge wire and a 1-ft. (30cm) piece of 24-gauge wire.
[2] Make a bend ½ in. (1.3cm) from one end of the 24-gauge wire, and place the 18-gauge wire against the bend. Wrap the 24-gauge wire around the 18-gauge wire for a total of three wraps.
[3] With the tips of your roundnose pliers, grasp the 18-gauge wire next to the wraps you just made. Go under the lower jaw of the pliers with the 24-gauge wire, and wrap it around the 18-gauge piece three times (photo a).

[4] Repeat step 3 eight times to make a total of nine loops. Trim the excess wire.
[5] Center the nine-loop segment on the 18-gauge wire, and bend the wire into a teardrop shape, with the ends crossing about ¾ in. (1.9cm) from the top (photo b).
[6] Where the wires cross, bend one end straight up, then use roundnose pliers to bend it into a loop (photo c).
[7] Wrap the other wire around the first. Trim the excess wire (photo d).

Fringe dangles

[1] Cut a 1½-in. (3.8cm) piece of 24-gauge wire. Fold over the tip to make a head pin (photo e).

[2] String a 3mm color A bead, and make a wrapped loop above the bead (see Basics, p. 10 and photo f).
[3] Repeat steps 1 and 2 to make a total of 18 color A dangles.
[4] Repeat steps 1 and 2 to make a total of nine 3mm color B dangles, making only the first half of a wrapped loop above the beads (photo g).
[5] Repeat steps 1 and 2 to make a total of ten 3mm color C dangles, making only the first half of a wrapped loop.
[6] Slide an A dangle into the loop of a B or C dangle (photo h). Repeat until you've connected all the A dangles to a B or C dangle. You'll have one C dangle left over.

[7] Cut a 2-in. (5cm) piece of 24-gauge wire, and fold the tip over to make a head pin. String a 6mm round bead or an 8mm rondelle, a spacer, and a 3mm B. Make the first half of a wrapped loop (photo i). Make a total of two round/rondelle accent dangles.
[8] Make one dangle with a teardrop, a spacer, and one or two Cs as in step 7 (photo j).

> **EDITOR'S NOTE:**
> Making the loops at the bottom of the earring is the trickiest part of this project. Practice with copper or craft wire until you're comfortable with the technique.

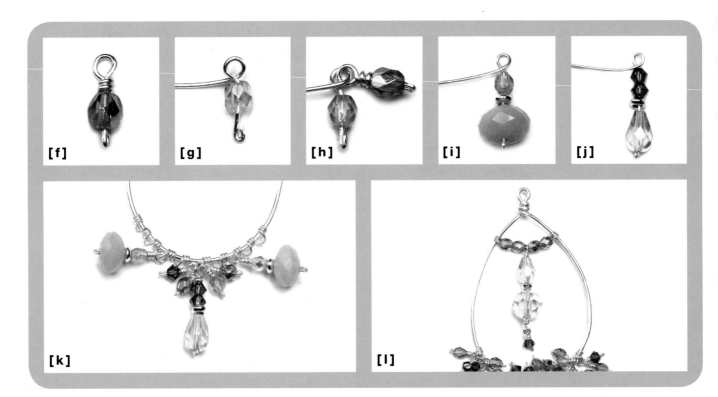

[f]　[g]　[h]　[i]　[j]

[k]　[l]

Center dangle

[1] Cut a 2½-in. (6.4cm) piece of 24-gauge wire, and make a wrapped loop at one end. Slide this loop into the loop of the leftover C dangle from step 6 of "Fringe dangles," and finish the wraps.

[2] String an 8mm round crystal, a spacer, and a teardrop. Make a wrapped loop above the beads.

Assembly

[1] Attach the teardrop dangle from step 8 to the middle loop on the nine-loop segment, and finish the wraps. Skip a loop on either side, and attach one of the round/rondelle dangles to each.

[2] Attach a B and a C dangle to the loop on each side of the teardrop accent dangle, and finish the wraps. Repeat for the round/rondelle accent dangles (photo k). Attach a B and a C dangle to each remaining loop.

[3] Cut a 2-in. piece of 24-gauge wire, and wrap one end three times around the wire frame about ½ in. from the top.

[4] String two 3mm As, the center dangle, and two 3mm As. Wrap the wire around the other side of the frame. Trim the excess wire (photo l).

[5] Open the loop on an earring finding, and attach the earring. Close the loop.

MATERIALS

one pair of earrings

- 4 6 x 9mm or 5 x 7mm teardrops, color A
- 2 8mm round beads, color B
- 4 6mm round beads or 8mm rondelles, color B
- 3mm beads
  44 color A
  22 color B
  24–26 color C
- **8** 3mm flat spacers
- 14 in. (36cm) 18-gauge wire
- 13 ft. (4m) 24-gauge wire
- pair of earring findings
- chainnose pliers
- roundnose pliers
- wire cutters

[6] Make a second earring to match the first.

The author offers kits for these earrings. See page 255 for more information.

Triangle dangles

Make great shapes with
crystals, chain, and wire

by **Melody MacDuffee**

A clever arrangement of chain and wire
gives these earrings an unusual flair. Crystals
bring color and sparkle to any outfit.

Follow the pattern below to make a flower spring to life amidst the crystals, as in the earrings on p. 59.

MATERIALS

one pair of earrings

- **74** 4mm bicone crystals
- 1g size 11º Japanese cylinder or seed beads
- 24 in. (61cm) 22-gauge wire
- 30 in. (76cm) fine chain (about 20 links per inch)
- **16** 1-in. (2.5cm) head pins (optional)
- pair of earring findings
- chainnose or flatnose pliers
- roundnose pliers
- wire cutters

step*by*step

[1] Cut the chain into two 87-link sections, two 53-link sections, two 47-link sections, and two 41-link sections. Cut the length of wire in half.

[2] Attach an earring finding to the middle link of an 87-link chain.

[3] Make a small plain loop (see Basics, p. 10) at the end of the wire and flatten it with flatnose or chainnose pliers (photo a). String a cylinder or 11º seed bead.

[4] Go through the seventeenth link from the earring finding (don't count the link attached to the earring finding). Pick up a 4mm bicone crystal, and go through the corresponding link on the other half of the chain (photo b).

[5] Pick up an 11º, and cut off the remaining wire, leaving just enough to make a matching plain loop. Make a plain loop (photo c). Set aside the remaining wire for the next row.

[6] For the following rows, prepare the wire as in step 3, and string an 11º. Finish each row as in step 5.

Row 2: Skip two links, and go through the next link in the 87-link chain. Pick up a crystal, the middle link of the 53-link chain, and a crystal. Go through the corresponding link on the other half of the 87-link chain (photo d).

Row 3: Skip two links, and go through the next link on the 87-link chain. Add a

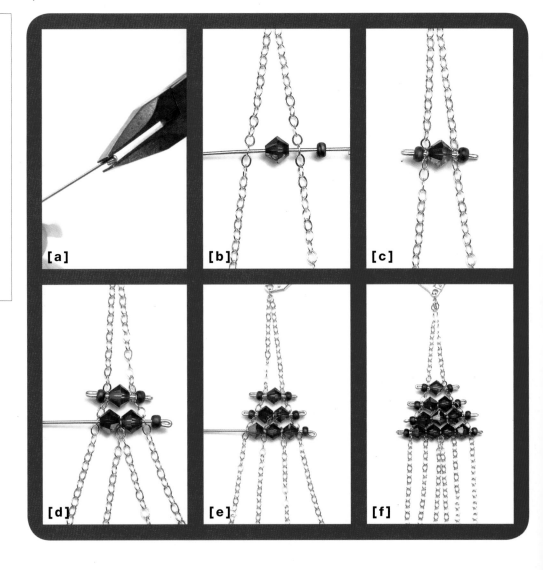

[a]

[b]

[c]

[d]

[e]

[f]

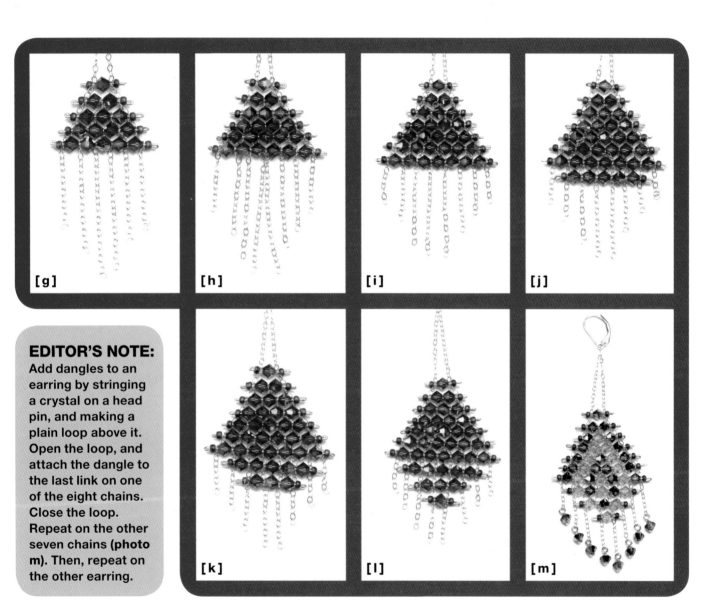

[g]

[h]

[i]

[j]

[k]

[l]

[m]

EDITOR'S NOTE:
Add dangles to an earring by stringing a crystal on a head pin, and making a plain loop above it. Open the loop, and attach the dangle to the last link on one of the eight chains. Close the loop. Repeat on the other seven chains (photo m). Then, repeat on the other earring.

crystal between the next three chains (photo e).
Row 4: Skip two links, and go through the next link on the 87-link chain. Pick up a crystal, and go through the corresponding link on the 53-link chain. Pick up a crystal, the middle link of the 47-link chain, and a crystal. Go through the corresponding link on the 53-link chain. Pick up a crystal, and go through the

corresponding link on the 87-link chain (photo f).
Row 5: Skip two links, and add a crystal between each chain (photo g).
Row 6: Skip two links, and add a crystal between each chain, increasing the middle as in rows 2 and 4 with the 41-link chain (photo h).
Row 7: Repeat row 5 (photo i).
Row 8: Skip two links, and add a crystal between the

six inner chains (photo j), omitting the two outer chains.
Row 9: Skip two links, and add a crystal between the four inner chains (photo k).
Row 10: Skip two links, and add a crystal between the two inner chains (photo l).
[7] Make a second earring to match the first.

Delicate drops

Dangle crystal briolettes from chain for a dainty necklace-and-earrings set

by **Helene Tsigistras**

Sparkling crystals add character to a basic chain necklace. It's simple enough for everyday wear, so you'll find yourself reaching for it often.

stepbystep

Necklace

[1] Make a 45-degree bend ¾ in. (1.9cm) from the end of the wire with your chainnose pliers. Slide a crystal next to the bend, and make another 45-degree bend on the other side of the crystal **(photo a)**.

Make two wraps above the crystal with the wire remaining from the first bend **(photo b)**. Trim the excess wire. Cut the long wire 1½ in. (3.8cm) above the wraps. Repeat for a total of eight dangles.

[2] Make the first half of a wrapped loop (see Basics, p. 10) above the wraps on one of the dangles.

[3] Repeat step 2 with the remaining dangles.

[4] Attach the loop to the twelfth large link from one

MATERIALS

both projects
- chainnose pliers
- roundnose pliers
- wire cutters

necklace 19 in. (48cm)
- **8** 5 x 10mm briolette crystals
- toggle clasp
- 25 in. (64cm) 22-gauge wire
- 18 in. (46cm) figure 8 chain, 5mm links
- **2** jump rings

one pair of earrings
- **6** 5 x 10mm teardrop crystals
- **4** 4mm bicone crystals
- 10 in. (25cm) 22-gauge wire
- 2½ in. (6.4cm) figure 8 chain, 5mm links
- **4** 24-gauge head pins
- pair of earring findings

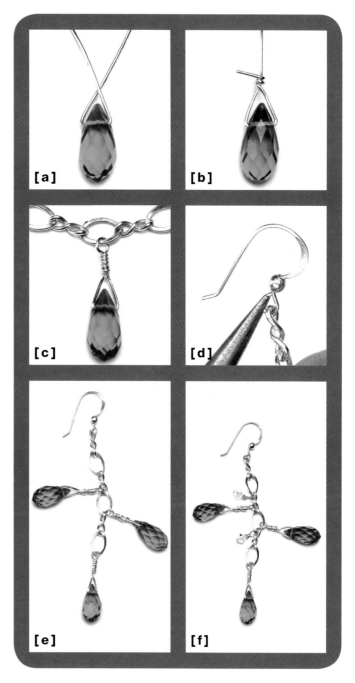

[a] [b] [c] [d] [e] [f]

end of the chain. Finish the wraps **(photo c)**. Trim the excess wire.

[5] Skip a large link and attach a dangle to the next large link. Finish the wraps.

[6] Repeat step 5 with the remaining dangles.

[7] Open a jump ring (Basics), and connect the last link of the chain to one clasp half. Repeat on the other end with the other clasp half.

Earrings

[1] Cut two pieces of chain with three figure 8 links and three large links each. Attach the earring finding to the end figure 8 link of one piece **(photo d)**.

[2] Make three dangles as in step 1 of the necklace. Attach the first dangle to the bottom half of the second figure 8 link with a wrapped loop. Repeat with the other two dangles, attaching one to the second large link and one to the third large link **(photo e)**.

[3] String a 4mm bicone crystal on a head pin, and make the first half of a wrapped loop. Attach the loop to the top half of the second figure 8 link, and finish the wraps. Repeat with a second 4mm, and attach it to the top half of the third figure 8 link **(photo f)**.

[4] Make a second earring to match the first.

Charming glass spirals

Coiled wire loops
highlight glass charms

by **Cheryl Phelan**

MATERIALS

bracelet 8 in. (20cm)

- **13–16** 12–15mm disk-shaped glass beads (Family Glass, familyglasskc.com)
- **14–16** 10mm round stone or glass beads
- **4** 3mm round silver spacers
- **4** 4mm flat silver spacers
- toggle clasp
- 4 ft. (1.2m) 24-gauge sterling silver wire, half-hard
- **13–16** 6.8 x 4.7mm, 18-gauge oval jump rings (Rio Grande, riogrande.com)
- 2 crimp beads
- 2 crimp covers (optional)
- flexible beading wire, .014
- chainnose pliers
- crimping pliers (optional)
- roundnose pliers
- wire cutters

The unusual shape and radiant colors of these disk-shaped glass beads are irresistible. Showcase them in this sophisticated version of the classic charm bracelet.

step*by*step

Charms

[1] Cut a 3-in. (7.6cm) piece of 24-gauge wire. Using roundnose pliers, start at one end of the wire, and roll a loop large enough to accommodate an oval jump ring **(photo a)**.

[2] Hold the loop with chainnose pliers. Apply pressure to the straight wire with your index finger while turning the loop with the pliers to form a spiral **(photo b)**.

[3] Continue coiling the wire around the initial loop for two or three revolutions. Then bend the straight wire at a right angle below the coiled spiral **(photo c)**.

[4] Slide a disk-shaped glass bead on the wire. Bend the wire so the spiral is slightly higher than the edge of the bead. Then bring the wire up against the back of the bead so it is parallel with the straight wire under the spiral **(photo d)**.

[5] Trim the straight wire to 1 in. (2.5cm) above the spiral. Start at the end of the wire, and make a second spiral to match the first **(photo e)**.

[6] Open an oval jump ring (see Basics, p. 10), and slide it through the center loop of both spirals **(photo f)**. Close the jump ring.

[7] With chainnose pliers, make bends in the straight wire that resemble a zigzag or lightning bolt **(photo g)**. These decorative bends will snug the wire against the bead.

[8] Repeat steps 1–7 with the remaining disk beads.

Assembly

[1] Cut a 12-in. (30cm) length of flexible beading wire, and tape one end to your work surface. Starting with a 10mm round bead, string a charm between 10mm rounds **(photo h)** until your bracelet is about 1½–2 in. (3.8–5cm) short of the desired length.

[2] String a flat spacer, a 3mm spacer, a flat spacer, a crimp bead, and a 3mm spacer. Bring the wire through the loop of a clasp half and back through the beads just strung **(photo i)**.

[3] Remove the tape from the other end of the beading wire, and repeat step 2 with the other clasp half. Leave a little slack between the beads so the charms hang freely on the wire.

[4] Carefully check the fit of the bracelet, and add or remove beads as necessary. Crimp the crimp beads (Basics), and trim the excess wire. Cover each crimp bead with a crimp cover if desired.

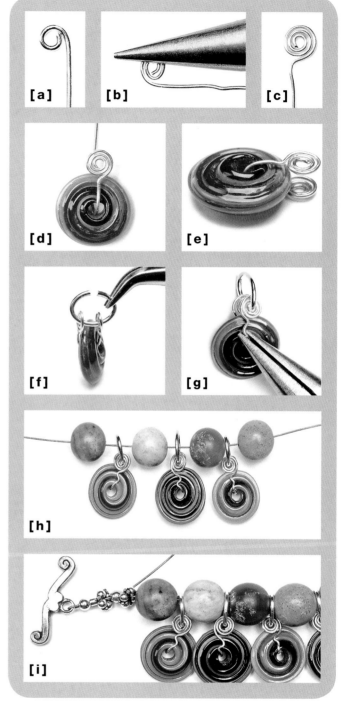

[a] [b] [c] [d] [e] [f] [g] [h] [i]

Uptown charm bracelet

Crystal pearls dance and swing on this charming bracelet with matching earrings

by **Maryann Scandiffio-Humes**

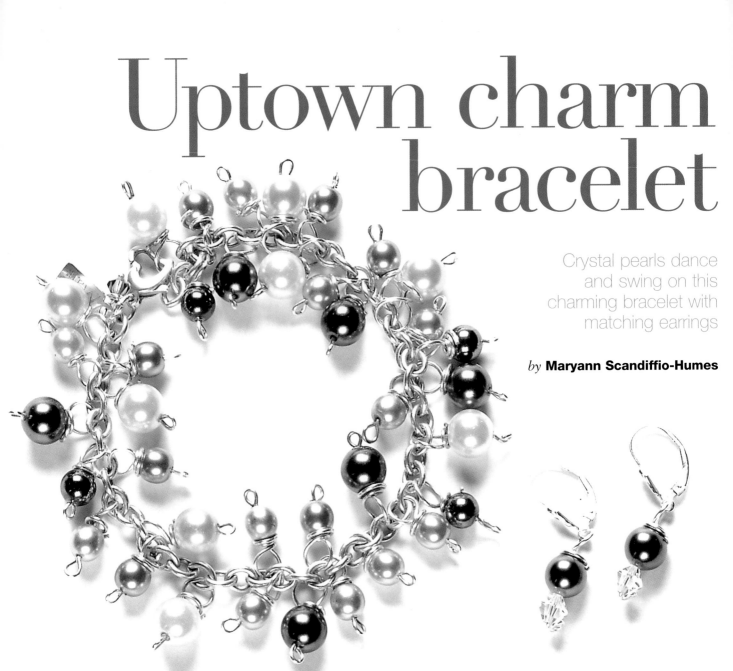

For another alternative to the traditional charm bracelet, try pearls. Embellished with spiraling wire caps, they take the look from casual to upscale.

step*by*step

The wrapped loops used in these projects are larger than standard wrapped loops and should have little or no stem at the base. This allows you to begin the wraps right on top of the bead, producing a spiraling cap. Be sure to get comfortable with the technique using craft or copper wire before beginning the project.

Bracelet

[1] Cut a 2½-in. (6.4cm) piece of wire, and make a plain loop (Basics, p. 10 and **photo a**) at one end.

[2] String a pearl, and bend the wire at a right angle (**photo b**).

[3] Using the wide part of the roundnose pliers, make the first half of a large wrapped loop (Basics) right above the bead (**photo c**). Repeat, making a total of 37 pearl dangles.

[4] Slide the loop of a pearl dangle into the end chain link (**photo d**). Repeat with the remaining pearls,

[a]

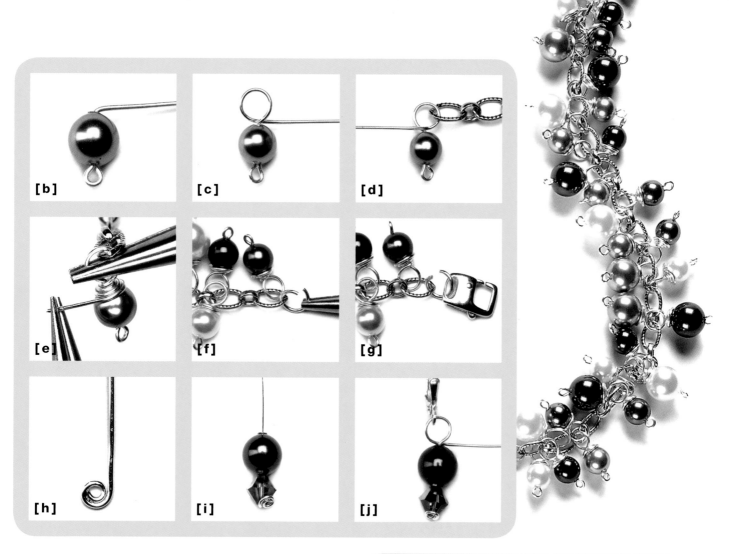

distributing the colors and sizes evenly along the length and on both sides of the chain.

[5] When you're pleased with the placement of the pearls, grasp the wire tail on a dangle, and wrap it around the base of the loop. Continue wrapping two or three times around the top of the pearl, forming a spiral cap **(photo e)**. Trim the excess wire. Repeat with the remaining pearl dangles.

[6] Open a jump ring (Basics), and attach it to the end link at one end of the chain **(photo f)**. Attach the clasp **(photo g)**, and close the jump ring.

[7] If desired, make a crystal dangle, and attach it to one end of the bracelet.

Earrings

[1] Cut a 3-in. (7.6cm) piece of wire, and make a small coil at one end **(photo h)**. String a crystal and a pearl, and press the coil up against the crystal **(photo i)**.

[2] Make the first half of a large wrapped loop above the bead, as in steps 2 and 3 of the bracelet.

[3] Slide the dangle through the loop on an earring finding **(photo j)**, and finish the spiraling wraps, as in step 5 of the bracelet. Trim the excess wire.

[4] Make a second earring to match the first.

EDITOR'S NOTE:

To adapt this design, try one of the following options:
- **Combine a colorful assortment of glass beads for casual wear.**
- **Mix Bali silver or vermeil with crystals for a glamorous look.**
- **Use only white pearls for classic appeal.**

MATERIALS

both projects
- chainnose pliers
- roundnose pliers
- wire cutters

bracelet 7½ in. (19.1cm)
- **15** 8mm round crystal pearls in **3** colors
- **22** 6mm round crystal pearls in **5** colors
- 4mm bicone crystal (optional)
- clasp

- 8 ft. (2.4m) 22-gauge wire, half-hard
- 7¼ in. (18.4cm) cable chain, 6mm links
- 4–5mm jump ring

one pair of earrings
- **2** 8mm round crystal pearls
- **2** 5–6mm bicone crystals
- 6 in. (15cm) 22-gauge wire, half-hard
- pair of earring findings

Cluster bangle

Gemstone clusters highlight
a lampworked focal bead

by **Jennifer Cook**

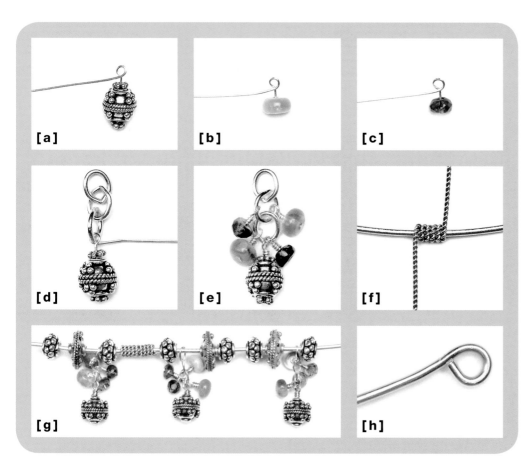

[a]

[b]

[c]

[d]

[e]

[f]

[g]

[h]

MATERIALS

bracelet 8 in. (20cm)

- 10 x 15mm lampworked focal bead* (Jennifer Cook, jmcglassart.com)
- 6 6–8mm round silver beads
- gemstone rondelles 8-in. (20cm) strand 6mm 8-in. strand 4mm
- silver spacers
  6 4 x 17mm disk*
  10–12 4 x 9mm*
  12 3mm daisy (optional)
- S-hook clasp or 4½ in. (11.4cm) 14-gauge sterling silver wire
- 2 12–14mm bead caps*
- sterling silver wire
  1 ft. (30cm) 14-gauge
  1 ft. 18-gauge, twisted
  5 ft. (1.5m) 28-gauge, dead-soft
- 5 in. (13cm) cable chain, 6–8mm links
- 30 1½-in. (3.8cm) 24-gauge sterling silver head pins)
- permanent marker
- chainnose pliers
- roundnose pliers
- wire cutters

* holes must be large enough to fit over 14-gauge wire

Combine sterling silver, gemstones, and an art glass bead in this stunning wire bangle. A hand-fashioned clasp completes the design.

step*by*step

Components

[1] Measure your wrist, add 2¼ in. (5.7cm), and cut the 14-gauge wire to this length.
[2] String a 6–8mm round silver bead on a head pin, and make the first half of a wrapped loop (see Basics, p. 10 and photo a). If the bead's hole is large, string a 3mm daisy spacer on each end, as shown. Repeat with the remaining five 6–8mm beads.
[3] String a 6mm rondelle on a head pin, and make the first half of a wrapped loop

(photo b). Make a total of 12 6mm rondelle dangles.
[4] Repeat step 3 using 4mm rondelles (photo c).
[5] Cut six three-link pieces of chain.
[6] Attach the loop of a silver-bead dangle to an end link of one chain piece (photo d). Finish the wraps. Attach one silver dangle to each of the five remaining chain pieces.
[7] Attach a 6mm dangle and a 4mm dangle to the same link as the silver dangle. Attach a 6mm dangle and a 4mm dangle to the middle chain link

(photo e). Repeat with the remaining five chain pieces.
[8] Fold the twisted wire in half, and place the 14-gauge wire in the fold. Wrap one end of the twisted wire around the 14-gauge wire to make a coil (photo f). When you've finished coiling one end, repeat with the other end. Remove the coil from the 14-gauge wire. Cut the coil in half.

Assembly

[1] On the 14-gauge wire, center a bead cap, the focal bead, and a bead cap.

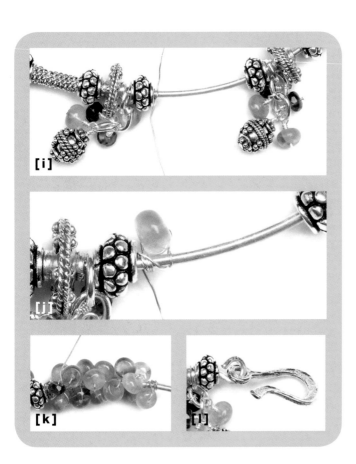

[i]

[j]

[k]

[l]

EDITOR'S NOTE:
The gemstone clusters on the bracelet below are closer to the focal bead than to the clasp. To achieve this placement, string the focal bead, bead caps, and the first four components in step 2 of "Assembly." Skip the twisted-wire coil, and string the next four components. String the coil, and complete the stringing sequence.

TEMPLATE

the 6mms (photo k) and filling any gaps as desired. Secure the 28-gauge wire by carefully wrapping back toward the cluster a few times. Trim the excess wire, and press the end close to the 14-gauge wire. Repeat on the other side.

Clasp and finishing
[1] If desired, refer to the template (at left) to make a hook clasp with a 4½-in. (11.4cm) piece of 14-gauge wire.
[2] Open the loop (Basics) on one end of the bracelet, attach the clasp, and close the loop (photo l).
[3] Gently shape the bracelet to fit your wrist, and try it on. If it's too big, undo the loops, and remove a few beads or snip off a bit of the coils. Replace any desired beads, and redo the loops.

[2] On each end, string a 4 x 9mm spacer, a disk spacer, the top link of a dangle chain, a 4 x 9mm, a twisted-wire coil, a 4 x 9mm, a dangle chain, a disk, two 4 x 9mms, a disk, a dangle chain, and a 4 x 9mm (photo g).
[3] With the widest part of your roundnose pliers, make a simple loop at one end of the 14-gauge wire (photo h). Repeat on the other end.
[4] You'll have a lot of free space on the 14-gauge wire for the gemstone clusters. To determine where they'll go, center the focal bead and bead caps, and arrange the rest of the beads so there is a gap between the pairs of 4 x 9mm spacers on each end. Mark the wire with a permanent marker where the clusters will start and stop.

Gemstone clusters
[1] Cut the 28-gauge wire in half. On one piece, make a bend about 1 in. (2.5cm) from one end. Place the bend on one of the marks, and wrap the 28-gauge wire around the 14-gauge wire several times (photo i). Cross over the tail at least once. Trim the tail close to the 14-gauge wire, and press it down with chainnose pliers.
[2] String a 6mm rondelle on the 28-gauge wire, and, holding the bead in place, wrap the 28-gauge wire around the 14-gauge wire once to the right of the bead, once to the left of the bead (photo j), and again to the right of the bead. Repeat, attaching 6mm rondelles until you reach the marked point. Do not trim the wire.

[3] Make a cluster of 6mms on the other side of the bracelet with the remaining piece of 28-gauge wire.
[4] Continuing with the same piece of 28-gauge wire, string a 4mm rondelle, and, working in the other direction, repeat step 2, interspersing 4mms among

Chandelier
ensemble

Hand-fashioned wire components
frame faceted beads

by **Julia Gerlach**

Make a delicate pendant-
and-earring ensemble
with tiers of wire arches.
Accented with small,
faceted dangles, this set is
light as a feather and oh,
so wearable.

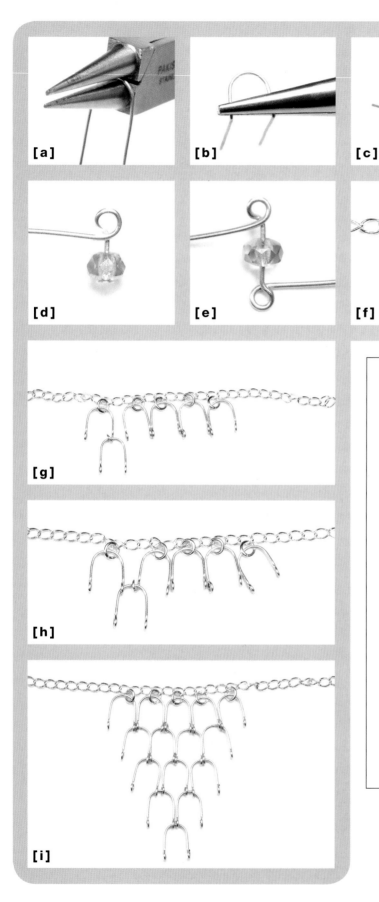

[a]

[b]

[c]

[d]

[e]

[f]

[g]

[h]

[i]

step*by*step

Necklace
Components

[**1**] Cut 15 1½-in. (3.8cm) pieces of 22-gauge wire.
[**2**] Curve a piece of wire around the widest part of one jaw of your roundnose pliers, forming an arch (**photo a**).
[**3**] Using your chainnose pliers, bend each wire end into a right angle $5/16$ in. (8mm) from the curve (**photo b**).
[**4**] Trim the wire ends to $5/16$ in., and make a small plain loop (see Basics, p. 10 and **photo c**) on each.
[**5**] Repeat steps 2–4 with the remaining 14 wires.
[**6**] String a 3 x 5mm rondelle on a head pin, and make the first half of a wrapped loop (Basics and **photo d**). Repeat with the remaining 24 head pins.
[**7**] Cut a 2½-in. (6.4cm) piece of wire, and make the first half of a wrapped loop on one end. String a rondelle, and make the first half of a wrapped loop on the other end (**photo e**). Make a total of six wrapped-loop units.
[**8**] Cut six 1¾-in. (4.4cm) pieces of chain.

Assembly

[**1**] Cut a 3¾-in. (9.5cm) piece of chain with an odd number of links.
[**2**] Open a 4mm jump ring (Basics), and slide it through the center chain link. Attach a wire arch, and close the jump ring (**photo f**).
[**3**] On each side of the first arch, skip two or three links, and repeat step 2 with another wire arch, making sure that the loops at the base of the arches all face the same way.

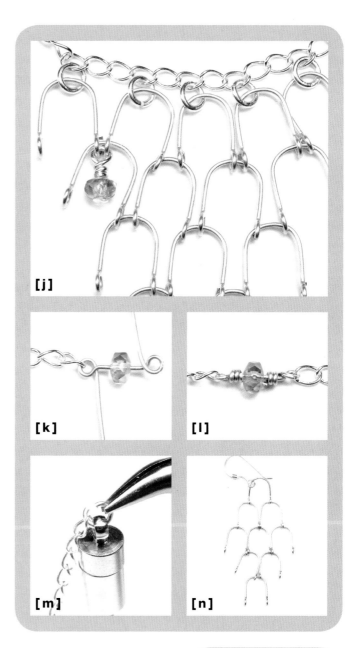

[j]

[k]

[l]

[m]

[n]

Repeat. Make any necessary adjustments so that the five arches hang side by side without overlapping or leaving gaps.

[4] Open the inner loop of an end arch, and attach the curved part of an arch **(photo g)**. Close the loop. Open the loop of the adjacent arch, and attach it to the same arch **(photo h)**.

[5] Continue connecting arches in this manner until you have five rows: five arches in the first row, four in the second, three in the third, two in the fourth, and one in the final row **(photo i)**.

[6] Attach the loop of a rondelle dangle to two adjacent arch loops. Finish the wraps **(photo j)**. Repeat to attach a rondelle dangle at each single loop and pair of loops. Also, attach one rondelle dangle to each jump ring that connects the pendant to the chain.

[7] Attach one loop of a wrapped-loop unit to the end chain link **(photo k)**. Finish the wraps on this loop.

[8] Attach an end link of a 1¾-in. piece of chain to the other wrapped loop. Finish the wraps **(photo l)**.

[9] Repeat steps 7 and 8 twice.

[10] Repeat steps 7–9 on the other end.

[11] Open a jump ring, and connect the end chain link to the clasp **(photo m)**. Close the loop. Repeat on the other end.

Earrings

[1] Make 18 wire arches as in steps 1–4 of the necklace components.

[2] Make 28 rondelle dangles as in step 6 of the necklace components.

[3] Open the loop of an earring finding, and attach it to one wire arch. Close the loop.

[4] Connect the wire arches so you have five rows: one arch in the first row, two in the second, three in the third, two in the fourth, and one in the final row **(photo n)**.

[5] Attach the rondelle dangles as in step 6 of the necklace assembly.

[6] Repeat steps 3–5 to make a second earring.

EDITOR'S NOTE:
When you're not wearing these pieces, hang them up to prevent tangling.

Clever petals

MATERIALS

one pair of earrings

- 6mm bicone crystals
  2 color A
  2 color B
- 4mm bicone crystals
  2 color C
  2 color D
- **6** 3–6mm silver spacers
  or bead caps
- 10 in. (25cm) 18-gauge
  wire, dead-soft
- 8 in. (20cm) 24-gauge
  wire, dead-soft
- pair of earring findings
- hammer
- steel block or anvil
- drill with diamond bit
  (optional)
- chainnose pliers
- roundnose pliers
- wire cutters

Bring the garden indoors with a pair of easy flower earrings. This whimsical summertime accessory blooms all year long.

step*by*step

[1] Cut a 5-in. (13cm) piece of 18-gauge wire. Using roundnose pliers, roll one end of the wire into a small loop **(photo a)**.
[2] Refer to the template in **figure 1**, and continue bending the wire into a flower shape **(photo b)**. Trim any excess wire.
[3] Place the flower shape on a steel block or anvil, and use a hammer to flatten and harden it **(photo c)**. Adjust the flower shape with pliers as needed.

To give the wire a textured surface, you can carve a design into the head of a hammer **(photo d)** using a drill with a diamond bit before you hammer the wire.
[4] Cut a 4-in. (10cm) piece of 24-gauge wire. Roll one end of the wire into a small loop as in step 1. Continue rolling until you have two loops **(photo e)**.

Add a burst of color to wire flowers

by **Wendy Witchner**

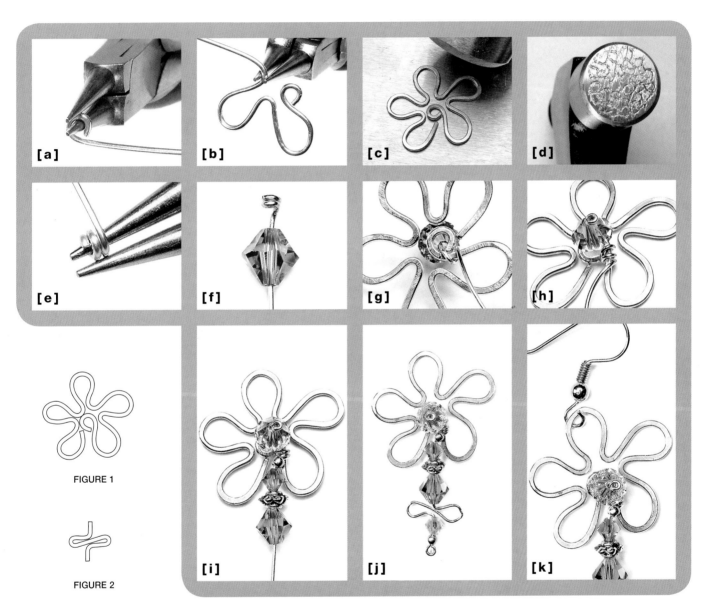

[a]

[b]

[c]

[d]

[e]

[f]

[g]

[h]

FIGURE 1

[i]

[j]

[k]

FIGURE 2

[5] Make a bend in the wire directly below the loops, and string a 6mm color A crystal on the wire **(photo f)**.
[6] Bring the end of the wire through the flower's center loop. Secure the crystal in the loop by wrapping the wire around the side of the petal below the loop **(photo g)**.

Make a couple more wraps, and end with the wire crossing over the front of the petal **(photo h)**.
[7] String a silver spacer or bead cap, a 4mm color C crystal, a silver spacer or bead cap, and a 6mm color B crystal **(photo i)**.
[8] Position these beads

against the flower, and bend the wire directly below the beads as shown in **figure 2**.
[9] String a 4mm color D crystal and a silver spacer or bead cap. Make a small loop (see Basics, p. 10) or coil, and trim the excess wire **(photo j)**.
[10] Open the loop on an earring finding, and connect it

to the middle petal **(photo k)**. Close the loop.
[11] Make a second earring to match the first.

75

Sculptural art

glass necklace

An innovative wire frame supports a harvest of art beads

by **Alice St. Germain**

Like many lampworkers, Alice St. Germain is always on the lookout for interesting shapes and color combinations to turn into beads. During a trip to a farmers market, she was unexpectedly inspired by a bushel of colorful squash known as pattypans. After creating beads based on these strange and wonderful vegetables, she developed an interlocking wire structure that allows many stylish combinations of the disk-shaped beads.

step*by*step

Glass beads

[1] Cut a 12-in. (30cm) piece of 18-gauge wire. Place flatnose pliers at the center of the wire, and fold half the wire over the jaw of the pliers **(photo a)**. Pinch the bend closed **(photo b)**.

[2] Use roundnose pliers to turn the bend into a loop **(photo c)**. Adjust the placement of the pliers, make a second loop, and make a bend under both loops to create an S shape in the wire **(photo d)**.

[3] Slide a glass bead over both wire ends and against the S shape. With flatnose or chainnose pliers, bend both wires against the back of the bead to hold it in place **(photo e)**.

[4] Make a slight bend in one of the wires approximately 2 in. (5cm) from the bead's hole. Form the wire around a pencil or other mandrel to make a large loop. Then, bend the wire where it meets the first bend **(photo f)**.

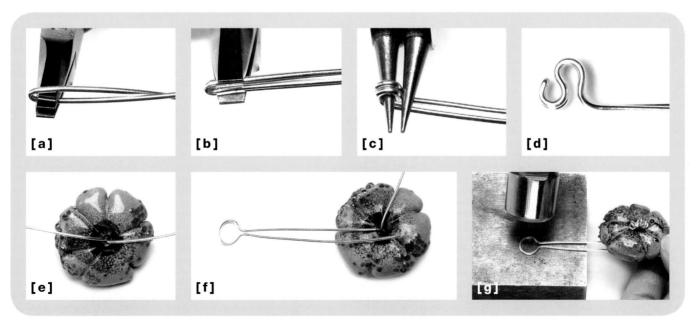

[a]   [b]   [c]   [d]

[e]   [f]   [g]

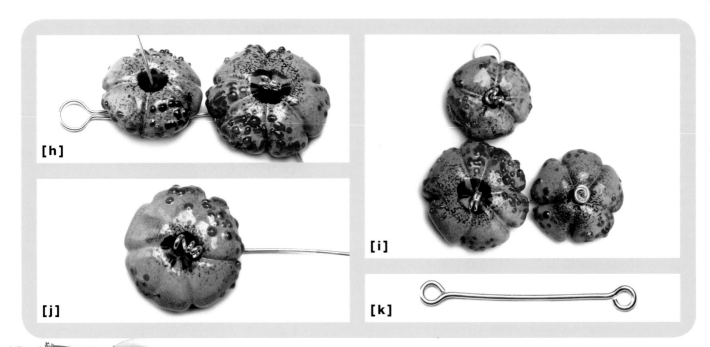

[h]

[j]

[i]

[k]

Behind the scenes
The key steps to connecting the glass-bead components are hidden on the back of the necklace. Refer to **points a–b** as you work step 11 and **points c–d** as you work step 12.

a

b

d

c

[5] Place the loop on an anvil or steel block, and hammer the loop to flatten and harden it **(photo g)**.
[6] Grasp the wire end halfway between the loop and the bead with flatnose pliers, and make a right-angle bend in the wire so it is pointing up. Slide a glass bead on the wire **(photo h)**.
[7] Using roundnose pliers, make a free-form coil in the wire as close to the bead as possible. Trim the excess wire.

MATERIALS
necklace 19 in. (48cm)
- 5 28–35mm disk-shaped glass beads (Succulent Glass, 410-746-7046)
- **5–7** 4mm bicone crystals
- **2** 3mm round silver beads
- **2** 4mm flat spacers
- clasp
- **2** silver cones
- sterling silver wire
  10–16 in. (25–41cm) 26- or 24-gauge, dead-soft
  6 in. (15cm) 22-gauge, half-hard
  29 in. (74cm) 18-gauge, half-hard
- 24–48 in. (61–120cm) ¼–½ in. (6–13mm) ribbon
- anvil or steel block
- hammer
- chainnose pliers
- flatnose pliers
- roundnose pliers
- wire cutters

[l]   [m]   [n]   [o]

[p]   [q]   [r]   [s]

[8] Repeat steps 6 and 7 with the other wire end to add a third glass bead. Adjust the wires so the placement of the beads resembles a V or L shape **(photo i)**.
[9] Cut an 8-in. (20cm) piece of 18-gauge wire. Using roundnose pliers, make a few coils at one end of the wire. String a glass bead against the coils, and bend the wire against the bead to hold it in place **(photo j)**.
[10] Repeat steps 4–7 to make a second large loop and connect a glass bead.
[11] Cut a 2-in. piece of 18-gauge wire, and make a loop at each end (see Basics, p. 10 and **photo k**). Open each loop. Connect one loop to the wire on the center bead of the three-bead section, and connect the other loop to the second bead of the two-bead section. Close the loops (p. 78, **a–b**).
[12] Cut a 3-in. (7.6cm) piece of 18-gauge wire and make a small free-form coil at one end of the wire. Slide the wire through the third bead on the three-bead section so the coil is on the front side of the bead. Bend the wire against the back of the bead to hold it in place. Trim the wire as necessary, make a loop, and connect it to the loop on the two-bead section (p. 78, **c–d**).

Crystal accents
[1] Cut a 6-in. (15cm) piece of 24- or 26-gauge wire, and fold the tip of the wire back with chainnose pliers. If you are using 26-gauge wire, you may need

to bend the end of the wire a second time to keep the crystal from sliding off. String a crystal on the wire **(photo l)**. Slide the wire through the center of one of the glass beads.
[2] Wrap the 24- or 26-gauge wire around the 18-gauge wire on the back of the glass bead **(photo m)**. These wraps secure the crystal and give added support to the glass beads and 18-gauge wire form. Trim the excess wire.
[3] Continue adding crystals to the other glass beads as desired. If a glass bead needs extra support, or if you need to fill the hole, string a crystal to the center of a 10-in. (25cm) piece of 26-gauge wire. Bend both ends of the wire down and against the sides of the crystal **(photo n)**. Working one end of the wire at a time, wrap it around an 18-gauge wire on the back of the glass bead, as in step 2.

Finishing
[1] For a 19-in. (48cm) necklace, cut two 12-in. pieces of ribbon. Center the ribbon in one of the large wire loops. When using ¼-in. (6mm) ribbon, use two 12-in. pieces of ribbon on each side.
[2] Cut a 2-in. piece of 18-gauge wire. Place flatnose pliers ½-in. (1.3cm) from the end of the wire, and fold the wire over one jaw of the pliers, as in **photo a**. Adjust the placement of the pliers, and continue wrapping the long wire over one jaw of the pliers until there are two

wraps on the bottom and three wraps on the top **(photo o)**.
[3] Trim the end of the wires to ⅜ in. (1cm) so both wire ends are the same length.
[4] Use roundnose pliers to make a loop at one end of the wire, and center it above the wraps **(photo p)**. Repeat with the other end so the second loop coils in the opposite direction of the first.
[5] Slide the wire coil over both ends of the ribbon and close to the large loop **(photo q)**.
[6] Cut a 3-in. piece of 22-gauge wire, and make the first half of a wrapped loop at one end (Basics). Fold in the ends of the ribbon about ¼–1 in., depending on the desired finished length of the necklace. Pierce the fold in the ribbon with the wire, and slide the ribbon onto the loop **(photo r)**. Finish the wrap.
[7] String a cone, a flat spacer, and a round silver bead on the wire. Make the first half of a wrapped loop, and slide a clasp half onto the loop **(photo s)**. Finish the wraps.
[8] Repeat steps 1–7 on the other end of the necklace.

EDITOR'S NOTE:
You can use long, decorative head pins to add crystals to the glass beads.

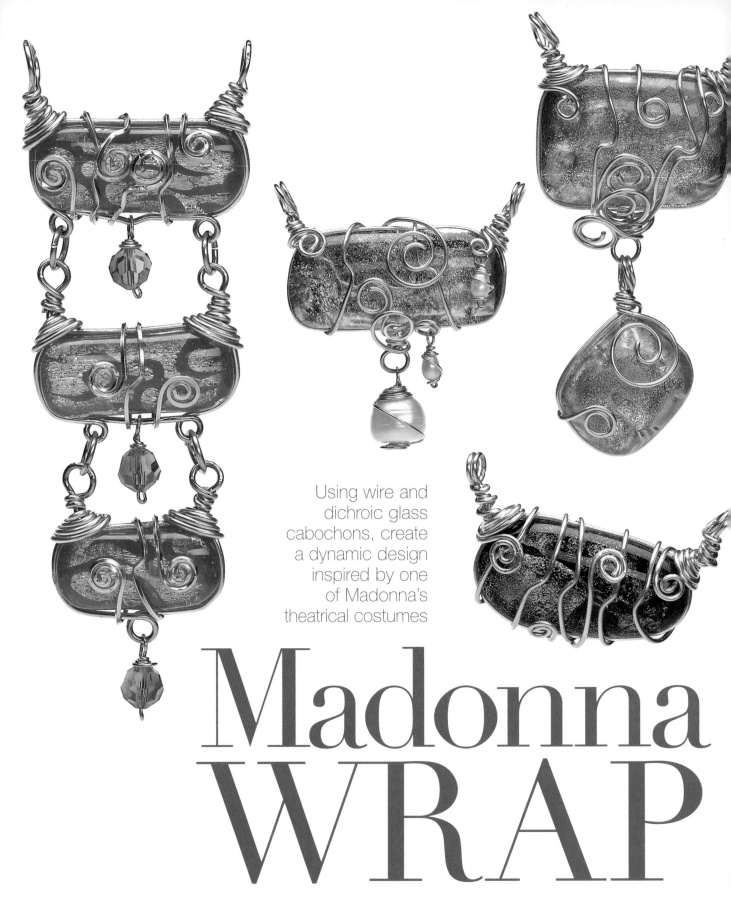

Using wire and
dichroic glass
cabochons, create
a dynamic design
inspired by one
of Madonna's
theatrical costumes

Madonna
WRAP

by Julia Coale Freeform wire wraps and spirals turn a glass
cabochon into a fabulous pendant. Add beads
or more cabs for even more pizzazz.

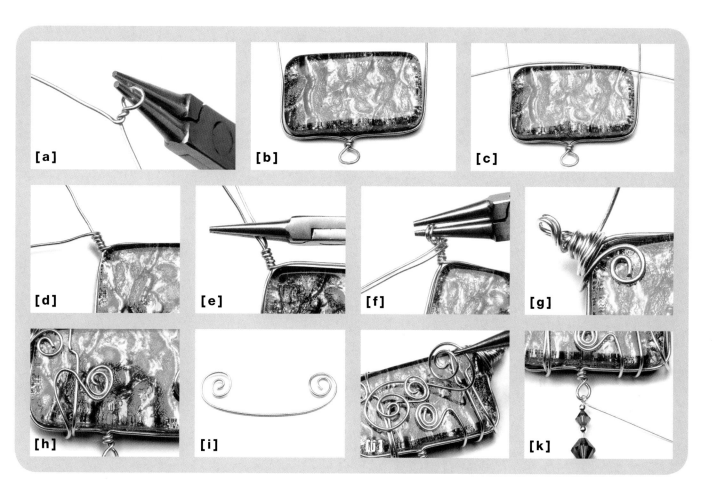

stepbystep

[1] Cut a 2-ft. (61cm) length of 20-gauge wire. Holding the center of the wire in your roundnose pliers, make a loop and twist the two ends together (photo a).

[2] Center the loop along the bottom edge of the cabochon and bend the wires along the sides until both ends are sticking straight up (photo b).

[3] Cut an 18-in. (46cm) length of wire. Lay it across the top of the cab (photo c).

[4] Twist the intersecting wires together several times to create a ¼-in. (6mm) join (photo d). Repeat at the other corner.

[5] To make a loop, place both wires in the pliers (photo e). Bring the wires over the top and underneath the pliers. Reposition them as shown, and bring the wires around the twisted stem once (photo f). Repeat at the other corner.

[6] Wrap the shorter wire around the twisted stem. Finish with a spiral, and press it down onto the cab (photo g). Repeat at the other corner.

[7] Wrap the long wire vertically around the cab twice, ending with a spiral (photo h). Press the spiral onto the face of the cab. Tighten any loose wires by gripping the wire in the pliers, and pulling it away from the cab while twisting slowly.

[8] Make a loose spiral at each end of the remaining 6-in. (15cm) piece of 20-gauge wire (photo i). Link one end to another spiral on the face of the cab. Use your pliers to manipulate it into the desired design, and press it into place (photo j).

[9] Use 24-gauge wire or head pins to add dangles to the pendant (photo k) with wrapped loops (see Basics, p. 10). You can also use the 24-gauge wire or jump rings (Basics) to attach additional cabs (p. 80).

EDITOR'S NOTE:
Julia, along with close friends Pam Hall and Juliana Bendt, fuse their own wire-friendly glass cabochons. The artists rout grooves along the perimeter of the glass to give the wire an extra foothold. While you can use regular cabs for this project, the routed cabs make the initial wrapping much easier.

MATERIALS
cabochon pendant
1½ x 1 in. (3.8 x 2.5cm)
- fused dichroic glass cabochon (Julia Coale, 615-746-2253, galswithglass.com)
- assortment of beads for embellishment (optional)
- 4 ft. (1.2m) 20-gauge sterling silver or gold-filled wire, dead soft
- 24-gauge sterling silver wire, half-hard (optional)
- head pins (optional)
- jump rings (optional)
- ruler
- roundnose pliers
- wire cutters

Coiled wire

ensemble

Coils and spirals put a spin on wirework

by **Wendy Witchner**

Link spiraling wire components to make a bracelet that converts into a necklace. Make two more units for a great pair of earrings.

step*by*step

Bracelet

[1] Cut a 9-in. (23cm) piece of 20-gauge wire and a 16-in. (41cm) piece of 24-gauge wire. Fold the 24-gauge wire in half, and place the 20-gauge wire in the fold. Hold the wires in place with your nondominant hand, and tightly wrap the 24-gauge wire around the 20-gauge wire **(photo a)**.

[2] Working one end at a time, continue wrapping the 24-gauge wire around the 20-gauge wire to form a coil **(photo b)**. Approximately 8 in. (20cm) of 24-gauge wire makes a 1-in. (2.5cm) coil. Slide the coil off the 20-gauge wire, and cut the ends of the wire so they are flush against the coil.

EDITOR'S NOTE:
If you are having trouble forming the spirals, try 22-gauge wire as the core wire. The spirals won't be as stiff, but you can form the spiral shape easily using a round mandrel such as a pen.

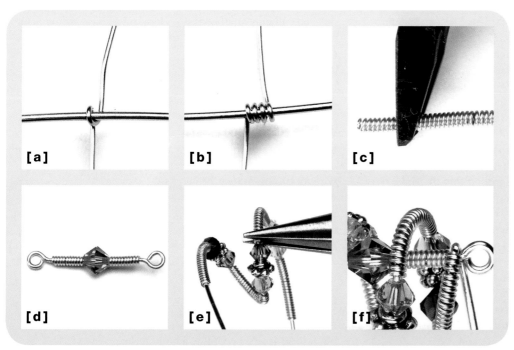

[a]

[b]

[c]

[d]

[e]

[f]

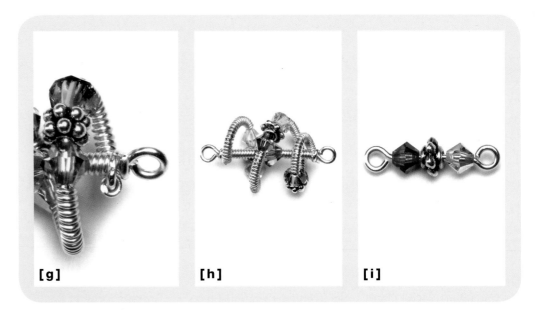

[g] [h] [i]

[3] Using the same piece of 20-gauge wire, repeat steps 1 and 2 with the remaining 24-gauge wire. Then set the 9-in. piece of 20-gauge wire aside until step 6.

[4] Cut ten ¼-in. (6mm) and 20 ½-in. (1.3cm) coils as shown in **photo c**.

[5] Cut a 1½-in. (3.8cm) piece of 20-gauge wire, and make a plain loop at one end (see Basics, p. 10). Slide a ¼-in. coil, a 6mm crystal, and a ¼-in. coil on the wire. Make a second loop in the same plane as the first, leaving a small space between the coils and the loops **(photo d)**. Make five crystal-and-coil components.

[6] Cut the 9-in. 20-gauge wire in half. On one of the 4½-in. (11.4cm) wires, string a ½-in. coil, a 4mm crystal, a 4–5mm spacer, and a 4mm crystal. Repeat the pattern twice more (three times total), then string another ½-in. coil.

[7] Using your fingers, gently form the wire into a spiral. Since the crystals fit snugly on the wire, hold the wire next to the crystals with a pair of pliers as you work to keep the crystals from cracking **(photo e)**.

[8] Bend the 20-gauge wire on each end into small hooks, just past the end coils. Slide the hooks onto a crystal-and-coil component, in the space between the coils and the loops **(photo f)**. Working one end at a time, wrap the wire end of the spiral around the component to hold it in place, and trim the excess wire **(photo g)**. Adjust the shape of the spiral as necessary so the crystal-and-coil component is centered in the spiral **(photo h)**.

[9] Repeat steps 6–8 four times, using the remaining 20-gauge wire.

[10] Cut a 1-in. piece of 20-gauge wire, and make a plain loop at one end. Slide a

4mm crystal, a 6–8mm flat spacer, and a 4mm crystal on the wire. Make a second plain loop in the same plane as the first **(photo i)**. Make four crystal components.

[11] Open a loop (Basics) on a crystal component from step 10, and connect it to a loop on a spiral component. Close the loop (Basics and **photo j**). Continue connecting the spirals with crystal components.

[12] Attach a jump ring to one of the end spiral loops. Connect the hook clasp to the remaining end spiral loop with the second jump ring.

Necklace extension

Make a chain extension that converts the bracelet to a 16-in. necklace, or wear it on its own as a second bracelet. (Make the extension 9½ in./24.1cm, and it can be worn as an ankle bracelet.)

[1] Repeat step 10 of the bracelet.

[j]

MATERIALS

both projects
- chainnose pliers
- roundnose pliers
- wire cutters

bracelet 8 in. (20cm)
- **5** 6mm bicone crystals
- **38** 4mm bicone crystals
- **4** 6–8mm flat silver spacers
- **15** 4–5mm flat silver spacers
- hook clasp
- 3 ft. (.9m) 20-gauge sterling silver wire, dead-soft
- 11 ft. (3.4m) 24-gauge sterling silver wire, dead-soft
- **2** 5mm jump rings

**necklace extension
8 in. (20cm)**
- **8** 4mm bicone crystals
- **4** 4–5mm flat silver spacers
- hook clasp
- 6–8 in. (15–20cm) chain, large links

one pair of earrings
- **4** 6mm bicone crystals
- **12** 4mm bicone crystals
- **6** 4–5mm flat silver spacers
- **2** 6mm silver bead caps
- 18 in. (46cm) 20-gauge sterling silver wire, dead-soft
- 6 ft. (1.8m) 24-gauge sterling silver wire, dead-soft
- **2** head pins
- pair of earring findings

[2] Cut three 1½-in. pieces of chain, and connect them with the crystal components.
[3] Cut two ½-in. pieces of chain, and connect them to the end crystal components.
[4] Connect the hook clasp to the end link on one of the ½-in. chains.
[5] Attach the chain extension to the bracelet as shown in the photo on p. 82.

Earrings

[1] Make four 1-in. (2.5cm) and two ¼-in. (6mm) coils.
[2] Repeat step 5 of the bracelet.
[3] Repeat steps 6–8 of the bracelet, using the 1-in. coils and a 6½-in. (16.5cm) piece of 20-gauge wire. The crystals will line up in a row down the side of the spiral.
[4] Slide a 6mm crystal and a bead cap on a head pin. Make a plain loop.
[5] Connect the head pin component to one end of the spiral and an earring finding to the other end.
[6] Make a second earring as the mirror image of the first.

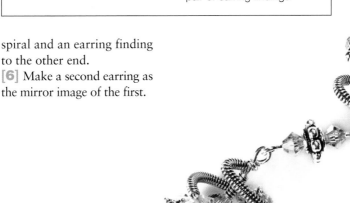

Coils & crystals

by **Wendy Witchner**

A few beads and a little wire are all it takes to make these easy earrings

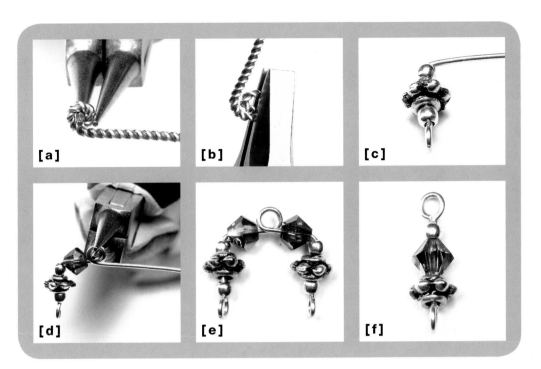

[a]

[b]

[c]

[d]

[e]

[f]

Coiled wire components give these earrings an ethnic flair. Crystals give them sparkle and verve.

step*by*step

[1] Cut a 4½-in. (11.4cm) piece of 20-gauge round or 22-gauge twisted wire. Grasp the tip of the wire with roundnose pliers and roll the end of the wire into a small loop **(photo a)**.

[2] Hold the loop with flatnose or chainnose pliers as shown in **photo b**. Place your index finger on the straight wire next to the loop, and add pressure with your finger while turning the loop with the pliers. Continue wrapping the wire around the initial loop until you have a flat coil **(figure 1)**.

[3] Refer to the template in **figure 2**, and, working from the bottom left coil to the right, bend the wire into the triangular shape.

[4] Place the triangular shape between two steel blocks, and hammer the top

block to flatten and stiffen the wire. Adjust the shape of the form with your pliers as needed.

[5] Cut a 2-in. (5cm) piece of 22-gauge wire, and make a loop at one end (see Basics, p. 10). String a 2mm round silver bead, a 4mm decorative silver bead, and a 2mm round bead. Working just above the beads, make a bend in the wire that is perpendicular to the loop **(photo c)**.

[6] String a 4mm color A crystal. With roundnose pliers, hold the wire next to the crystal, and bring the wire up and over the top jaw of the pliers. Reposition the pliers, and continue forming the wire around the bottom jaw **(photo d)**.

[7] Work the second half of the component as the mirror image of the first: String a 4mm A, and make a bend in the wire just past the crystal.

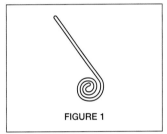

FIGURE 1

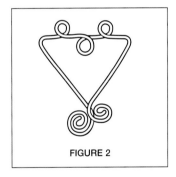

FIGURE 2

String a 2mm round bead, a 4mm decorative silver bead, and a 2mm round bead. Make a loop perpendicular to the bend and parallel to the first loop **(photo e)**.

[8] Cut a 1-in. (2.5cm) piece of 22-gauge wire, and make a loop at one end (Basics). String a 4mm decorative silver bead, a 4mm color B crystal, and a 2mm round bead. Make a loop above the

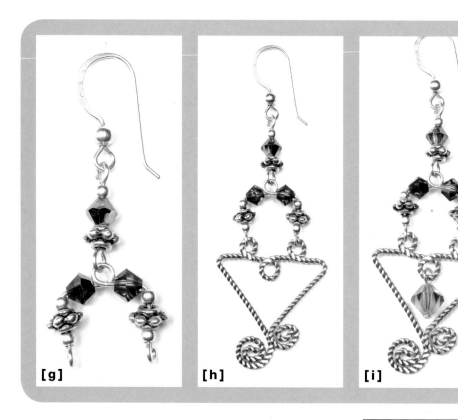

[g] [h] [i]

beads perpendicular to the first loop (photo f).

[9] Open the loop (Basics) next to the 2mm round bead on the component made in the previous step, slide it onto the loop of an earring finding, and close the loop (Basics). Open the other loop on the component, connect it to the loop between the crystals on the component shown in photo e, and close the loop (photo g).

[10] Open the bottom loops on the component, and connect them to the top loops of the coiled wire component. Close the loops (photo h).

[11] String a 6mm crystal on a head pin, and make a loop above the crystal. Open the loop, connect it to the center loop on the triangular shape, and close the loop (photo i).

[12] Make a second earring as the mirror image of the first.

MATERIALS
one pair of earrings

- bicone crystals
  2 6mm
  4 4mm, color A
  2 4mm, color B
- **6** 4mm decorative silver beads
- **10** 2mm round silver beads
- 9 in. (23cm) 20-gauge round or 22-gauge twisted sterling silver wire, half-hard
- 6 in. (15cm) 22-gauge round sterling silver wire, half-hard
- **2** head pins
- pair of earring findings
- hammer
- **2** steel blocks
- flatnose or chainnose pliers
- roundnose pliers
- wire cutters

Tips & Techniques

Cleaning tarnished spacers

Cleaning tarnished spacers thoroughly can be difficult because they're so small, so I devised the following method: To polish spacers on a finished piece, spray a cotton swab liberally with Hagerty's Silversmith's Spray Polish (or other spray polish), and rub the swab over each spacer until it's shiny. To polish loose spacers, place them on a cloth diaper or cotton rag, spray them with polish, and rub in a circular motion until shiny.
– Kelli Peduzzi, Poughkeepsie, N.Y.

Bead traveler

Empty travel sized baby-wipe containers make great storage for bead projects. They're lightweight, the right depth to hold tubes of beads and projects, and fit easily into a purse or carry-on. Best of all, you can recycle something that would otherwise end up in the garbage.

I line mine with a beading surface cut to fit. In fact, the container seals so tightly, you don't have to put the beads back in the tubes if you're in a rush to close up your beading. You won't lose anything.
– Sherry Magid, Skokie, Ill.

Cute-as-a-button pendant

Make your own pendant by attaching a button to a drilled donut. On a head pin, string a small bicone crystal, a button through its shank, and two or three seed beads. Insert the head pin through the donut hole from inner to outer edge, and make a wrapped loop (see Basics, p. 10) above the outer edge. String a second head pin through the donut's other hole. Make the first half of a wrapped loop, string a dangle, then complete the wraps.
– Pam O'Connor, Vienna, Va.

Works like clockwork

My blind grandfather accomplished his tasks easily by laying his tools out in a preplanned order. I use that approach with my beading tools. By placing them in a circle as if they were clock numbers, I always pick up the right tool without looking. It's efficient and easy to learn.
– Bonnie Elliott, Columbus, Ohio

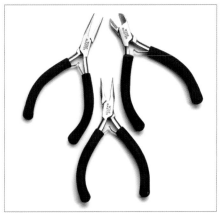

Design platforms

I found that the little racks used in Scrabble games to hold tiles are approximately 7 in. (18cm) long – perfect for designing a bracelet. The beads rest on the ledge, allowing them to be seen in an upright position – a better perspective than on a flat bead board. Three or four racks can be positioned side by side for necklaces also.
– Louise Lessing, via e-mail

stitching

Crystal tier

Easy-to-make earrings are long on style

by **Noriko Romanko**

Create earrings that reflect your personal style with an easy cross-needle stitch. Pair bicone crystals with faceted beads for an artsy flair, or with pearls for aristocratic elegance.

step*by*step

To make the longer version of these earrings, refer to the Editor's Note.

[1] Thread a needle on each end of 20 in. (51cm) of Fireline.

[2] Pick up one 6mm bead and one 15º seed bead. Repeat three times, and center the beads on the thread **(figure 1)**.

[3] Pull the beads into a ring, and tie a square knot (see Basics, p. 10). With one needle, go back through the first 6mm picked up, and tug gently to hide the knot inside the bead.

[4] With each needle, pick up a 15º, a 5mm bicone crystal, and a 15º **(figure 2)**.

[5] Pick up a 5mm on one needle, and cross the other

needle through it in the opposite direction **(figure 3)**.

[6] Repeat step 4.

[7] Pick up a 3mm bicone crystal on one needle, and cross the other needle through it in the opposite direction **(figure 4)**.

[8] With one needle, pick up six 15ºs, and sew back through the 3mm to make a loop **(figure 5, a–b)**. With the

earrings

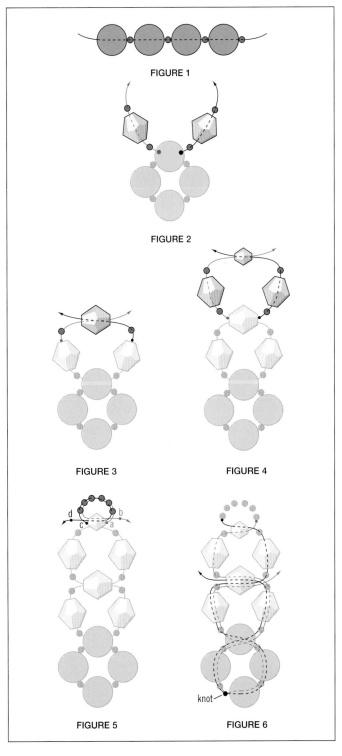

FIGURE 1

FIGURE 2

FIGURE 3

FIGURE 4

FIGURE 5

knot

FIGURE 6

other needle, sew through the six 15ºs and the 3mm in the opposite direction **(c–d)**.
[9] Retrace each thread path to the bottom 6mm, and tie a square knot on one side. Continue up through the 6mms and the bottom tier of 4mms **(figure 6)**. Trim the tails.

[10] Open the loop on an earring finding (Basics), and slide it through the loop of 15ºs.
[11] Make a second earring to match the first.

EDITOR'S NOTE: To make the longer version of the earrings (opposite right, and above), use 5mm bicone crystals for steps 4 and 5, then repeat steps 4–6 with 4mm bicones to add an extra tier of crystals for length and drama.

Cocktail ring

Dress up your fingers with sparkling rings

by **Anna Elizabeth Draeger**

Want to add a little glitz for a special occasion? These crystal rings work up fast and dress up any outfit.

step*by*step

Ring top

[1] On 2 yd. (1.8m) of Fireline, pick up an alternating pattern of four 4mm color A bicone crystals and four 3mm color C bicone crystals. Leaving a 24-in. (61cm) tail, tie them into a ring with a square knot (see Basics, p. 10). Sew through the next A and C (figure 1, a–b).

[2] Pick up a 3mm color D bicone crystal, an A, and a D. Sew back through the C, then continue on through the next A and C in the ring (b–c).

[3] Repeat step 2 three times, then continue through the next D and A (c–d).

[4] Pick up a 15º seed bead, a 4mm color B bicone crystal, and a 15º. Sew through the next A (d–e).

[5] Repeat step 4 three times (e–f), then reinforce the new bottom ring by retracing the thread path. Set the working thread aside, and pick up the tail, making sure the tail is exiting an inner A.

[6] Pick up a 15º, a D, a C, a D, and a 15º. Sew back through the A that the thread is exiting, and continue around the ring, exiting the opposite A (figure 2, a–b).

[7] Pick up a 15º and a D. Sew through the C from step 6 (b–c). Pick up a D and a 15º, and sew back through the A. Continue on through the next C and A (c–d). Secure the tail using half-hitch knots (Basics) between a few beads. Trim the tail.

Ring band

[1] With the working thread exiting a B, pick up a 15º, a C, a 15º, an A, a 15º, a C, and a 15º. Sew back through the B from the ring top (figure 3, a–b). Then sew through the 15º, the C, the 15º, and the A (b–c).

[2] Repeat step 1, using Ds instead of Cs and a B instead of an A (c–d).

[3] Repeat steps 1 and 2 nine times or until you reach the desired size.

[4] To connect the last row of the band, pick up a 15º, a C, and a 15º. Sew through the opposite B on the ring top. Then pick up a 15º, a C, and a 15º. Sew through the D from the ring band.

[5] Reinforce the band with another thread path, and secure the tail as before.

MATERIALS

one ring
- 4mm bicone crystals
  13 color A
  8 color B
- 3mm bicone crystals
  17 color C
  20 color D
- 1g size 15º Japanese seed beads
- Fireline 6 lb. test
- beading needles, #12

Note: For a larger ring top, substitute 6mm crystals for colors A and B and 4mm crystals for colors C and D in steps 1–5. Keep the crystals the same in steps 6 and 7.

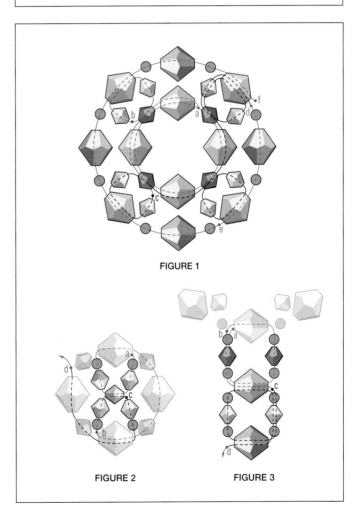

FIGURE 1

FIGURE 2

FIGURE 3

Vintage button bracelet

Bring your button collection to life when you make this bracelet using a quick two-needle technique

by **Melody MacDuffee**

Whether made of cut glass, metal, or Bakelite, the special qualities of vintage buttons imbue this bracelet with the glamour of a bygone era. An easy two-needle weave makes this project come together quickly

step*by*step

Base

[1] Thread a needle on each end of 4 ft. (1.2m) of Fireline or Power Pro. With one needle, pick up three color A 11º seed beads, the large button, three A 11ºs, a color B 11º seed bead, a 4mm color C fire-polished bead, and a B 11º. Center the beads and the button. Using the other needle, cross through the last three beads **(figure 1, a–b)**.

[2] On each needle, pick up four A 11ºs, a B 11º, and a color C 11º seed bead **(b–c, l–m)**. Cross both needles through the shank on a small button **(c–d, m–n)**.

[3] Pick up a C 11º, a B 11º, two A 11ºs, and three 3mm fire-polished beads on each needle **(d–e, n–o)**. Go back through the last four beads before the shank, cross through the shank, and continue through the first four beads after the shank **(e–f, o–p)**.

[4] Pick up an A 11º, a B 11º, and a C 11º on each needle **(f–g, p–q)**. Cross both through a 4mm C **(g–h, q–r)**.

[5] Pick up a C 11º, a B 11º, an A 11º, and a 4mm color A fire-polished bead on each needle **(h–i, r–s)**. Go back through the last three beads before the 4mm C, cross through the 4mm C, then continue through the three beads after the 4mm C **(i–j, s–t)**.

[6] Repeat step 2, but pick up two A 11ºs instead of four **(j–k, t–u)**.

[7] Repeat steps 3–6 six times. Make more or fewer repeats to alter the length by 1-in. (2.5cm) increments.

[8] Repeat step 3.

[9] Pick up an A 11º, a B 11º, a C 11º, a 4mm C, a C 11º, a B 11º, and an A 11º **(figure 2, a–b)**. Cross through these beads with the other needle **(c–d)**. Pick up enough beads to form a loop that will fit over the end button **(d–e)**. Go into the bracelet, back through the last four beads before the shank, through the shank, and continue through the four beads after the shank **(e–f)**. Go back through the loop to reinforce it **(f–g)**.

[10] To end each thread, tie half-hitch knots (see Basics, p. 10) between beads, dab them with glue, then trim the tails.

Embellishment

[1] Start 4 ft. of thread at the loop end. Secure the thread with knots and glue, then exit at **figure 3, point a**.

[2] Pick up an A 11º, a C 11º, a D 11º, a C 11º, and an A 11º **(a–b)**. Go through the 3mm below this bead group **(b–c)**.

[3] Go through the next 3mm. Pick up an A 11º, a C 11º, a D 11º, and a C 11º, then go through the first A 11º from the previous step. Go back through the 3mm **(c–d)**. Repeat **(d–e)**.

[4] Pick up two A 11ºs, and sew through the next 4mm **(e–f)**. Pick up two more A 11ºs, and go through the next 3mm **(f–g)**.

[5] Repeat steps 2–4 along both edges of the bracelet.

[6] For additional embellishment, add pairs of D 11ºs as shown in **figure 4**. Repeat along both edges, then secure the thread.

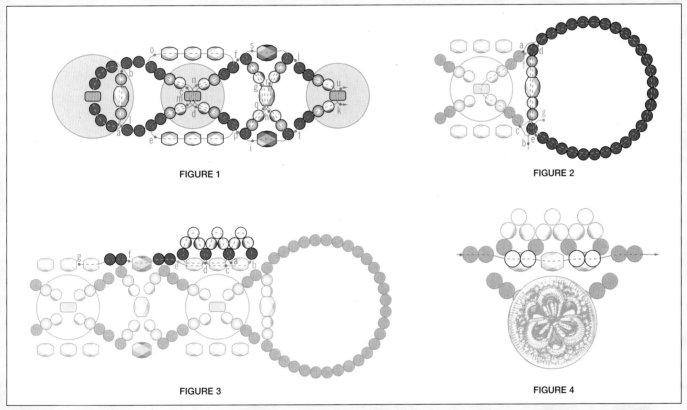

FIGURE 1

FIGURE 2

FIGURE 3

FIGURE 4

MATERIALS

bracelet 7 in. (18cm)

- shank buttons
  ⅝ in. (1.6cm) or ¾ in. (1.9cm)
  8 ⅜ in. (1cm) or ½ in. (1.3cm)
- fire-polished beads
  14 4mm black, color A
  9 4mm silver, color C
  48 3mm silver, color C

- 2g each of size 11º seed beads
  black, color A
  hematite, color B
  silver, color C
  silver-lined crystal, color D
- Fireline 4 lb. test, or
  Power Pro 10 lb. test
- beading needles, #12
- G-S Hypo Cement

Beaded watch-band

Go beyond the basics
with a bead-woven band

by **Julia Gerlach**

Stitch an easy watchband using
two-needle weave. Elastic thread
gives it a perfect fit.

step*by*step

[1] Measure your wrist and
subtract the length of the
watch face.
[2] Cut two 1-yd. (.9m)
pieces of elastic, and thread
a twisted-wire needle on

each of the four ends. Set
one piece aside.
[3] Go through two
adjacent holes on the watch
face from the inside out,
and center the watch face
on the strand **(photo a)**.
[4] String a 4mm color A

MATERIALS
watchband 6½ in. (16.5cm)
- **2** 16-in. (41cm) strands
  4mm beads, **1** in each of **2**
  colors, A and B
- 2g size 15º seed beads
- 1-in. (2.5cm) three-strand
  watch face (Fire Mountain

Gems, 800-355-2137,
firemountaingems.com)
- Gossamer Floss elastic
- **4** twisted-wire needles,
  medium
- G-S Hypo Cement

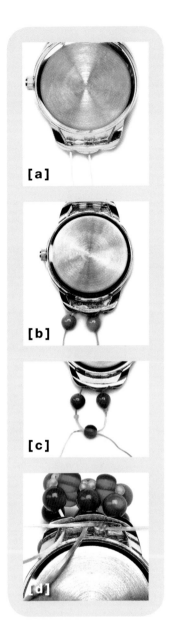

[a]

[b]

[c]

[d]

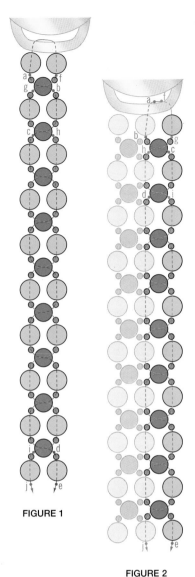

FIGURE 1

FIGURE 2

FIGURE 3

EDITOR'S NOTE: Make this band with a clasp if you prefer. Use Fireline 10 lb. test instead of Gossamer Floss, and stitch one side at a time. To determine how long each stitched section should be, subtract the length of the watch face and the clasp from the total length, and divide by two. Refer to figure 3 to attach a clasp half to each end. Finish off all tails with a few half-hitch knots (Basics) between beads, and trim.

bead on each strand (photo b). Pick up a 15º seed bead with each needle, and cross through a 4mm color B bead (figure 1, a–b, f–g, and photo c).

[5] Pick up a 15º, an A, and a 15º on each needle, and cross through a B (b–c, g–h). Repeat until you are ³⁄₁₆ in. (5mm) from the length established in step 1 (c–d, h–i). Pick up a 15º and an A on each needle (d–e, i–j).

[6] Working with the other piece of elastic, go through the middle hole of the watch face and the top right A with one end (figure 2, a–b). Go through the remaining hole

with the other end, and string an A (f–g).

[7] Pick up a 15º with each needle, and cross through a B (b–c, g–h).

[8] With the edge needle, pick up a 15º, an A, and a 15º. With the other needle, pick up a 15º, go through an A on the previous column, and pick up a 15º. Cross the needles through a B (c–d, h–i). Repeat until the second column is the same length as the first (d–e, i–j).

[9] With the middle two strands, go through the center hole on the other side of the watch face. With

each edge strand, go through the corresponding hole.

[10] Tie two adjacent strands together with a square knot (see Basics, p. 10 and photo d). Repeat with the other two strands. For additional security, tie all four strands together with a square knot. Dab the knots with glue, and let them dry. Trim the ends.

Colorful lentil

by **Carol Perrenoud**

While you're most likely to see lentil beads at the end of a dangle, they really stand up and get noticed in this project. Add them to a simple spiral rope for a lavish, jewel-toned necklace.

step*by*step

Rope

[1] Using a comfortable length of Fireline, pick up four color A 11º seed beads, one color B 11º seed bead, one color A lentil, and one B 11º. Leaving a 10-in. (25cm) tail, tie a surgeon's knot (see Basics, p. 10). Go back through the four A 11ºs **(figure 1, a–b)**.

[2] Pick up an A 11º, a B 11º, a color B lentil, and a B 11º **(figure 2, a–b)**. Go through the top three A 11ºs and the new A 11º just added **(b–c)**. Move

the new lentil group over to the left so it's next to the first.

[3] Repeat step 2, rotating your lentil colors, until your necklace is the desired length. This necklace is 30 in. (76cm).

Finish the ends

[1] To make the loop closure, pick up 21 A 11ºs. Go back through several As in the rope **(figure 3, a–b)**.

[2] Tie a half-hitch knot (Basics), and retrace the thread path. Secure the Fireline, and trim the tail.

[3] On the other end of the necklace, thread a needle on the tail.

MATERIALS

necklace 30 in. (76cm)

- **125** each of 6mm lentil beads
  (Beadcats, 503-625-2323,
  orders@beadcats.com,
  beadcats.com)
  olive green, color A
  purple, color B
  amber, color C
  cranberry, color D
- 30g each of size 11º seed beads
  olive green, color A
  purple, color B
- Fireline, 6-lb. test
- beading needles, #12

necklace

Lentil beads add color and texture to a spiral rope necklace

[4] To make the flower, pick up three A 11ºs, a B 11º, an A lentil, and a B 11º (figure 4, a–b).

[5] Go through the last A 11º in the core and the three new A 11ºs (b–c).

[6] Pick up a B 11º, a B lentil, and a B 11º (figure 5, a–b). Go back through the top three A 11ºs (b–c).

[7] Stitch three more lentil groups (rotating colors), always going through the top three A 11ºs. By going through the same As, the lentils will fan out into flower petals. The top of the flower is shown in figure 6.

[8] Go back down the core, and reinforce the connection by going through several petals and at least the first five core beads. Secure the Fireline, and trim the tail.

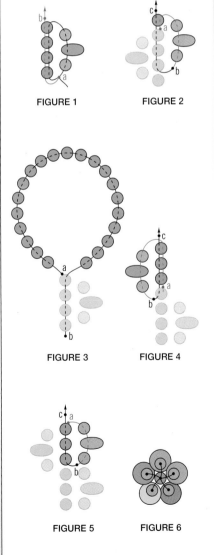

FIGURE 1

FIGURE 2

FIGURE 3

FIGURE 4

FIGURE 5

FIGURE 6

EDITOR'S NOTE: Wear your necklace at different lengths by making an easy extension. Make a spiral rope the desired length by following steps 1–3, but substitute color B 11ºs for the lentil beads. By finishing with a loop on one end and a flower on the other, you can connect the extension to the larger rope as shown in the photo, or wear it as a bracelet or anklet.

Embellished
ladder stitch bracelets

Two quick stitches combine to create fun and easy bracelets

by **Julz**

Whip up a ladder stitch base, and prepare to be delighted at how quickly you can create a casual, comfortable bracelet that you embellish with colorful 11º seed beads.

step*by*step

[1] On 4 yd. (3.7m) of Fireline, leaving a 10-in. (25cm) tail, use 8º seed beads to stitch a three-bead ladder (see Basics, p. 10 and **figure 1**). This one is 54 rows long. (To alter the length of your bracelet, stitch fewer or more rows.)

[2] Exit the last row of the ladder, and pick up two color A 11º seed beads, an 8º, three As, half the clasp, and three As. Sew back through the 8º **(figure 2, a–b)**. Pick up two As, and sew back through the last row of the ladder **(b–c)**. Reinforce the beads just added with a second and third thread pass. Exit at **point c**.

[3] Pick up five As, and sew through the middle 8º on the base, two rows from where your thread is exiting **(figure 3, a–b)**. Pick up five As, and

sew through the first row of 8ºs **(b–c)**. Then sew through the next row **(c–d)**.

[4] Repeat step 3 with color B 11ºs, reversing the direction of the thread path, as shown in **figure 4**.

[5] Repeat steps 3 and 4 with the color C, D, and E 11ºs, making a repeating pattern with the five colors.

[6] When you reach the first row, repeat step 2, using the other half of the clasp. Secure the working thread in the last few rows by weaving in the thread and tying half-hitch knots (Basics) between a few beads. Trim the thread.

[7] Secure the tail in the same manner as the working thread.

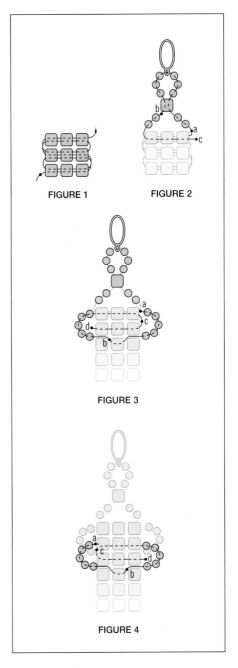

FIGURE 1

FIGURE 2

FIGURE 3

FIGURE 4

MATERIALS
bracelet 7½ in. (19.1cm)
- Japanese seed beads
  5g size 8º
  1g of size 11º, in each of **5** colors:
  A, B, C, D, E
- toggle clasp
- Fireline 6 lb. test
- beading needles, #12

EDITOR'S NOTE: You can use another shape or size of seed bead instead of the 8º Japanese seed beads, but you may need to alter the number of 11ºs it will take to make the embellishment across the top of the base.

Springtime
delight
necklace

by **Sandra D. Halpenny**

Stitch a collar of flowers, and experience spring any time of the year. For an array of colors, get out those seed beads, and vary the petal hues randomly as you work.

step*by*step

Flowers

[1] Using a comfortable length of conditioned thread (see Basics, p. 10) string a stop bead (Basics) to 8 in. (20cm) from the end. Pick up 11 color A 11º seed beads and ten color B 11º seed beads.

[2] Slide the beads next to the stop bead, and sew through the first B again to form a small ring **(figure 1, a–b)**. Pick up a 3mm fire-polished bead. Sew through the sixth B, the 3mm, and the first B **(b–c)**.

[3] Pick up seven color C 11º seed beads, and sew through the third B on the ring **(figure 2, a–b)**. Pick up seven Cs, skip a bead on the ring, and sew through the next B **(b–c)**. Repeat three times for a total of five petals **(c–d)**.

[4] Pick up three color D 11º seed beads, and sew through the third, fourth, and fifth Cs on the first petal **(figure 3, a–b)**. Pick up three Ds, skip a bead on the ring, and sew through the next B **(b–c)**. Repeat with the remaining four petals **(c–d)**. Sew through the ring of Bs, and continue through five As on the stem **(d–e)**.

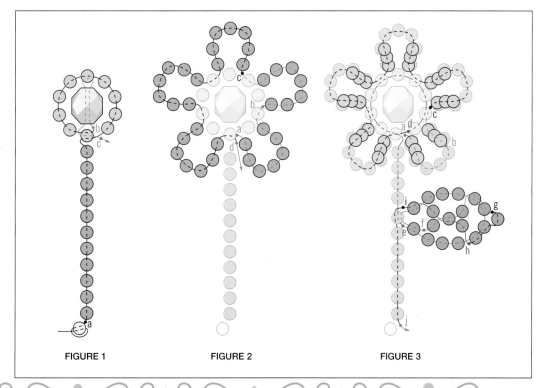

FIGURE 1   FIGURE 2   FIGURE 3

FIGURE 4

FIGURE 5

[5] Pick up 12 As. Sew through the stem bead again in the same direction and then go through first new A **(e–f)**. Pick up three As. Sew through the eighth and seventh As **(f–g)**. Pick up an A, and sew through the sixth and fifth As **(g–h)**. Pick up an A, sew through the center A, pick up an A, and sew through the 12th A **(h–i)** and the remaining stem beads **(i–j)**.

[6] Pick up two As, and sew through the first two stem beads and the two new As again **(figure 4, a–b)**. Pick up two As, and sew up through the previous two As. Pick up an A, and sew down through the two As just added **(b–c)**. Continue working a two-bead ladder (Basics) for a total of ten pairs, adding a single bead on every other pair, as shown **(c–d)**.

[7] Pick up nine As and ten Bs. Repeat step 2 **(d–e)**.

[8] Work the first three petals as in step 3 **(e–f)**. For the fourth petal, pick up three Cs, sew through the end bead on the second petal of the previous flower, pick up three Cs, and sew through the B on the ring **(f–g)**. Add the fifth petal **(g–h)**, and repeat step 4, but only sew through four As on the stem.

[9] Pick up 12 As. Sew through the stem bead in the same direction and the first new A **(figure 5, a–b)**. Pick up three As. Sew through the eighth and seventh As, the end A on the leaf on the previous flower, and the sixth and fifth As **(b–c)**. Pick up an A, sew through the center A, pick up an A, and sew through the 12th A and two As on the stem **(c–d)**.

[10] Repeat step 5 to add a second leaf.

[11] Repeat steps 6–10 until you reach the desired length minus 1 in. (2.5cm) for the clasp. This necklace has 23 flowers and is 16 in. (41cm) long

without the clasp. Remove the stop bead, secure the tail and working thread in the beadwork with half-hitch knots (Basics) between a few beads, and trim.

Clasp

[1] Working with 1 yd. (.9m) of conditioned thread, string a stop bead to 12 in. (30cm) from the end. Pick up four Cs, a 3mm, and four Cs. Work in odd-count peyote (Basics) using Cs for a total of five rows. Treat the 3mm as one 11º.

[2] Remove the stop bead, and thread a needle on the tail. Work five rows of odd-count peyote on the other side of the 3mm, counting the 3mm row as row 1. You will end with five beads on the top and bottom edges of the peyote strip **(photo a)**.

[3] Fold the peyote strip, aligning the end rows, and zip it up (Basics) to form a tube. Secure the tail in the beadwork,

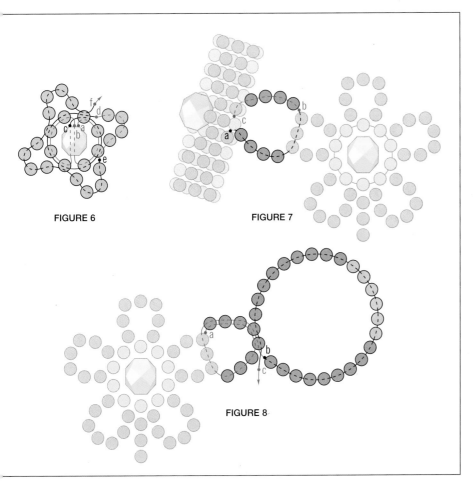

FIGURE 6

FIGURE 7

FIGURE 8

[a]

[b]

EDITOR'S NOTE:
If you are uncomfortable working in odd-count peyote for the toggle clasp, pick up five Cs, a 3mm, and four Cs in step 1. Then follow the steps, working in flat, even-count peyote (Basics). Your toggle will be one row longer, and the flower will be slightly off center, but it won't even be noticeable when it is worn.

MATERIALS

necklace 17 in. (43cm)
- **24** 3mm Czech fire-polished beads
- size 11º Japanese seed beads
  20g green, color A
  5g gold, color B
  7g purple, color C
  5g light purple, color D
- Nymo D or C-Lon, conditioned with beeswax
- beading needles, #11 or #12

and trim. Weave the working thread through the beadwork so it exits the 3mm (photo b).

[4] Pick up four Bs, and sew through the 3mm (figure 6, a–b). Pick up four Bs, and sew through the 3mm again (b–c). Sew through all eight Bs, go through the first B again, and pull them into a tight circle around the 3mm (c–d). Pick up four Ds, skip a B in the ring, and sew through the next B (d–e). Repeat around the ring for a total of four small petals (e–f).

[5] Secure the thread in the peyote tube, and exit a bead on the other side of the tube about four beads from the edge (figure 7, point a). Pick up four Cs, and sew through three Cs on the edge petal as shown (a–b). Pick up four Cs, and sew into the adjacent bead on the peyote tube (b–c). Weave through to point a, and reinforce the thread path with a few more passes. Secure the thread, and trim.

[6] Secure an 8-in. thread in the other end flower, and exit the edge petal (figure 8, point a). Pick up eight Cs, and sew through the three end Cs on the petal, ending back at point a. Retrace the thread path again, then sew through the next five Cs, and exit at point b.

[7] Pick up nine Cs, six Ds, and nine Cs. Sew through the fourth and fifth Cs from the previous step (b–c). Check the fit of the loop, and add or remove beads as necessary so it fits over the toggle bead. Retrace the thread path, secure the thread, and trim.

Subtle
stripes
band

Take an Ndebele herringbone bracelet from flat to fabulous with a mix of matte and shiny triangle beads

by **Perie Brown**

This sophisticated bracelet covers all the angles. Glinting triangle beads give the surface a fabric-like texture when stitched into a herringbone band. Up the ante with the designer's touch of slanting stripes to create a bracelet with unbeatable appeal.

step*by*step

Herringbone band

[1] Assign each of the eight triangle bead colors a letter from A–H. Determine the finished length of the bracelet and subtract the length of your clasp. This will give you the length of the beaded band.

[2] Start with 2 yd. (1.8m) of conditioned thread (see Basics, p. 10). Leaving a 12-in. (30cm) tail, use the color pattern in **figure 1** to construct a ladder (Basics) with two beads per stack for 16 stacks.

[3] Work a row of flat herringbone (Basics) off the ladder row, referring to the pattern **(figure 2, a–b)** for the color changes. At the end of the row, turn without adding an edge bead, as shown in **figure 2, b–c.**

[4] Continue working in herringbone, following the pattern, until you reach the desired length.

[5] Reinforce the last row with a second thread path, but don't cut the thread.

Clasp

[1] With the working thread, sew through the first loop on the clasp and under the thread bridge between the first two beads in the last row **(figure 3, a–b).**

[2] Continue sewing through the loops on the clasp and the thread bridges until the clasp is secure. Retrace the thread path to reinforce the join.

[3] Repeat on the other end of the bracelet using the 12-in. tail.

FIGURE 1

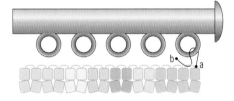

FIGURE 3

MATERIALS

bracelet 7½ in. (19.1cm)

- size 11º triangle beads, 2.5g in each of **8** colors
- five-strand slide clasp
- Nymo D conditioned with beeswax
- beading needles, #12

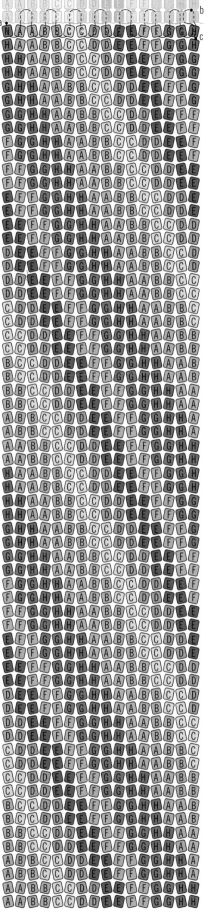

FIGURE 2

PEARL
spikes

Lustrous pearls reach out from
a herringbone cuff and grab
your attention

by **Lisa Olson Tune**

What better way to accent a special outfit than
with a dramatic bracelet? This impressive display
of richly colored pearls works best when paired
with a band of seed beads in a similar hue and
accent beads in a bright metallic finish.

step*by*step

[1] Working with a 2 yd. (1.8m) length
of conditioned thread (see Basics, p.
10), pick up six color A 11° seed beads.
Sew through the beads again in the
same direction, leaving a 6-in. (15cm)
tail. Arrange the beads into two stacks
of three **(figure 1, a–b)**.

[2] Pick up three As. Sew through the
three beads on the previous stack from
top to bottom, and through the new
stack from bottom to top **(b–c)**.
Continue working in ladder stitch
(Basics and **c–d**) for a total of 82 stacks
for a 7½-in. (19.1cm) bracelet. Adjust
the length of the bracelet by adding or
removing four stacks.

[3] Turn your work so the thread exits
the top left bead of the ladder. Work
in flat Ndebele herringbone as follows:
Pick up four As, and sew down
through the second edge bead on the
ladder **(figure 2, a–b)**. Sew up through
the third edge bead, pick up four As,
and sew down through the fourth edge

bracelet

FIGURE 1

FIGURE 2

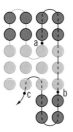

FIGURE 3

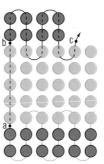

FIGURE 4

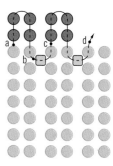

FIGURE 5

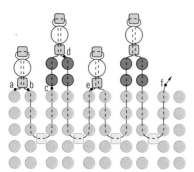

FIGURE 6

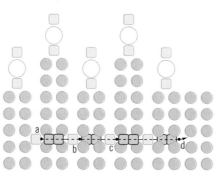

FIGURE 7

MATERIALS

bracelet 7½ in. (19.1cm)

- 16-in. (41cm) strand 4–5mm rice pearls or stone chips
- 18g size 11º Japanese seed beads, color A
- 8g hex-cut Japanese cylinder beads or size 13º seed beads, color B
- two-strand box clasp
- 4 4mm jump rings
- Nymo B conditioned with beeswax
- beading needles, #12

bead (b–c). Sew up through the next edge bead (c–d). Repeat along the edge of the ladder.

[4] When you add the last stack of beads, sew through all three beads on the ladder's last stack (figure 3, a–b). Pick up four beads, and continue working in herringbone along the other edge (b–c).

[5] Once you've added the last stack of beads, sew through all three ladder beads and the two end herringbone beads (figure 4, a–b). Work a second row of herringbone along the top edge (b–c), sew through the beads on the end of the band after adding the last stack, and stitch a second row of herringbone along the bottom edge.

[6] Work a third row along both edges as follows: Pick up four As, and sew

down through the next bead on the previous row (figure 5, a–b). Pick up a color B cylinder bead, and sew up through the next bead (b–c). Repeat across the row (c–d). After stitching the third row along the bottom edge, end with your thread exiting the top left bead of the band.

[7] Pick up a B, a pearl, and a B. Sew back through the pearl and the first B (figure 6, a–b). Sew down through the three As in the next stack, the B, and up through the next three As (b–c).

[8] Pick up two As, a B, a pearl, and a B. Sew back through the pearl and the first B (c–d). Pick up two As, and sew down through three As in the next stack, the B, and up through three As in the next stack (d–e).

[9] Repeat steps 7 and 8 along both edges of the band, alternating between short and long pearl fringes (e–f). As you work the second edge, make sure it is the mirror image of the first – a short fringe across from a short fringe, and a long fringe across from a long fringe.

[10] Weave through the beadwork so your thread exits the first B between the herringbone rows (figure 7, point a).

Pick up two Bs, positioning them in front of the long herringbone stack, and sew through the next B (a–b).

[11] Pick up two Bs, position them behind the short herringbone stack, and sew through the next B (b–c).

[12] Repeat steps 10 and 11 across the band (c–d), sewing through each B. When you reach the end, weave through the beadwork, and exit the first B between the herringbone rows on the other side. Repeat steps 10 and 11 as you did on the first side.

[13] Secure your working thread and tails with half-hitch knots (Basics) between a few beads, and trim. Connect the clasp to the end rows of beads with jump rings.

Fiesta bangle

Liven up a herringbone tube with hundreds of colorful loops

by **Marcia Katz**

This bangle really makes a statement in color and movement. With a few simple stitches and seed beads, you can watch this plain tubular herringbone bracelet evolve into a vibrant accessory that will complement your next festive outfit.

step*by*step

Bangle with single-colored loops

[**1**] Cut a piece of plastic tubing long enough to fit loosely over the largest part of your hand. Cut a ¾-in. (1.9cm) piece of tubing, then cut it in half lengthwise (**photo a**). Discard one half. Dab glue inside one end of the long tubing. Push the ¾-in. tubing halfway into the long piece, smearing the glue around. Set the tubing aside to dry.

[**2**] Work with comfortable lengths of thread, as you will have to add thread many times. Secure your tails by sewing into previous rows and tying half-hitch knots (see Basics, p. 10). Stitch a ladder (Basics) 14 beads long, using size 11º seed beads. Connect the ladder into a ring (**photo b**).

[**3**] Using 11ºs, work a round of tubular herringbone (Basics). Step up through the first 11º in the new round. (You may want to put your work over the long tubing as you stitch so you know your work will fit over the tubing when you assemble the bangle.)

[**4**] Modify the remaining rounds as follows to add colorful loops to each round: Work a stitch in herringbone with 11ºs, but do not sew through the first bead in the next stack. Pick up 20 color A Charlottes. Sew back through the first Charlotte, making a loop (**photo c**). Then sew up through the first bead in the next stack (**photo d**). Complete the round, adding herringbone stitches with 11ºs and loops with Charlottes in colors B–H. Work the next round in the same manner, using colors I–N for the loops.

[**5**] Repeat step 4 until the bangle is 1½ in. (3.8cm) short of the desired length.

[**6**] Center the herringbone tube on the plastic tubing. Dab glue on the exposed end of the ¾-in. tubing (**photo e**). Then push the open end of the long tubing over the remainder of the ¾-in. piece. Hold the two together until the glue sets (**photo f**).

[**7**] Work as many rounds of herringbone as needed to cover the tubing, but don't add loops to the last two rounds. Twist the herringbone tube, then pick up an 11º, and sew into the corresponding 11º in the first round (**photo g**). Pick up another 11º, and sew into the corresponding bead in the last round (**photo h**). Repeat to complete the round.

[**8**] Add colorful loops to the last few rounds of the herringbone tube to cover the join.

Bangle with multicolored loops

[1] To begin the multicolored-loops bangle, follow steps 1–3 of the single-colored-loops bangle.

[2] Work step 4, but modify it by using the following bead pattern. You will make loops that have 26 beads instead of 20 per stitch.

Loop 1: 3A, 2B, 2C, 2D, 2E, 2F, 1G, 2F, 2E, 2D, 2C, 2B, 2A.

Loop 2: 3B, 2C, 2D, 2E, 2F, 2G, 1A, 2G, 2F, 2E, 2D, 2C, 2B.

Loop 3: 3C, 2D, 2E, 2F, 2G, 2A, 1B, 2A, 2G, 2F, 2E, 2D, 2C.

Loop 4: 3D, 2E, 2F, 2G, 2A, 2B, 1C, 2B, 2A, 2G, 2F, 2E, 2D.

Loop 5: 3E, 2F, 2G, 2A, 2B, 2C, 1D, 2C, 2B, 2A, 2G, 2F, 2E.

Loop 6: 3F, 2G, 2A, 2B, 2C, 2D, 1E, 2D, 2C, 2B, 2A, 2G, 2F.

Loop 7: 3G, 2A, 2B, 2C, 2D, 2E, 1F, 2E, 2D, 2C, 2B, 2A, 2G.

[3] Repeat loops 1–7 on each round until the bangle is 1½ in. (3.8cm) short of the desired length.

[4] Work the remainder of the bangle as in steps 6–8 of the single-colored-loops bangle.

EDITOR'S NOTE:
Charlottes have holes with inconsistent sizes. If you pick up a bead that seems to be a tight fit, discard it since it is unlikely that you'll be able to make a second pass through it.

[a] [b]

[c] [d]

[e] [f]

[g] [h]

Fiery blooms necklace

by **Debbie Nishihara**

Bicone crystals provide a marvelous setting for a gorgeous hibiscus bead. Adding a dramatic twist to the herringbone rope allows the crystals to nestle together.

step*by*step

Herringbone tubes

The number of crystals in the materials list makes two 7-in. (18cm) herringbone tubes for an overall necklace length of 18 in. (46cm). This necklace used approximately 32 crystals per inch (2.5cm), so if you want to lengthen or shorten the tubes, be sure to adjust the number of crystals accordingly.

[1] Using a comfortable length of beading cord, make a ladder (see Basics, p. 10) following the color pattern shown in **figure 1, a–b**.
[2] Join the beads into a ring by coming up the first color A, down the last B, and back up the first A **(figure 2, a–b)**. The bicone shape prevents this row from lining up as usual, so be sure to note which are the tops of the beads.
[3] Pick up an A and a B, and go down through the next B **(figure 3, a–b)**. Come

up the next A, pick up an A and a B, and go down the next B **(b–c)**.
[4] To add a gentle spiral to the herringbone tube, modify the stitch slightly, as follows: Come up through both As in the next stack, pick up an A and a B, and go down through the first B in the next stack **(figure 4, a–b)**. Come up through both As in the next stack, pick up an A and a B, and go down through the next B **(b–c)**. Repeat until the tube is 7 in. long. When you finish

117

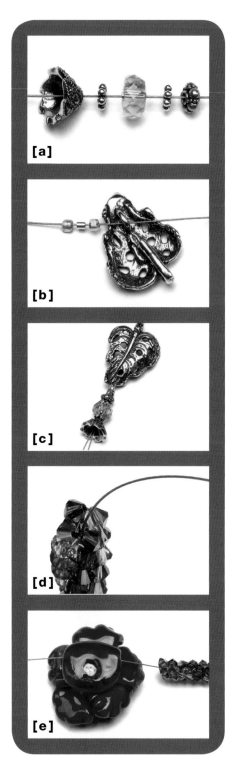

[a]

[b]

[c]

[d]

[e]

MATERIALS

necklace 18 in. (46cm)

- hibiscus bead (Alethia Donathan, DACS Beads, 808-842-7714, dacsbeads.com)
- **2** 8mm faceted citrine rondelles
- **2** 6mm silver accent beads
- 4mm Swarovski bicone crystals
  224 fire opal, color A
  224 green tourmaline AB, color B
- **4** size 5º triangles, lime with copper
- **4** 5mm daisy-shaped silver spacers
- linked-leaves sterling toggle clasp (Candice Wakumoto, 808-625-2706, candicewakumoto@msn.com)
- **2** 10mm marcasite cones
- **2** crimp beads
- DandyLine beading cord, .008
- flexible beading wire, .014–.015
- beading needles, #12
- crimping pliers
- wire cutters

the tube, leave the needle on the working thread. Secure the beginning thread with a few half-hitch knots (Basics) between beads, and trim. Make a second herringbone tube.

Assembly

[**1**] Add 6 in. (15cm) to the combined measurement of your two tubes, and cut a piece of flexible beading wire to that length. This beading wire is 20 in. (51cm) long.

[**2**] String a cone, a spacer, a rondelle, a spacer, and an accent bead (**photo a**). Then string a triangle, a crimp bead, a triangle, and a clasp half (**photo b**). Go back through all the beads and the cone, and crimp the crimp bead (Basics). With the clasp face-up, the end components should look like those in **photo c**.

[**3**] Hold the tube vertically, trimmed-end first, and drop the beading wire down into it in small increments (**photo d**). Slide the tube into the cone.

[**4**] Using the thread with the needle still attached, sew through several beads to close the tube around the beading

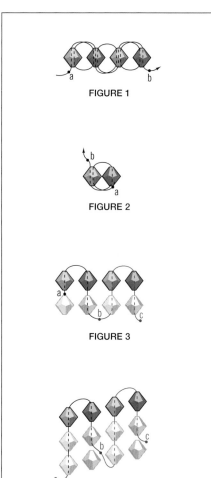

FIGURE 1

FIGURE 2

FIGURE 3

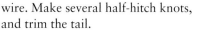

FIGURE 4

wire. Make several half-hitch knots, and trim the tail.

[**5**] String the focal bead and the other herringbone tube (**photo e**). Close the other end of the tube around the beading wire as in step 4.

[**6**] Repeat step 2 to finish the other end of the necklace. Do not pull the wire too tightly before you crimp, or the herringbone tubes will buckle.

EDITOR'S NOTE:

Keeping your tension fairly tight throughout the herringbone rope produces a consistent spiral. However, if your tension is too tight, the tubes will be inflexible.

by **Deborah Staehle**

A supple spiral herringbone base
supports a graceful embellishment

Falling
leaves
bracelet

This lavish bracelet is much easier to make than it looks. Simply stitch a spiral herringbone base of 8º seed beads, and embellish it with leaves as you work. This time-saving step will have you wearing a flattering fringe around your wrist in no time at all.

MATERIALS

bracelet 9 in. (23cm)

- Japanese seed beads
  15g size 8º, color A
  15g size 8º, color B
  15g size 8º, color C
  15g size 8º, color D
  15g size 11º, color E
  15g size 11º, color F
- 12mm flat flower with a single hole, or a shank button
- Power Pro 10 lb. test
- beading needles, #12

step*by*step

[1] Using a 3-yd. (2.7m) length of Power Pro, leave a 20-in. (51cm) tail, and stitch a three-bead ladder four rows long (see Basics, p. 10). Use 8º seed beads, and follow the color sequence in **figure 1**.

[2] Sew through the first, last, and first rows again to connect the ladder into a tube. Exit the top of a stack of color A 8º s.

[3] Work in spiral herringbone as follows: Pick up an A and a color B. Sew down through the top bead in the B stack and up through the two top beads on the color C stack **(figure 2, a–b)**.

[4] Pick up a C and a color D. Sew down through the top bead in the D stack and up through the three top beads on the A stack **(b–c)**.

[5] Pick up an A, eight color E 11º seed beads, and four color F 11º seed beads. Skip an F, and sew back through the next F **(figure 3, a–b)**. Pick up two Fs and three Es. Skip two Fs and three Es, and sew through the next three Es **(b–c)**.

[6] Pick up six Es and four Fs. Skip an F, and sew through the next F **(c–d)**. Pick up two Fs and three Es. Skip two Fs and three Es, then sew through five Es **(d–e)**.

[7] Pick up a B, and sew down through the top B on the B stack **(e–f)**. Then sew up through the two top beads on the C stack.

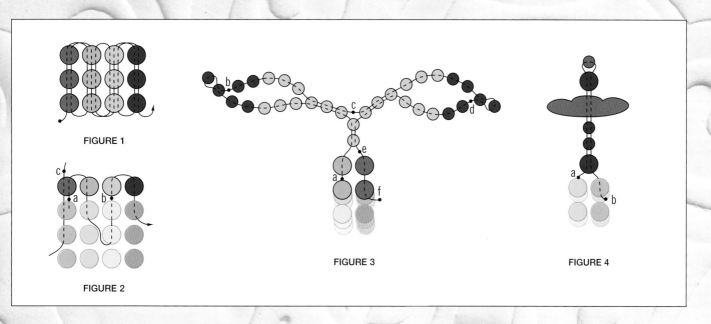

FIGURE 1

FIGURE 2

FIGURE 3

FIGURE 4

[8] Pick up a C and a D, and sew down through the top bead in the D stack. Then sew up through the three top beads in the A stack.

[9] Pick up an A and a B. Sew down through the top bead in the B stack and up through the two top beads in the C stack.

[10] Repeat steps 5 and 6, but pick up a C instead of an A.

[11] Pick up a D, and sew down through the top bead on the D stack and up through the three top beads on the A stack.

[12] Repeat steps 3–11 until you reach the desired length.

[13] Exit the top bead in the A stack, pick up an D, two Fs, a flat flower or button, an D, and an F. Skip the F, and sew back through the beads to the bracelet (figure 4, a–b). Retrace the thread path to reinforce the clasp.

[14] Secure the tails in the beadwork with half-hitch knots (Basics), and trim.

[15] On the tail, pick up enough 8°s to accommodate the clasp. Go into the bead opposite where the thread is exiting. Retrace the thread path to reinforce the loop. Make three sets of leaves on the loop.

[16] Secure the tail as before.

EDITOR'S NOTE: Lengthen the bracelet to make a choker. Stitch a few leaf fringes near the back of the necklace, and gradually make it fuller near the front. Add crystals to the base, if desired.

Bezeled stone rings

by **Hatsumi Oshitani**

Make settings for small cabochons using modified Ndebele herringbone, netting, and circular peyote. These settings can be perfectly fitted to any size ring. They are fun to make, and they work up so quickly, you may find yourself running out of fingers to wear them on!

step*by*step

As you work, keep the tension tight so the beads curve into a dome shape instead of staying flat.

Side one

[1] On 2 yd. (1.8m) of Fireline, center three color A 8º seed beads. Sew back through the beads again, and tie them into a ring using a surgeon's knot (see Basics, p. 10 and **figure 1, point a**). Sew through the next bead **(a–b)**.

[2] Work in flat, circular herringbone by picking up two As and sewing through the next bead **(b–c)**. Repeat two more times. Step up through the first bead added in this step **(c–d)**.

[3] Pick up two As, and sew through the next bead **(d–e)**. Then work an increase by picking up a color B 11º seed bead and sewing through the next bead (e–f). Repeat two more times to complete the round, and end by stepping up through the first bead added in this step (f–g).

[4] Work a total of five rounds, referring to **figure 1** for the color changes (g–h).

[5] Work one more round, without adding new As (h–i). Reinforce the section of Bs, and make a half-hitch knot (Basics) where the working thread is exiting. Set the working thread aside.

[6] Thread a needle on the tail, and sew through one of the stacks of As opposite the section of Bs. This tail will be used later to make the band. Set it aside.

Side two

[1] Repeat steps 1–5 of side one, but use 1 yd. (.9m) of Fireline, and leave an 8-in. (20cm) tail.

[2] Go through the outer round again, and add one more row of Bs (**figure 2, a–b**). Set the working thread aside.

[3] Secure the 8-in. tail with half-hitch knots, and trim.

Connect the sides

Line up the two sections of color B seed beads and pick up the working thread from side two. Connect the two sides by sewing back and forth between edge beads (**figure 3, a–b**). Retrace the thread path to reinforce the join. Secure the working thread, and trim.

Beaded bezel

[1] Pick up the working thread from side one, pick up two color E 15º seed beads, a color F 15º, and two Es. Sew through the next A (**figure 3, c–d**). Repeat around, skipping As as shown, and step up through the first three beads added in this step (d–e). Place the cabochon in the center of the ring, and hold it in place (or glue it) as you work the next steps.

[2] Pick up an E, an F, and an E. Sew through the next F on the previous round (e–f). Keep a fairly tight tension on your thread so the beads snug up

MATERIALS
beaded ring
- 10 x 14mm cabochon (Rio Grande, 800-545-6500, riogrande.com)
- Japanese seed beads
  5g size 8º, color A
  5g size 11º, color B
  5g size 11º, color C
  3g size 11º, color D
  3g size 11º, color G
  3g size 15º, color E
  3g size 15º, color F
- Fireline 6 lb. test
- beading needles, #12–#13
- E6000 adhesive (optional)

around the cabochon, and repeat around the top of the ring. Exit through the first E added in this step (f–g).

[3] Pick up an F, and sew through the next E on the previous round (g–h). Repeat around the previous row, and exit through the first F added in this step (h–i). Go through the beads in the last round again to tighten them against the cabochon. Secure the tail, and trim.

Size the ring

[1] On the tail from side one, pick up two color G 11º seed beads, and sew through the A next to where the thread is exiting (**figure 4, a–b**). Then sew through the A and the first new G (b–c).

[2] Pick up two Gs, sew back through the previous row of Gs, and continue through the new G (c–d).

[3] Repeat step 2 until the band is long enough to make your ring the desired size. Sew through the As on side two, connecting the two sides. Secure the tails, and trim.

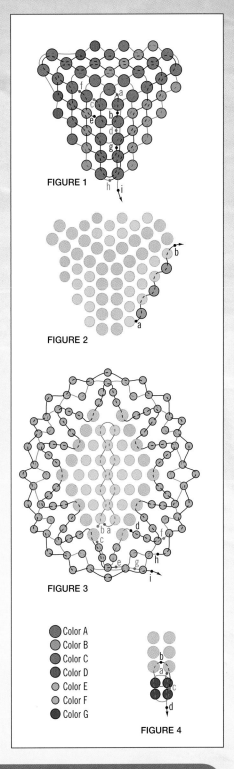

FIGURE 1

FIGURE 2

FIGURE 3

● Color A
○ Color B
○ Color C
● Color D
○ Color E
○ Color F
● Color G

FIGURE 4

EDITOR'S NOTE: Cabochons may vary somewhat in shape and size, so you may have to adjust the tension or bead count in your beaded bezel to accommodate your stone.

Peyote channel bracelet

Crystals accentuate flowers in a peyote bracelet

by **Jennifer Creasey**

Peyote stitch is a pattern lover's
dream – it gives you a finished piece
that looks intricate but works up
quickly. In this project, crystals
connect bands with a repeating
floral pattern in a bracelet
that's deceptively simple.

step*by*step

Toggle bead

[1] On 1 yd. (.9m) of conditioned thread (see Basics, p. 10), position a stop bead (Basics) 6 in. (15cm) from the end. Pick up ten color A cylinder beads, and work in flat, even-count peyote (Basics) for a total of 12 rows.

[2] Remove the stop bead. Fold the peyote strip in half so the first and last rows are aligned, and zip up the end rows (Basics) to form a tube (photo a).

[3] Sew through a few rows on the tube to stiffen it. Position the thread so it exits the middle of the peyote tube instead of an edge bead.

[4] Pick up a 4mm bicone crystal and an A. Sew back through the crystal and the peyote tube (photo b).

[5] Repeat step 4 on the other end of the tube. Secure the threads in the beadwork with a few half-hitch knots, and trim.

Peyote band

[1] Using 2 yd. (1.8m) of conditioned thread, start at **point a** on the pattern, and work part 1 in flat, odd-count peyote (Basics), leaving an 8-in. (20cm) tail.

[2] Weave through the bead-work, and exit at **point b**. Continue in flat, even-count peyote, and work part 2 of the pattern.

[3] Turn the pattern, start a new thread, and work part 3 as you did part 1.

[4] Align the last row of part 2 and the first row of part 3, and stitch them together, sewing through the up-beads.

[5] Position your needle so it exits at **point c**, and work part 4 of the pattern. Stitch the last row of part 4 to the first row of part 1.

Attach the clasp

[1] Thread a needle on the tail, and weave through to the single bead on the end row (**point d**). Pick up three As, sew through a bead at the center of the toggle bead, and pick up three As. Sew through the center bead on the end of the band to attach the toggle with a loop of beads.

[2] Retrace the thread path a few times, secure the thread, and trim.

[3] Secure a thread at the other end of the band, and exit the single bead on the end row. Pick up 24 As. Sew through the center end bead in the same direction. Adjust the number of beads in the loop as necessary so it fits around the toggle bar. Retrace the thread path a few times, secure the thread, and trim.

Crystal accents

[1] Start a new thread, secure it in the band, and exit the bead at **point e**.

[2] Pick up an A, a 6mm crystal, and an A. Sew through the bead at **point f**.

[3] Weave through the band and exit at **point g**. Pick up

an A, a 6mm crystal, and an A. Sew through the bead at **point h**.

[4] Continue adding crystal embellishments along the center of the band as indicated by the arrows on the pattern.

[5] Secure the thread in the beadwork, and trim.

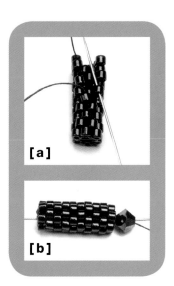

[a]

[b]

MATERIALS

bracelet 7 in. (18cm)

- **16** 6mm bicone crystals
- **2** 4mm bicone crystals
- Japanese cylinder beads
  6g black, color A
  3g dark pink, color B
  3g green, color C
  1g yellow, color D
  1g purple, color E
  1g orange, color F
- Nymo D conditioned with beeswax, or SoNo
- beading needles, #12

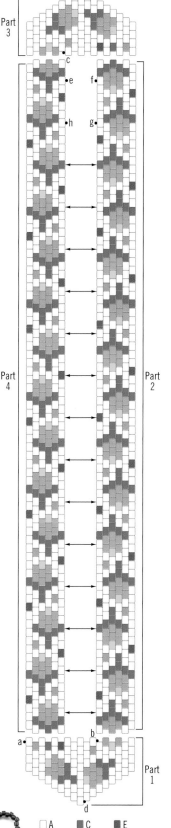

Part 3

Part 4

Part 2

Part 1

☐ A	■ C	■ E
■ B	☐ D	■ F

Sumptuous *but* simple peyote necklace

Deep, lustrous colors pair with sparkling dangles in this embellished peyote stitch necklace

by **Aasia Hamid**

The traditional clothing and gold jewelry worn in Aasia Hamid's native country, Pakistan, are rich in both color and texture. This sparkling combination of faceted drops with hex-cut cylinder beads in metallic and pearl finishes recalls those gorgeous visuals. This necklace is a piece that's perfect for any special occasion.

step*by*step

Garnet necklace
Peyote band

[1] Thread a needle on 1 yd. (.9m) of Fireline, and attach a stop bead (see Basics, p. 10) about 6 in. (15cm) from the end.

[2] Pick up one color A and two color B 8º hex-cut beads. Go back through the A in the opposite direction **(figure 1, a–b)**. Pick up an A, and go through the last B added **(b–c)**.

[3] Continue stitching in flat, even-count peyote (Basics) until your band is approximately 15 in. (38cm). Use an even number of Bs, and end with a B.

[4] Remove the stop bead, secure the tails in the peyote band with a few half-hitch knots (Basics) between beads, and trim.

FIGURE 1

FIGURE 2

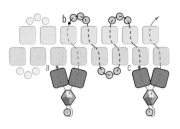

FIGURE 3

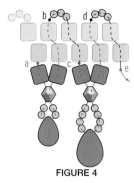

FIGURE 4

MATERIALS
both projects
- Fireline 6 lb. test
- Nymo B
- beading needles, #12

garnet necklace 16 in. (41cm)
- **9** 8 x 8mm garnet briolettes
- **10** 6 x 6mm garnet briolettes
- **41** 3mm bicone crystals
- size 8º Japanese cylinder or hex-cut beads
  10g color A
  15g color B
- 5g size 15º Japanese seed beads
- 15mm crystal button

green or bronze necklace 16 in. (41cm)
- **18** 6.5 x 13mm crystal teardrops or 5.5 x 11mm crystal briolettes
- **40** 3mm bicone crystals
- size 8º Japanese cylinder or hex-cut beads
  10g color A
  15g color B
- 5g size 15º Japanese seed beads
- 15mm crystal button

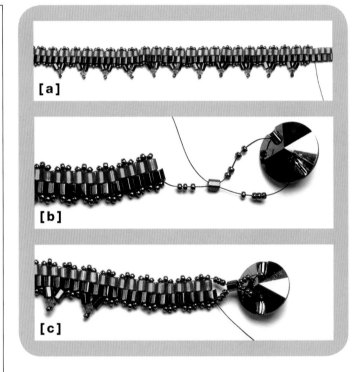

[a]

[b]

[c]

Embellishment
[1] Find the center point of the peyote band. Count 63 Bs in one direction, and slide a needle or other placeholder through that 63rd bead. This is where you'll begin the crystal picots in step 5.

[2] Secure 1 yd. of Nymo near the end with the marked B, and exit the end B.
[3] Pick up three 15º seed beads. Sew through the next B and the A above it to the right (figure 2, a–b).
[4] Pick up three 15ºs, and sew through the next A and B (b–c).

[5] Repeat steps 3 and 4 until you reach the marked B. Remove the needle or placeholder.
[6] Pick up a B, a bicone crystal, and a 15º. Go back through the crystal, pick up a B, and sew through the next B and A (figure 3, a–b).
[7] Stitch three three-bead groups as shown (b–c).
[8] Repeat steps 6 and 7 ten times to make a total of 11 crystal picots that alternate with three-bead groups (photo a).
[9] Pick up a B, a crystal, two 15ºs, a small briolette, and two 15ºs. Sew back through the crystal, pick up a B, and sew through the next B and A (figure 4, a–b). Pick up three 15ºs, and go through the next A and B (b–c).
[10] Pick up a B, a crystal, four 15ºs, a large briolette, and four 15ºs. Go back through the crystal, pick up a B, and go through the next B and A (c–d). Pick up three 15ºs, and go through the next A and B (d–e).
[11] Repeat steps 9 and 10 eight times, then repeat step 9 once more.
[12] Repeat steps 6 and 7 to make 11 crystal picots on the

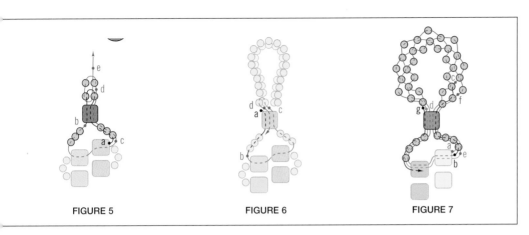

FIGURE 5   FIGURE 6   FIGURE 7

other end. Repeat steps 4 and 3 to the end.

[13] Secure the thread in the beadwork, and trim the tail.

Clasp

[1] Secure 18 in. (46cm) of Nymo at one end, and exit an end bead.

[2] Pick up three 15ºs, a B, four 15ºs, the button, and four 15ºs. Go back through the B (photo b). Pick up three 15ºs, and sew into the other edge bead (photo c). Retrace the thread path a few times for security. Secure the thread, and trim.

[3] Secure 1 yd. of Nymo at the other end, and exit an end bead.

[4] Pick up three 15ºs, a B, and two 15ºs. Go back through the B (figure 5, a–b). Pick up three 15ºs, and sew through the two end beads (b–c). Sew back through the three 15ºs, the B, and the first 15º above the B (c–d).

[5] Pick up two 15ºs, and go down through the 15º below. Go up through the adjacent 15º and the first 15º added in this step (d–e).

[6] Repeat step 5 until the strip is long enough to go around the button.

[7] Sew through the B at the base of the strip, and go through the three 15ºs as shown (figure 6, a–b). Go through both end beads, up through the three 15ºs, and back up through the B (b–c). Go up through the unattached 15º on the end of the loop and back down through the adjacent 15º (c–d). Retrace the thread path a few times. End the thread, and trim.

Green or bronze necklace

[1] Make a peyote band as in the garnet necklace.

[2] Follow steps 1–8 of "Embellishment," but begin the picots at the 62nd bead from the center.

[3] Follow step 9 of "Embellishment," but pick up a B, a crystal, three or four 15ºs, a teardrop bead or briolette, and three or four 15ºs for each dangle. Repeat for a total of 18 dangles.

[4] Embellish the other end of the band as you did the first. Secure the thread, and trim.

[5] Follow steps 1 and 2 of the clasp instructions for the garnet necklace to attach the button.

[6] For the loop, begin by picking up four 15ºs, an A, and enough 15ºs to go around the button. Go back through the A, pick up four 15ºs, and go through the two end hex-cut beads (figure 7, a–b).

[7] Go back through the four 15ºs, the A, and the first 15º of the loop. Pick up a 15º, skip a 15º, and go through the next 15º (b–c). Repeat around the loop to stitch a row of flat peyote (c–d), then go through the A, the four 15ºs, and the two end hex-cut beads (d–e).

[8] Sew through the beads as shown (e–f), then stitch one more row of flat peyote (f–g). Secure the thread, and trim.

Caterpillar cuff

Loops of beads cross over a
two-drop peyote band for a
luxurious, curved bracelet

by **Karmen Schmidt**

Embellishing a basic stitched band is a
classic beading technique that
can result in a lush and impressive
bracelet. Depending upon the approach,
however, it can be a time-consuming
undertaking. By using loops of beads,
you can add a rich fullness to beaded
projects without a lot of fuss.

FIGURE 1

FIGURE 2

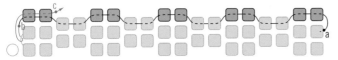

FIGURE 3

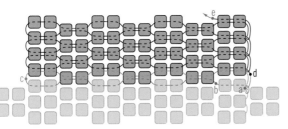

FIGURE 4

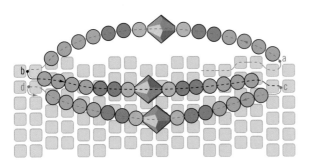

FIGURE 5

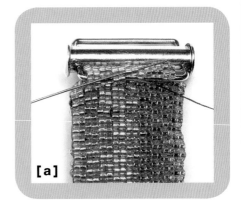

[a]

step*by*step

Two-drop peyote base

[1] Thread a needle with 2 yd. (1.8m) of conditioned Nymo (see Basics, p. 10), and attach a stop bead (Basics), leaving a 6-in. (15cm) tail.

[2] Pick up 18 cylinder beads (**figure 1, a–b**). Then pick up two cylinders, skip the last two, and go through the next two (**b–c**). Pick up two cylinders in each of the next three two-drop peyote (Basics) stitches (**c–d**).

[3] To secure the last stitch on this row, turn as in odd-count peyote (Basics): Go through the first two beads in row 1 (**d–e**). Pick up two cylinders, then go diagonally through the last stitch of row 2 and the second-to-last stitch of row 1 (**e–f**). Turn, and go diagonally through the second-to-last stitch of row 3 and the last on rows 2 and 1 (**f–g**). Go back through the two beads just added (**g–h**).

[4] Make four stitches to complete row 4 as shown in **figure 2**.

[5] For row 5, pick up two beads per stitch across the row (**figure 3, a–b**). Go under the thread bridge between the two rows below, and go back through the last two beads added in the opposite direction (**b–c**).

[6] Continue stitching in two-drop peyote until your band is about as long as the circumference of your wrist. Add new thread as needed (Basics).

[7] To make the flaps that will attach the band to the clasp, decrease by one stitch on each side of the band. Begin by exiting at **figure 4, point a**. Go under the thread bridge below, and go back through the two beads you just exited (**a–b**).

[8] Make three stitches to complete the first row (**b–c**).

MATERIALS

bracelet 7 in. (18cm)

- **200** (approximately) 4mm bicone crystals or fire-polished beads
- size 11º seed beads
  20g color A
  5g in each of **3** complementary colors: B, C, and D
- 10g Japanese cylinder beads
- tube-style clasp with 21mm side bar (Rio Grande, 800-545-6566, riogrande.com)
- Nymo B or D conditioned with beeswax or Thread Heaven
- beading needles, #11 or #12
- G-S Hypo Cement

EDITOR'S NOTE: If you can't find a clasp with a bar end, use a clasp with four loops instead. Stitch the band as indicated, but omit the flaps. Exit one end of the band between the two up-beads in the first column (photo b). Pick up four or five cylinder beads, go through an end loop on the clasp, and go back into the band in the same place (photo c). Retrace the thread path a few times for security, then sew through the beadwork to exit between the next two up-beads. Repeat to attach each loop to the band.

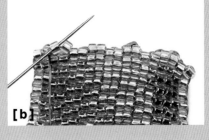

[b]

[c]

[9] Turn, and make four stitches to complete the second row of the flap. Go under the thread bridge below (c–d) and back through the last two beads added.

[10] Continue in two-drop peyote for six more rows (d–e). Do not finish off the tail yet.

[11] Repeat steps 7–10 on the other end of the band.

Loops

[1] Center a needle on 4 yd. (3.7m) of Nymo, and, working with doubled thread, secure it in the beadwork near one end of the band (not the flaps). Sew through the beadwork to exit the second bead from the edge in the first row (figure 5, point a).

[2] Pick up four color A 11º seed beads, a color B 11º, a color C 11º, a color D 11º, a crystal, a D, a C, a B, and four As. Cross the beads over the band, and go through the second bead from the other edge (a–b).

[3] Pick up the same bead sequence, cross the beads over the band, and go into the second bead from the edge in the next row (b–c). Repeat (c–d) for the length of the band. Secure the tail with a few half-hitch knots (Basics) between beads, and trim.

Clasp

[1] Slide one of the clasp bars onto a flap, and wrap the flap around the bar.

[2] Thread a needle on the tail from the flap, and stitch the flap to the underside of the first row of the band (photo a).

Retrace the thread path for strength. Secure the tail in the beadwork with half-hitch knots, dot them with glue, and trim.

[3] Making sure the band is not twisted and the clasp is properly oriented, repeat on the other end with the other clasp bar.

Bargello necklace

Staggered rows of two-drop peyote make a striking necklace

by **Rebecca Peapples**

Bargello, also called "flame stitch" because its characteristic zigzag pattern resembles flames, is an Italian upholstery and needlework stitch from the seventeenth century. This dramatic neckpiece gracefully imitates the bargello effect using two-drop peyote.

MATERIALS
necklace 20 in. (51cm)
- **23–30** 4mm round or drop-shaped glass, pearl, or gemstone beads
- 3g size 11º Czech seed beads, color A or B
- Japanese cylinder beads
  10g color A
  7g color B
  7g color C
- 3g size 15º Japanese seed beads, color C
- 10mm bead for clasp
- Nymo B or D conditioned with beeswax or Thread Heaven
- beading needles, #12

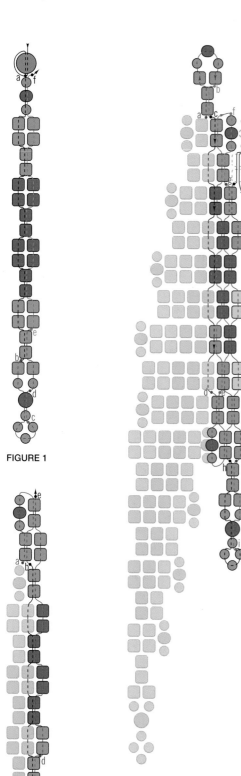

FIGURE 1

FIGURE 2

FIGURE 3

FIGURE 4

step*by*step

Getting started

[1] Thread a needle on 2–4 yd. (1.8–3.7m) of conditioned Nymo, and, leaving a 1–2-yd. (.9–1.8m) tail, attach a stop bead (see Basics, p. 10).

[2] Pick up a 15º seed bead, an 11º, a 15º, four color A cylinder beads, eight color B cylinders, and four As (figure 1, a–b).

[3] Pick up an A, a 15º, a 4mm round bead, and four 15ºs (b–c). Go back through the first of the four 15ºs and the 4mm (c–d). Pick up a 15º and an A, and go through the last two As from the previous step (d–e). (If you're using top-drilled drop beads, simply pick up an A, a 15º, a drop bead, a 15º, and an A, and go back through the last two As from the previous step.)

[4] Work four stitches in two-drop peyote (Basics), using a pair of As, a pair of Bs, a pair of Bs, and a pair of As. On the last stitch, go through the first three beads picked up in step 2 (e–f).

Necklace

[1] Pick up two As, a 15º, an 11º, a 15º, and two As, and go back through the first two As just picked up (figure 2, a–b). This sequence will be referred to as a long turn.

[2] Work four stitches in two-drop peyote using the same A, B, B, A sequence used in step 4 of "Getting started" (b–c).

[3] Pick up a 15º, an 11º, and a 15º, and go back through the last two As added in the previous step (c–d). This sequence will be referred to as a short turn.

[4] Work four stitches in two-drop peyote using the A, B, B, A sequence. After picking up the last two As, go through the second pair of As from the long turn (d–e).

[5] Repeat steps 1–4 three times.

[6] Pick up three As, a 15º, an 11º, a 15º, and an A

(figure 3, a–b), and go through the first two As just picked up (b–c). This sequence will be referred to as an apex unit.

[7] Work four stitches in two-drop peyote, using the A, B, B, A sequence (c–d). Make a long turn (d–e), and work four two-drop stitches using the A, B, B, A sequence (e–f).

[8] Work a short turn (f–g), then work four two-drop stitches using the A, B, B, A sequence (g–h).

[9] Pick up three As, a 15º, a 4mm, and four 15ºs (h–i). Go back through the first of the four 15ºs and the 4mm, pick up a 15º and an A, and go back through the first two As picked up in this step (i–j). This sequence will be referred to as a drop unit.

[10] Work four stitches in two-drop peyote, but substitute color C cylinders for the Bs (j–k). Repeat steps 1–9 using Cs instead of Bs. After making the next drop unit, switch back to using Bs. Continue working in this pattern, alternating Bs and Cs, until the first half of your necklace is the desired length. End with an apex unit, and embellish the edge with short-turn bead groups, if desired.

[11] To make the other half, flip your work, and remove the stop bead. Thread a needle on the tail, and repeat steps 1–10. After stitching two rows (figure 4, a–b), you may want to reinforce the center point. To do so, weave through the beadwork to exit the top of the 11º used in the first long turn of the first side (b–c). Pick up an 11º, and sew into the 11º and 15º of the first long turn made in this step (c–d). Retrace the thread path a few times, zig-zag back to where you left off, and resume stitching.

Clasp

[1] Exit an A near the top of either end. Pick up two 15ºs, an 11º, the clasp bead, a 15º, a 4mm, and an 11º. Skip the last 11º, and go back through the last four beads picked up. Pick up two 15ºs, and sew into the A adjacent to the one your thread is exiting. Retrace the thread path a few times. Secure the tail in the beadwork with a few half-hitch knots (Basics) between beads, and trim.

[2] Use the tail on the other end to make a loop. Pick up three 15ºs, an 11º, and enough 15ºs to fit around the clasp bead. Go back through the 11º (photo a). Pick up three 15ºs, and sew into the A adjacent to the one your thread is exiting (photo b). Retrace the thread path, secure the tail, and trim.

[a]

[b]

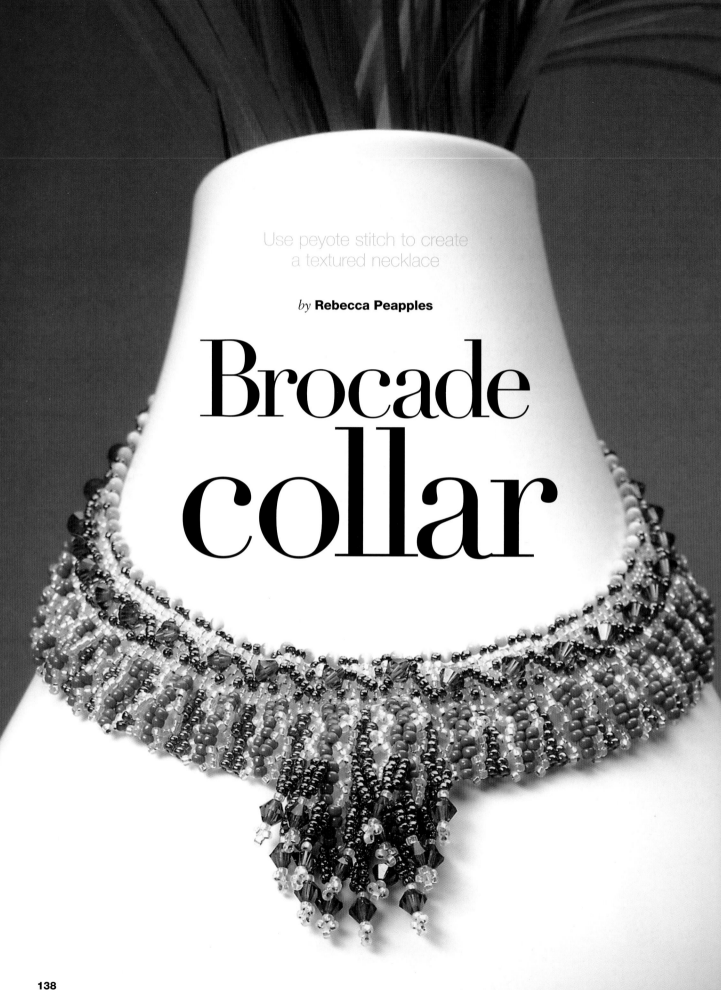

Use peyote stitch to create
a textured necklace

by **Rebecca Peapples**

Brocade
collar

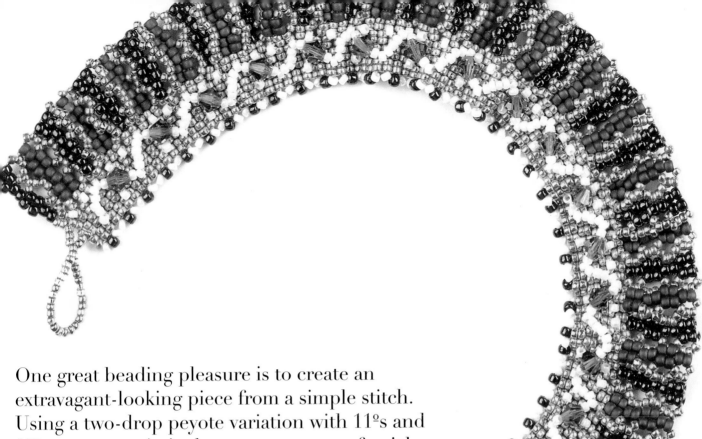

One great beading pleasure is to create an extravagant-looking piece from a simple stitch. Using a two-drop peyote variation with 11ºs and 15ºs, you can mimic the woven texture of a rich brocade. When people comment on your handsome neckpiece, just smile and enjoy the compliments.

step*by*step

Necklace

Make the base in flat, two-drop peyote stitch, working top to bottom and left to right. Keep the tension comfortably tight to help maintain the ruffled bottom. When you run out of thread, weave the working thread into the stitches on the ruffled bottom so you don't block any of the 15ºs, which will be embellished later. Begin a new thread where the old one left off.

[1] On 3 yd. (2.7m) of thread, pick up eight color A 15ºs and eight color C 11ºs (figure 1, a–b), leaving a 12-in. (30cm) tail. These beads form rows 1 and 2.

Row 3: Work in two-drop peyote (see Basics, p. 10): Pick up two Cs, skip two Cs on the previous row, and sew through the next two Cs (b–c). Work the next stitch with two Cs and the following two stitches with As (c–d).

Row 4: Two As, two As, four As, four As (d–e).

Row 5: Pick up four As. Sew through the second and third As on the previous

MATERIALS

necklace 16 in. (41cm)

- **100** 4mm glass beads or crystals
- **120** 2mm round glass or gemstone beads
- Japanese seed beads
  15g size 11º, color C
  15g size 11º, color D
  20g size 15º, color A
  10g size 15º, color B
- 8–10mm bead for clasp
- Nymo D or B
- beading needles, #12 or #13

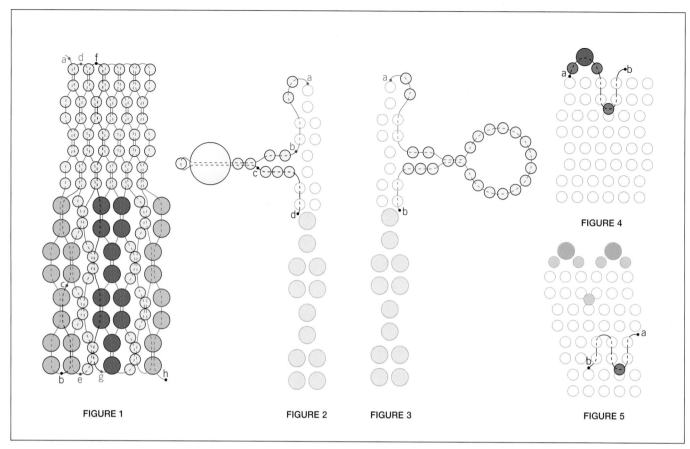

FIGURE 1

FIGURE 2

FIGURE 3

FIGURE 4

FIGURE 5

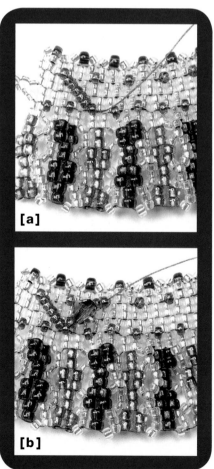

[a]

[b]

row. Repeat once. Two As, two As **(e–f)**.
Row 6: Two As, two As. Pick up two Ds.
Sew through the second and third As on
the previous row. Repeat once **(f–g)**.
Rows 7–12: Continue working as
shown **(g–h)**, alternating colors as you
add 11°s.

[2] Repeat rows 3–12 to the desired
length. You can stop in the middle of
the necklace base if you want to add the
optional centerpiece (shown on p. 138),
but complete the sequence so you end
with row 12. Don't cut the thread.

Closure

[1] Thread a needle on the tail left in
row 1. Pick up two As, skip two As in
the end row, and sew through the next
two As **(figure 2, a–b)**.

[2] Pick up four As, the clasp bead, and
an A. Sew back through the clasp bead
and two As **(b–c)**.

[3] Pick up three As, and sew through
the next two As on the end row **(c–d)**.
Retrace the thread path, secure the tail
with a few half-hitch knots (Basics)
between beads, and trim.

[4] Repeat step 1 with the working
thread, then pick up four As plus

enough As to make a loop large enough
to fit around the clasp bead. Sew through
the fourth and third As, pick up three As,
and sew into the next two As on the end
row **(figure 3, a–b)**. Retrace the thread
path, secure the tail, and trim.

Embellishment

[1] Start a new thread, and secure it in
the base 15°s, exiting at **figure 4, point a**.

[2] Pick up a B, a 2mm bead (or a C),
and a B. Skip a row, and sew down
through two As in the next base row.
Pick up a B and sew up the next two As
in the next base row **(a–b)**.

[3] Repeat step 2 until you reach the
other end of the necklace. Secure the
tails, and trim.

[4] Start a new thread and exit at **figure
5, point a**. Sew down two 15°s in the
first row, and pick up a B. Sew up
through the two 15°s in the next row
and down through the two 15°s in the
next row **(a–b)**. Pick up a B and go up
the next two 15°s. Repeat until you
reach the other end of the necklace, then
secure the thread.

[5] Start a new thread, and exit the first
B along the first row on the top of the

base. Pick up five Bs, and sew through the third B along the second row of Bs (**photo a**). Pick up a B, a 4mm crystal, and a B. Sew through the third B on the top edge (**photo b**). Repeat across the necklace base.

Centerpiece (optional)

To work the long rows in the center of the necklace, refer to **figure 6**.

[1] After row 12, pick up ten Cs. Skip two Cs, and sew through the next two Cs (**a–b**).

[2] Work the next stitch in Cs (**b–c**).

[3] Continue the centerpiece pattern (**c–d**), adding a total of 24 long rows (**photo c**) and ending at **point d**. Then switch back to the base pattern to mirror the first half of the base.

Centerpiece embellishment (optional)

To embellish the long rows of 11ºs, sew down through a pair of 11ºs, pick up three Bs, an A, a crystal, and four As. Sew back up through an A, the crystal, and an A. Pick up three Bs, and sew into the next two 11ºs on the base (**figure 7, a–b**). Sew through six 11ºs, exiting at **point c** (**photo d**). Repeat the bead sequence to make the next crystal fringe. Add as much fringe as desired.

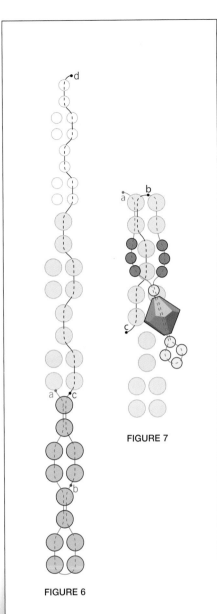

FIGURE 6

FIGURE 7

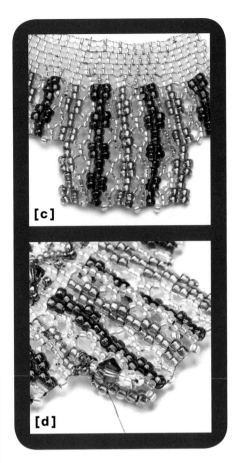

[c]

[d]

EDITOR'S NOTE:
Since the bottom curves more than the top of the base, it is important to keep steady tension on the separation between the top half and the bottom, otherwise there will be gaps between the stitches.

Totally tubular tassel

Three easy stitches add up to one great necklace for an art glass bead

by **Angela Sawyer**

Showcasing focal beads can be challenging when you want to do more than simply string them. This necklace supports a large bead while making tons of twists, turns, and loops with small ones.

step*by*step

Tassel

[1] Using a comfortable length of Fireline, pick up 16 color A 15º seed beads. Leaving a 10-in. (25cm) tail, tie them in a circle around the dowel **(photo a)** using a square knot (see Basics, p. 10).

[2] Working in tubular peyote (Basics), stitch 22 rounds **(photo b)**. Do not cut the thread.

[3] Stitch a strip that connects the tassel to the focal bead **(photo c)**: Pick up 15 As, skip two As, and go through the third bead from the end **(figure 1, a–b)**. Continue working in flat peyote stitch (Basics) across the row **(b–c)**. Go through the three nearest beads on the edge of the tube **(c–d)**. Work another row of peyote **(d–e)**. Do not cut the thread.

[4] Remove the tube from the dowel. To make the top

loop, attach the end of the strip to the other side of the tube by sewing through several beads. Secure the thread with a few half-hitch knots (Basics) between beads, and trim the tail.

[5] To cover the tube with loops of fringe, secure a new thread near the beginning end of the tube and exit any bead on round 1. Pick up 20 As, five Bs, a drop bead, five Bs, and 20 As. Go back

through the bead on the ring, the neighboring bead on round 2, and the next bead on round 1 **(figure 2, a–b)**. Make a total of eight loops.

[6] Weave through to round 3, and repeat. Continue adding eight loops to each odd-numbered round until you finish round 15. Make loops on the last three rounds as follows:

Round 17: 15 As, five Bs,

drop, five Bs, 15 As.

Round 19: ten As, five Bs, drop, five Bs, ten As.

Round 21: five As, five Bs, drop, five Bs, five As. Secure the thread.

Herringbone tubes

To add a spiral twist to a herringbone tube, distort the vertical bead stacks of conventional herringbone with the bead counts given in steps 2 and 3, below.

[a] [b] [c]

[d]

[e]

[f]

MATERIALS

necklace 18 in. (46cm)

- focal bead (beads p. 142 by Tom Boylan, Tom Boylan Glass Beads, 707-877-3578; bead p. 144 by Joanne Morash, Blue Iris Designs, 864-261-6368, blueirisdesigns.com)
- seed beads, size 15º
  60g matte emerald green, color A
  30g violet gold luster, color B
- 20g 4mm drop beads
- Fireline 8 lb. test
- flexible beading wire, .014
- beading needles, #12
- toggle clasp
- **2** crimp beads
- ⅛-in. (3mm) diameter dowel, 6 in. (15cm) long
- wire cutters
- crimping pliers

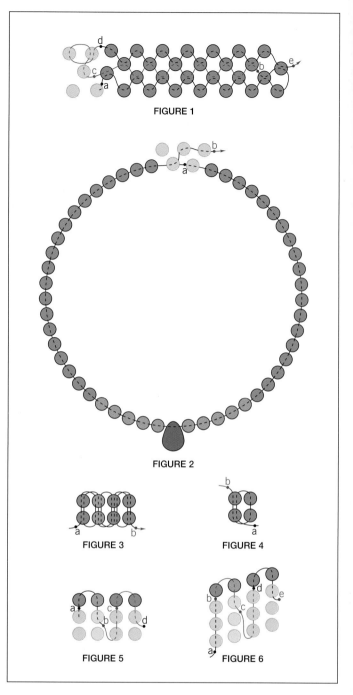

FIGURE 1

FIGURE 2

FIGURE 3

FIGURE 4

FIGURE 5

FIGURE 6

[**1**] Using a comfortable length of Fireline, make a four-stack ladder (Basics) with two beads per stack, arranging the colors as shown in **figure 3, a–b**. Connect the end beads to the first beads to join the ladder into a ring **(figure 4, a–b)**.

[**2**] Pick up one A and one B, and go down through the next B **(figure 5, a–b)**. Come up through two As in the next stack **(b–c)**. Pick up two As, and go down through the next A **(c–d)**.

[**3**] Come up through three As in the next stack **(figure 6, a–b)**. Pick up an A and a B, and go down through the next B **(b–c)**. Come up through three As in the next stack **(c–d)**. Pick up two As and go down through the next A **(d–e)**.

[**4**] Repeat step 3 until your tube is about 6 in. (15cm) long. Don't cut the thread.

[**5**] Finish the starting end by securing the tail with a few half-hitch knots between beads. Trim the tail. Make a second tube to match the first.

Assembly

[**1**] Determine the finished length of your necklace (This one is 18 in./46cm), add 6 in., and cut a piece of beading wire to that length.

[**2**] Center the tassel on the wire. String the focal bead over both ends **(photo d)**, and pull the tassel into the bead.

[**3**] String a herringbone tube, finished-end first, on one of the wire ends, and slide it against the focal bead **(photo e)**. Continue stitching the tube, if desired, to increase its length, but don't remove it from the wire. Secure the thread, and trim the tail.

[**4**] Repeat step 3 on the other wire end.

[**5**] On one end, string a crimp bead and half of the clasp. Go back through the crimp bead, and tighten the wire so the tube is right against the crimp bead. Crimp the crimp bead (Basics), and trim the excess wire **(photo f)**. Repeat on the other end of the necklace.

Dutch spiral necklace

by **Elaine Pinckney**

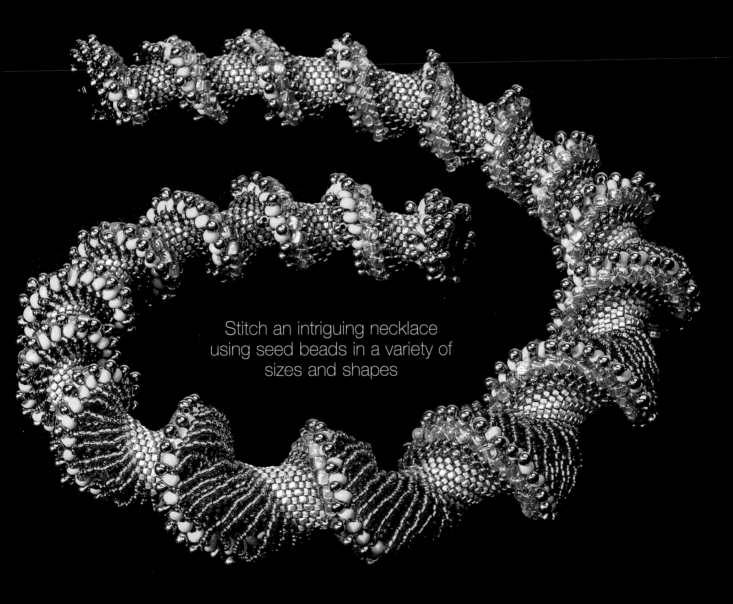

Stitch an intriguing necklace
using seed beads in a variety of
sizes and shapes

Many beaders love the serpentine look and feel of tubular peyote and really get a kick out of experimenting with its many variations. By enhancing it with the simple increases and decreases of the Dutch spiral stitch, an undulating wave of color completely transforms a sleek peyote tube into an entirely different animal.

step*by*step

[1] On a comfortable length of conditioned Nymo (use it doubled) or Fireline, pick up 20 seed beads in the following color sequence: an A, a B, two Cs, two Ds, two Es, four Fs, two Gs, two Hs, two Is, and two Js. Leaving a 6-in. (15cm) tail, tie the beads into a ring with a square knot (see Basics, p. 10). Sew through the first two beads again **(figure 1, a–b)**.

[2] Work round 3 in tubular peyote (Basics) as follows: Pick up a B, skip the first C, and sew through the second C. Pick up a C, skip the first D, and sew through the second D **(b–c)**. Continue the pattern around the ring, adding a D, an E, two Fs, a G,

an H, and an I **(c–d)**. To step up, pick up a J and an A, and sew through the B added on this round **(d–e)**.

[3] **Rounds 4–40:** Repeat step 2 **(figure 2, a–b)**.

[4] Continue working the pattern in tubular peyote as in rounds 1–40, but increase the number of As you pick up at the step-up of each round as follows:

Rounds 41–80: 2As
Rounds 81–100: 3As
Rounds 101–105: 4As
Rounds 106–110: 5As
Rounds 111–112: 6As
Rounds 113–114: 7As
Rounds 115–116: 8As
Rounds 117–118: 9As
Rounds 119–120: 10As
Rounds 121–122: 11As
Rounds 123–124: 12As

Rounds 125–126: 13As
Rounds 127–128: 14As
Rounds 129–247: 15As

[5] Rounds 129–247 form the center of the necklace. The finished necklace length is 19 in. (48cm). To increase the length of your necklace, continue adding rounds with 15 As until you have added the desired length.

[6] Decrease the number of As picked up for the following rounds so the second half of the necklace is the mirror image of the first.

Rounds 248–249: 14As
Rounds 250–251: 13As
Rounds 252–253: 12As
Rounds 254–255: 11As
Rounds 256–257: 10As
Rounds 258–259: 9As
Rounds 260–261: 8As

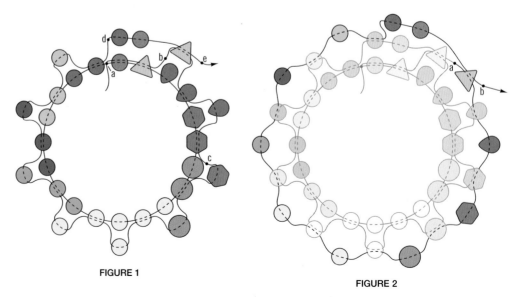

FIGURE 1

FIGURE 2

Rounds 262–263: 7As
Rounds 264–265: 6As
Rounds 266–270: 5As
Rounds 271–275: 4As
Rounds 276–295: 3As
Rounds 296–335: 2As
Rounds 336–375: 1A

[7] Sew a snap half to the first round of the spiral (photo a). Repeat on the other end. Make sure the snap halves are securely attached, and then hide the edges of the snap with a round of peyote, using one of the larger beads from the pattern (photos b and c). Secure the threads in the beadwork, and trim.

MATERIALS
necklace 19 in. (48cm)
- seed beads
  36g size 11º, color A
  40g size 5º triangles, color B
  24g size 6º or 16g size 8º hex-cuts or triangles, in **2** colors: C and D
  16g size 8º, color E
  16g size 8º or 8g size 11º, color F
  8g size 11º rounds, hex-cuts, or triangles in **4** colors: G, H, I, and J
- 40g drop beads (optional)
- 15mm metal snap
- Fireline 8 or 10 lb. test or Nymo B conditioned with beeswax
- beading needles, #12

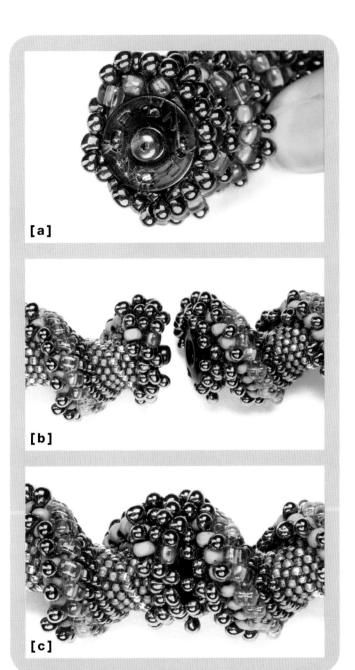

[a]

[b]

[c]

EDITOR'S NOTE: Small drop beads were added as an embellishment to this necklace and hide the snap on the necklace shown on p. 145. They are stitched between the Bs in the necklace to accentuate the spiral.

Peyote links

Use a favorite stitch to make a trendy piece of jewelry

by **Maiko Kage**

Large links of chain seem to be everywhere in fashion lately, and here's an interesting way to stitch them. Work around the circumference of a ring of beads as if making a wheel. Then do it again from the same base row. Sew the two halves together to form sturdy circular and oval links.

stepbystep

Circular link

Beads in the photos and illustrations are shown in several colors for clarity.

[1] On 2 yd. (1.8m) of thread, center 40 color A 11º seed beads. Tie the beads into a ring with a square knot (see Basics, p. 10). Sew through the next A (figure 1, a–b).

[2] Work in peyote stitch (Basics) by picking up an A, skipping an A on the ring, and sewing through the next A. Continue until you get back to the first A in this step. Sew through the first A added in this round to step up to the next round (b–c).

[3] Work an increase in the next round by picking up two As instead of one in every other stitch (c–d).

[4] Work the next round, using one A per stitch and sewing through both increase beads on the previous round (d–e and photo a).

[5] Set aside the working thread, and thread a needle on the tail. Work two rounds of peyote off the first row, remembering to step up (photo b).

[6] Repeat steps 3 and 4, making sure the increases match the increases on the existing rounds (photo c).

[7] With the thread exiting a single A on the last round, pick up two As, and sew through the next single A on the opposite edge (figure 2, a–b). Pick up one A, and sew through the next single A on the opposite edge (b–c and photo d).

[8] Continue around the ring until you reach the first As added in step 7. Sew through them, and continue, sewing through the As opposite the ones you sewed through in the last round.

[9] Secure the tails using half-hitch knots (Basics) between beads. Make six circular links.

MATERIALS

bracelet 8 in. (20cm)
- **6** 6–8mm round gemstone beads
- **12** 3mm bicone crystals
- size 11º Japanese seed beads
  30g color A
  30g color B
- Nymo B
- beading needles, #13

earrings
- **4** 4mm pearls
- **2** 6mm round crystals
- 5g 15º Japanese seed beads
- Nymo B
- beading needles, #13
- **2** 4mm soldered jump rings
- pair of earring findings
- chainnose pliers

[a]

[b]

[c]

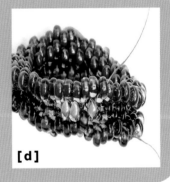

[d]

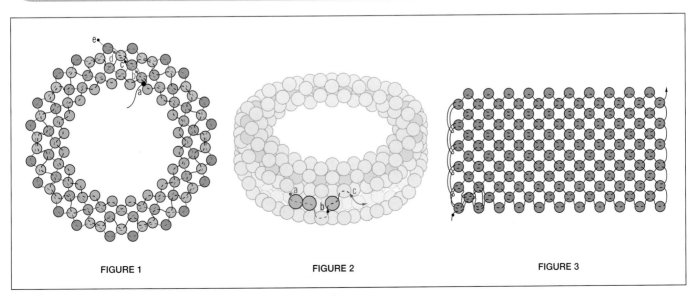

FIGURE 1

FIGURE 2

FIGURE 3

[e]

[f]

[g]

EDITOR'S NOTE:
If you prefer a more delicate bracelet, use 15° Japanese seed beads for the circular and oval links. Use a 4mm gemstone bead instead of a 6mm to connect the circular links.

Toggle

[1] On 2 yd. of thread, make a flat, odd-count peyote strip 21 As long and six rows wide (Basics and **figure 3**).

[2] Sew the first row to the last row by zipping up the edge beads (Basics).

Connecting the links

[1] Secure a 2-yd. length of thread in the first ring, and exit one of the single edge beads from step 7 of the circular link.

[2] Pick up a 3mm bicone crystal, a 6mm gemstone, and a 3mm crystal. Sew through a corresponding bead on a second chain link, back through the beads just added, and back into the bead from step 1 (photo e).

[3] Retrace the thread path to secure the connection. Then, sew around the outside edge of the second link to a single bead on the opposite side. Connect the remaining links in the same manner. Connect the toggle to the end link.

Oval link

Make oval links in the same manner as the circular links, with the following changes: Pick up 52 color B 11°s instead of 40 As. Sew through two circular links before tying the beads into a ring (photo f). Refer to **figure 4** for the increases and bead counts.

Earrings

[1] Make a circular link using 15° seed beads, but don't trim one of the tails.

[2] With the tail exiting an outer edge bead, pick up a 4mm pearl, a 6mm round crystal, a 4mm pearl, a 15°, and a 4mm soldered jump ring.

[3] Sew back through the beads and through the bead on the link where you started. Reinforce with a second thread path, tie a few half-hitch knots between beads, and trim the tails.

[4] Open the earring finding, and slide the soldered jump ring into it. Close the finding (photo g).

[5] Make a second earring to match the first.

FIGURE 4

Interlocking links

Weave peyote stitch links into a seamless cuff

by **Jacqueline Johnson**

[a]

This bracelet prompts the question "How did you do that?" By looking at the completed piece, you can't tell that the links are actually two colors. And if you don't know the secret, the illusion that these multiple rows of links have no beginning or end will keep you guessing to infinity and beyond!

MATERIALS

bracelet 7½ in. (19.1cm)

- 15g size 13º Charlottes, in each of **2** colors: A and C
- 15g size 15º Japanese seed beads, in each of **2** colors: B and D
- Nymo B or D conditioned with beeswax
- beading needles, #13

EDITOR'S NOTE:

As you make the links, count out the beads needed for each round listed in a step and line them up on your work surface. This will help you keep track of what round you are on, and when you run out of beads for the row, it will remind you to step up.

step*by*step

Links

[1] On 5 ft. (1.5m) of conditioned Nymo (see Basics, p. 10), pick up four color A 13º Charlottes. Sew through the first bead again to form a ring.

[2] Continue using As, and work in circular, even-count peyote (Basics) for a total of eight rows. Keep your tension consistent, but not too tight, so the links are soft and pliable.

[3] To form the first corner of the link, refer to **figures 1** and **2**, use As, and work an increase or a decrease on the second stitch of rounds 9–18 as follows. Sew through the first bead of each round to step up and through the first bead of each increase as you work each round.

Round 9: A, 2A, A, A **(figure 1, a–b)**
Round 10: A, 3A, A, A **(b–c)**
Round 11: A, 5A, A, A **(c–d)**
Round 12: A, 7A, A, A **(d–e)**
Round 13: A, 8A, A, A **(e–f)**
Round 14: A, 8A, A, A **(f–g)**
Round 15: A, 7A, A, A **(figure 2, a–b)**

Round 16: A, 5A, A, A **(b–c)**
Round 17: A, 3A, A, A **(c–d)**
Round 18: A, 2A, A, A **(d–e)**

[4] Continue working four beads per round in circular, even-count peyote **(e–f)**, for 19 rounds.

[5] Repeat step 3 to make the second corner.

[6] Repeat step 2 to complete the first half of a link.

[7] Repeat steps 2–6 using color B 15º seed beads **(photo a)**. Don't secure or cut the threads.

[8] Make a total of 18 links, nine in color A 13ºs and color B 15ºs, and nine in color C 13ºs and color D 15ºs.

Assembly

[1] Align the first and last rows on a color AB link, and zip up (Basics and **photo b**) the two ends to form a ring. Secure the tails in the beadwork, and trim.

[2] Twist the AB link so the 13º half of the link crosses over the 15ºs, forming a figure 8 **(photo c)**.

[3] Position a CD link as shown in **photo d** so the 15º half of the CD link is

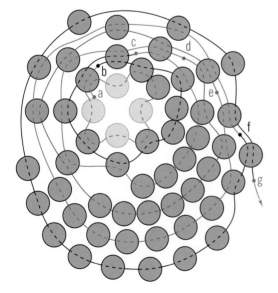

FIGURE 1

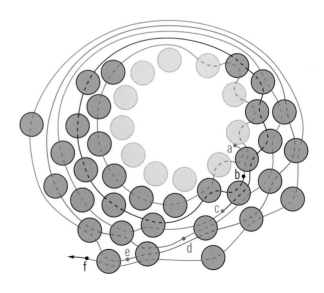

FIGURE 2

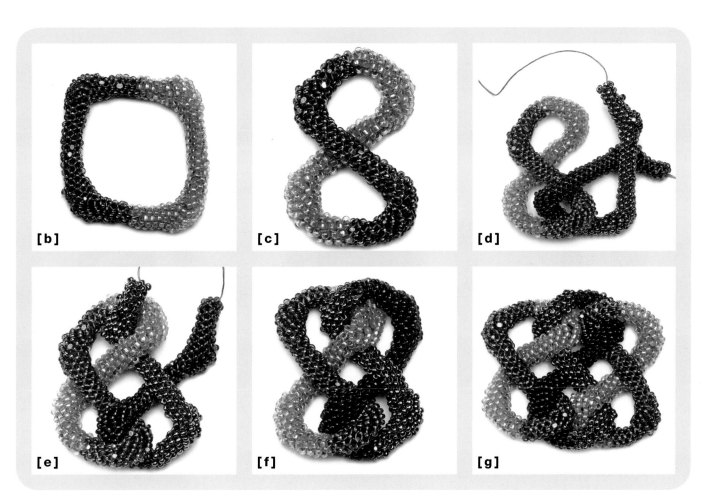

[b]

[c]

[d]

[e]

[f]

[g]

looped through the bottom ring of the
AB link.

[4] Form a figure 8 with the CD link so
the 13º half of the link loops through
the top ring of the AB link (photo e).

[5] Align the first and last rows of a CD
link, and stitch the two ends together as
you did in step 1. Secure the tails in the
beadwork, and trim (photo f).

[6] Repeat steps 3–5 with an AB link
(photo g).

[7] Continue connecting the links,
alternating between AB and CD links.
Join the 18th link to the 17th and to the
first link to complete the cuff.

Decorative vessels

Dress up peyote stitch containers with lively embellished lids

by **Wendy Ellsworth**

Colorful beaded containers with a slouchy-basket look work up rather quickly using size 8º Japanese seed beads. You'll be surprised to see how soon you have a cute little container for storing – what else? – more beads!

step*by*step

Container
Base

[1] Begin round 1 by picking up three color A 8º seed beads. Tie them into a ring with a square knot (see Basics, p. 10), and sew through the next bead (**figure 1, a–b**).

[2] Work the next round with a peyote increase by picking up two color B 8ºs per stitch. Step up through the first two Bs added in this step (**b–c**). Continue to add rounds, working in flat, circular peyote as follows, stepping up after each round:
Round 3: 6 As, adding a bead between each bead from round 2 (**c–d**).
Round 4: 2Bs per stitch (**d–e**).

Round 5: 1A per stitch, as in round 3 (**e–f**).
Round 6: 1B per stitch (**f–g**).
Round 7: Alternate between 2As and 1A per stitch (**g–h**).
Round 8: 1B per stitch, sewing through both increase beads from the previous round (**h–i**).
Round 9: 2As per stitch (**i–j**).
Round 10: Alternate between 1B and 2Bs per stitch (**j–k**).
Round 11: 2As per stitch (**k–l**).
Round 12: 2Bs per stitch (**l–m**).
Round 13: Alternate between 2As and 3As per stitch (**m–n**). This is the last row of the bottom of the vessel. (The bottom may not lie flat, but this can be addressed later.)

Walls
Work in two-, three-, and four-drop circular peyote as

follows, monitoring your tension for each row by not letting the thread show.
Round 14: 2Bs per stitch.
Round 15: 3As per stitch.
Round 16–23: Alternate between rounds 14 and 15 four times.
Round 24: Alternate between 2Bs and 3Bs per stitch.
Round 25: 3As per stitch.
Round 26: 3Bs per stitch.
Round 27–28: Repeat rounds 25 and 26.
Round 29: Alternate between 3As and 4As per stitch.
Round 30: 3Bs per stitch.
Round 31: 4Bs per stitch.
Round 32–35: Alternate between rounds 30 and 31 twice.
Round 36: Alternate between 3Bs and 4Bs per stitch.

Round 37: 4As per stitch.
Round 38: 4Bs per stitch.
Round 39–50: Alternate between rounds 37 and 38 six times.
Round 51: 4As per stitch.
Round 52: 3Bs per stitch.

MATERIALS
container with lid
- assortment of 4–8mm accent beads for lid
- **45** 4mm fringe beads
- 45g size 8º Japanese seed beads, in each of **2** colors: A and B
- Nymo D conditioned with beeswax, Power Pro, or Fireline 10 lb. test
- beading needles, #10

Round 53: 4As per stitch.
Round 54–65: Alternate between rounds of 3Bs per stitch and 3As per stitch six times. Secure the tail.

Lid

[1] Start a new thread, and alternate three As and three Bs 13 times. Tie the beads into a ring, and place them around the top rim of the container (photo a).
[2] Working in three-drop peyote, complete ten rounds, ending with As. Work these rounds on the container so the lid is the correct size. Adjust your tension as you work so the lid isn't too tight (photo b). Continue working in circular peyote. Begin with two- and three-drop, then decrease to single peyote as follows:
Round 11: 2Bs per stitch.
Round 12: 3As per stitch.
Round 13: 2Bs per stitch.
Round 14: 2As per stitch.
Round 15: 2Bs per stitch.
Round 16: 1A per stitch.
Round 17–26: Alternate rounds 15 and 16 five times.
Round 27: 1B per stitch.
Round 28: 1A per stitch.
Round 29: Decrease to ten beads in this round. Stitch the next four Bs, one bead per stitch (figure 2, a–b). Then skip a stitch by sewing through the next A (b–c). Work three Bs (one bead per stitch), skip a stitch, and work three Bs as before. Skip the last stitch, and step up

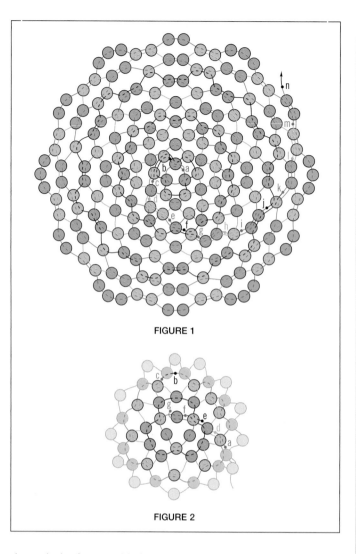

FIGURE 1

FIGURE 2

through the first B added in this step (c–d).
Round 30: Decrease to nine beads in this round. Stitch one A, skip a stitch, then work the remaining stitches with As (d–e).
Round 31: Decrease to three beads in this round. Stitch one B every third stitch (e–f).
Round 32: 1A per stitch (f–g). Reinforce the last round with a second thread pass.

Embellishment

[1] Start a new thread, and pick up enough accent beads to fit around the ledge of the

lid (photo c). Sew the beads into a ring, and secure the tails. If the ring is very loose, sew through a few beads on the lid to secure it.
[2] Exit the last round of the lid, and pick up one or two fringe beads (photo d), depending on how much space is between the beads. Sew through the next bead in the last round. Continue to add as many fringe beads as desired. Secure the tails, and trim. Push gently on the bottom to curve it inward (photo e).

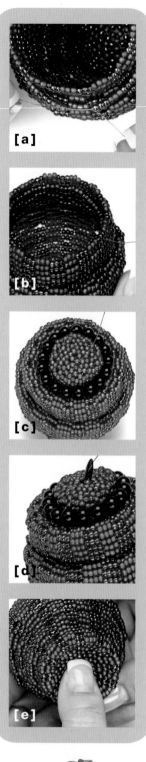

[a]

[b]

[c]

[d]

[e]

Peyote stitch
medallion necklace

The open feel of lacy
medallions lends a
lightness to this piece

by **Anna Elizabeth Draeger**

Crystals and seed beads sparkle in this delicate necklace with a floral motif. Combine small amounts of peyote stitch, stringing, and wirework for a piece that is a delight to make.

step*by*step

Pendant

[1] On 2 yd. (1.8m) of thread, pick up a repeating pattern of a 15º seed bead and a 4mm bicone crystal six times. Sew through the first 15º to form a ring (**figure 1, a–b**).

[2] Pick up 17 15ºs, and sew through the next 15º in the ring. Then sew back through the last three beads (**b–c**).

[3] Pick up 14 15ºs. Sew through the next 15º in the ring and back through the last three beads. Repeat three times (**c–d**).

[4] Pick up 11 15ºs, sew through the first three 15ºs from step 2, and sew through the next 15º in the ring. Sew back through the first four 15ºs from step 2 (**d–e**).

[5] Pick up a 15º, skip a 15º, and sew through the next 15º (**figure 2, a–b**). Continue in peyote stitch (see Basics, p. 10) for four stitches. Then sew through the next three beads, the next 15º in the ring, and back through the last three beads. Continue through the first 15º on the next loop (**b–c**). Repeat five times, exiting the first 15º added in this step (**c–d**).

[6] Work the next four stitches of peyote with 11ºs, and sew through to the next loop (**d–e**). Repeat on each loop, and exit the first 11º added (**e–f**).

[7] Sew through the next 15º and 11º. Pick up a 15º, a 4mm, a 15º, and a soldered jump ring. Skip the soldered jump ring, and sew back through the 15º, the 4mm, the 15º, and the next three beads (**figure 3, a–b**).

[8] Follow the thread path around the outer edge of the loops to the opposite side of the pendant, exiting at **point c**. Add three fringes to the bottom loop as follows:

Fringe 1: Pick up two 15ºs, a 4mm, and three 15ºs. Skip the last three 15ºs, and sew back through the 4mm and the two 15ºs. Sew through the next 11º (**c–d**).

Fringe 2: Pick up three 15ºs, a 4mm, a 15º, a 4mm, a 15º, a 4mm, and three 15ºs. Skip the last three 15ºs, and sew

MATERIALS

necklace 16 in. (41cm)
- Swarovski crystals
  8 6mm bicone
  68 4mm bicone
- **20** 6mm Swarovski pearls
- Japanese seed beads
  4g size 11º
  6g size 15º
- clasp
- 8 in. (20cm) 20- or 22-gauge wire
- **6** soldered jump rings
- **2** crimp beads
- Nymo D or Fireline 6 lb. test
- flexible beading wire, .014
- beading needles, #13
- chainnose pliers
- crimping pliers
- roundnose pliers
- wire cutters

back through these beads, skipping the first 15º (d–e). Pick up a 15º, and sew through the next 11º (e–f).

Fringe 3: Repeat fringe 1 (f–g).

[9] Follow the thread path back to the top loop, and reinforce the beads from step 7 with a second thread path (g–h).

Medallions

Make the medallions by following the steps for the pendant, but add a soldered jump ring on opposite sides and eliminate the fringe. Make two medallions.

Crystal links

Cut a 4-in. (10cm) length of wire. Make a plain loop (Basics) on one end. String a 4mm, a 6mm bicone crystal, and a 4mm. Make a plain loop on the other end. Make a second crystal link.

Assembly

[1] Open one loop on a crystal link, and attach it to the pendant's soldered jump ring. Close the loop. Open the loop on the other end, and attach it to a medallion. Repeat with the second crystal link and medallion.

[2] Cut a 16-in. (41cm) piece of beading wire. On the wire, center 17 15ºs and the available soldered jump ring of one medallion. String an 11º over both wire ends to create a loop of 15ºs around the soldered jump ring (photo a).

[3] On each strand, string a pleasing arrangement of seed beads, 4mm crystals, and 6mm pearls for ½ in. (1.3cm) (photo b). Then string a 4mm over both strands. Repeat until you are within ½ in. of the desired length of the

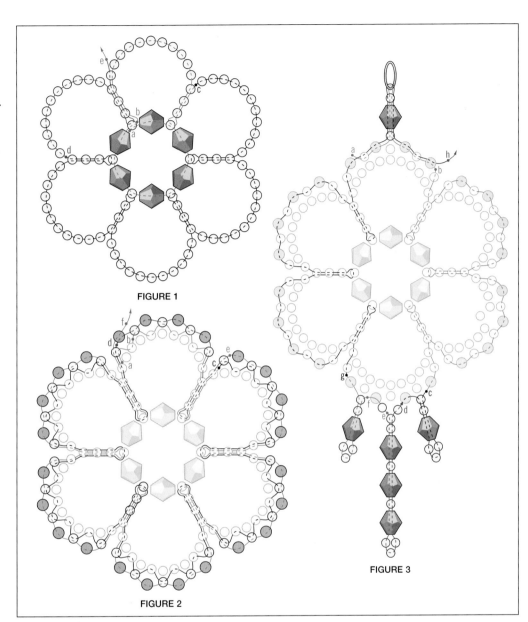

FIGURE 1

FIGURE 2

FIGURE 3

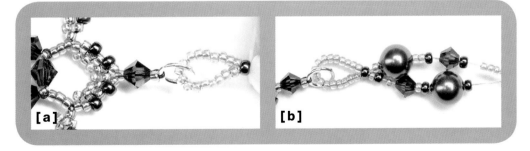

[a] [b]

necklace. If you wish, you can end each strand by stringing an alternating pattern of 6mm and 4mm crystals.

[4] String a crimp bead and one half of the clasp over both ends. Take both ends back through the crimp bead, and tighten the loop. Crimp the crimp bead (Basics).

[5] Repeat steps 2–4 on the other side of the necklace.

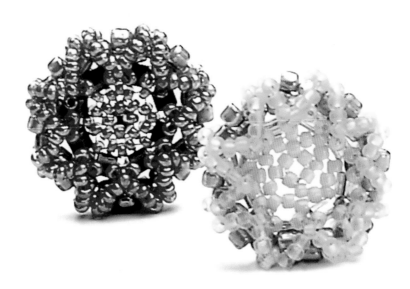

Beaded buttons

Enhance your jewelry with decorative seed bead buttons

by **Nancy Sathre-Vogel**

Button-and-loop closures are secure and easy to use. Rather than choosing a store-bought button, though, you can easily make your own to complement your designs. Use them on bracelets, necklaces, or sweaters; or, add a loop to transform your button into an earring.

MATERIALS

one button ⅞ in. (2.2cm)
- 2g size 8º seed beads
- 1g size 8º hex-cut beads
- 2g size 11º seed beads
- 3–4mm round or bicone crystal or fire-polished bead (optional)
- Nymo D, or Fireline 6 lb. test
- beading needles, #12

EDITOR'S NOTE: To make an earring instead of a button, make a small loop for hanging, and substitute a 3–4mm crystal or fire-polished bead for the shank bead, if desired. To make the loop, sew through the beadwork to exit an edge 8º bead. Pick up seven or eight 11ºs, and go back through the 8º in the same direction. Retrace the thread path a few times, then sew into the beadwork. Make a few half-hitch knots, and trim.

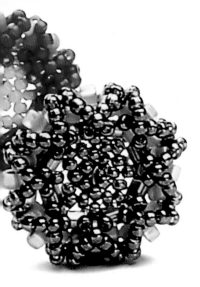

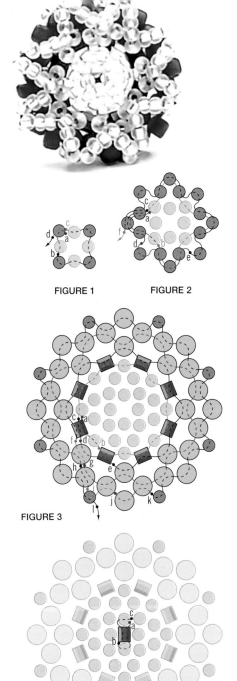

step*by*step

Base

[1] Thread a needle with 1 yd. (.9m) of Fireline or Nymo, and, leaving a 10-in. (25cm) tail, pick up four 11º seed beads. Tie the beads into a ring using a square knot (see Basics, p. 10). Go through the first 11º, and gently tug the thread to hide the knot inside the bead.

[2] Pick up an 11º, and go through the next 11º on the ring (**figure 1, a–b**). Repeat around, inserting an 11º between each 11º on the ring (**b–c**). Step up through the first 11º added in this round (**c–d**).

[3] Pick up three 11ºs, and go through the next 11º of the previous round (**figure 2, a–b**). Repeat around (**b–c**). To get in position for the next round, sew through the first three 11ºs added in this step (**c–d**).

[4] Pick up an 11º, and sew through the next group of three 11ºs added in the previous step (**d–e**). Repeat around to add a total of four beads in this round. Step up through the first two beads of the first three-bead group (**e–f**). You now have eight up-beads.

[5] Pick up an 8º hex-cut bead, and go through the next up-bead (**figure 3, a–b**). Working in peyote stitch (Basics), repeat around to add a total of eight hex beads (**b–c**). Step up through the first hex bead added (**c–d**).

[6] Pick up an 8º seed bead, and go through the next hex bead (**d–e**). Repeat to stitch a round of peyote using 8ºs (**e–f**), stepping up through the first 8º added in this round (**f–g**).

[7] For the next round, begin a peyote increase by placing two 8ºs between each 8º in the previous round (**g–h**). Step up through only the first 8º of the first pair added (**h–i**).

[8] For the final round on the base, complete the peyote increase by picking up an 11º and going through the next 8º (**i–j**). Pick up an 8º, and go through the first 8º of the next pair of 8ºs (**j–k**). Repeat around, picking up an 11º in the middle of each pair of 8ºs from the previous round and adding an 8º between stitches (**k–l**).

[9] To add a shank, thread a needle on the 10-in. tail, pick up a hex bead, and go through the 11º opposite the one your thread is exiting (**figure 4, a–b**). Go back through the hex bead and the 11º on the first side (**b–c**). Retrace the thread path several times. Sew into the beadwork, make a few half-hitch knots (Basics) between beads, and trim.

Surface embellishment

[1] Sew through the beadwork to exit a hex bead. Pick up three 11ºs, and go through the next hex bead (**figure 5, a–b**). Repeat around, making a total of eight three-bead picots between hex beads (**b–c**). Flip the piece over, and repeat on the other side.

[2] Step up through the first two 11ºs of the first picot (**c–d**). Pick up three 11ºs, and go through the nearest 11º on the outer edge (**d–e**). Pick up three 11ºs, and go through the middle 11º on the next three-bead picot (**e–f**). Repeat around, stepping up through the first three 11ºs added in this step and the edge 11º (**f–g**). Repeat on the other side. Retrace the thread path of the star design at least once, switching from side to side at the edge.

FIGURE 1　　**FIGURE 2**

FIGURE 3

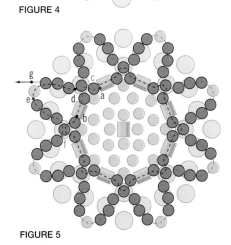

FIGURE 4

FIGURE 5

Harvest

Highlight a bevy of fall-colored lampworked beads in a fringed bracelet

by **Carol Cypher**

loops bracelet

Don't relegate small lampworked beads in autumn's richest hues to the humble role of spacers. Look for scrumptious beads the size of M&Ms, then choose an assortment of seed beads to complement them. Hidden underneath these playful loops is a simple peyote strip with a picot edge. Stitch a matching toggle closure to give your bracelet a perfect finish.

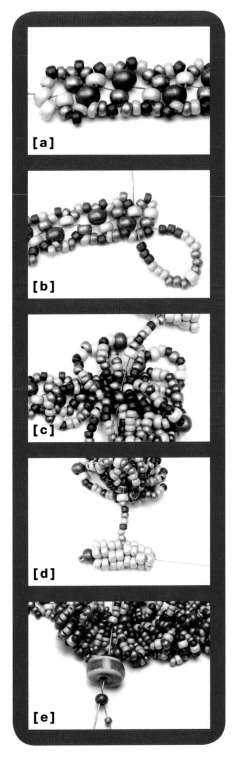

[a]

[b]

[c]

[d]

[e]

stepbystep

Base

[1] Using 2 yd. (1.8m) of thread, attach a stop bead (see Basics, p. 10), leaving a 10-in. (25cm) tail (figure 1, a–b).

[2] Pick up three 8º seed beads and sew through the first 8º in the opposite direction (b–c).

[3] Pick up three 11ºs and an 8º or 6º. Then sew through the third 8º picked up in the previous step (c–d).

[4] Continue working a two-bead peyote band with a picot edge (figure 2 and photo a) for approximately 6 in. (15cm) for a bracelet 6½–8 in. (16.5–20cm) long, or 7 in. (18cm) for a bracelet 7½–9 in. (19.1–23cm) long.

[5] Tie half-hitch knots (Basics) between a few beads to secure the thread. Trim the excess.

[6] Remove the stop bead. Thread a needle on the tail. Pick up 19 11ºs, and sew through the two 8ºs on the end of the band (figure 3, a–b).

[7] Sew through the first 12 11ºs just picked up (b–c). Then pick up 15 11ºs, and sew back through five 11ºs on the previous loop (c–d).

[8] Sew through ten beads on the new loop (d–e). Pick up 15 11ºs, and sew back through five beads on the previous loop (e–f). These three loops make the length of your bracelet adjustable.

[9] Retrace the thread path through the loops to reinforce them. Secure the tail, and trim.

Loops

[1] Secure a new length of thread in the base near either end. Exit an 8º or 6º at the end of the base.

[2] Pick up nine 11ºs, an 8º or a 6º, and nine 11ºs. Sew through an adjacent 8º or 6º on the base (photo b).

[3] Continue adding loops to the base, sewing through every 8º and 6º. Keep the loops similar in size, but change the color combinations as desired.

[4] Secure the thread, and trim.

Toggle bead

[1] Using 1 yd. (.9m) of thread, attach a stop bead 12 in. (30cm) from the end.

[2] Pick up ten 8ºs (figure 4, a–b). Skip the last four beads, and sew through the next two (b–c). Continue working in two-drop peyote (Basics) for a total of eight rows (c–d).

[3] Remove the stop bead. Fold the peyote strip in half so the first and last rows are aligned. Zip up (Basics) the end rows of the strip to form a tube to use as a toggle bead.

[4] Sew through a few rows in the toggle to stiffen it. Secure the working thread, and trim.

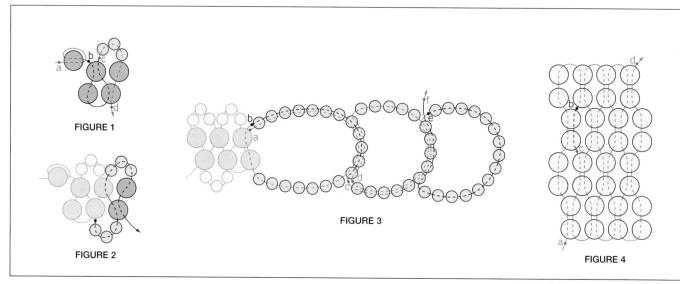

FIGURE 1

FIGURE 2

FIGURE 3

FIGURE 4

[5] Thread a needle on the tail. Sew through four beads on the next row so you exit at the middle of the toggle.

[6] Pick up seven 11°s and an 8°. Sew into an 8° or 6° on the base about ½ in. (1.3cm) from the end without the closure loops (photo c).

[7] Sew back through the 8° and 11°s and the next four beads on the toggle.

[8] Pick up a 6° and an 11°. Skip the 11°, and sew back through the 6° and the center of the toggle bead (photo d).

> **EDITOR'S NOTE:**
> Sew through the base beads carefully when adding the loops and embellishments so you don't catch your needle on the previous stitches.

[9] Repeat step 8 at the other end of the toggle bead. Secure the thread.

Accent beads

[1] Arrange the glass or porcelain beads on your work surface to determine how you will embellish your bracelet.

[2] Secure 1½–2 yd. (1.4–1.8m) of Power Pro in the base of the bracelet near the toggle bead. Exit an 8° or 6° where you want to add the first accent bead.

[3] Pick up a 6°, an accent bead, a 6°, and an 11°. Sew back through the 6°, the accent bead, the 6°, and an adjacent 8° or 6° on the base (photo e).

[4] Repeat step 3 across the length of the bracelet, working around the fringe loops.

MATERIALS
adjustable bracelet 6½–9 in. (16.5–23cm)

- **12–16** 10mm glass or porcelain accent beads
- seed beads
  8–10g size 6°, **1–3** colors
  6–8g size 8°, **1–3** colors
  18–20g size 11°, **1–3** colors
- Fireline 8 lb. test, or Nymo D conditioned with beeswax
- Power Pro 10 lb. test
- beading needles, #10 or #12

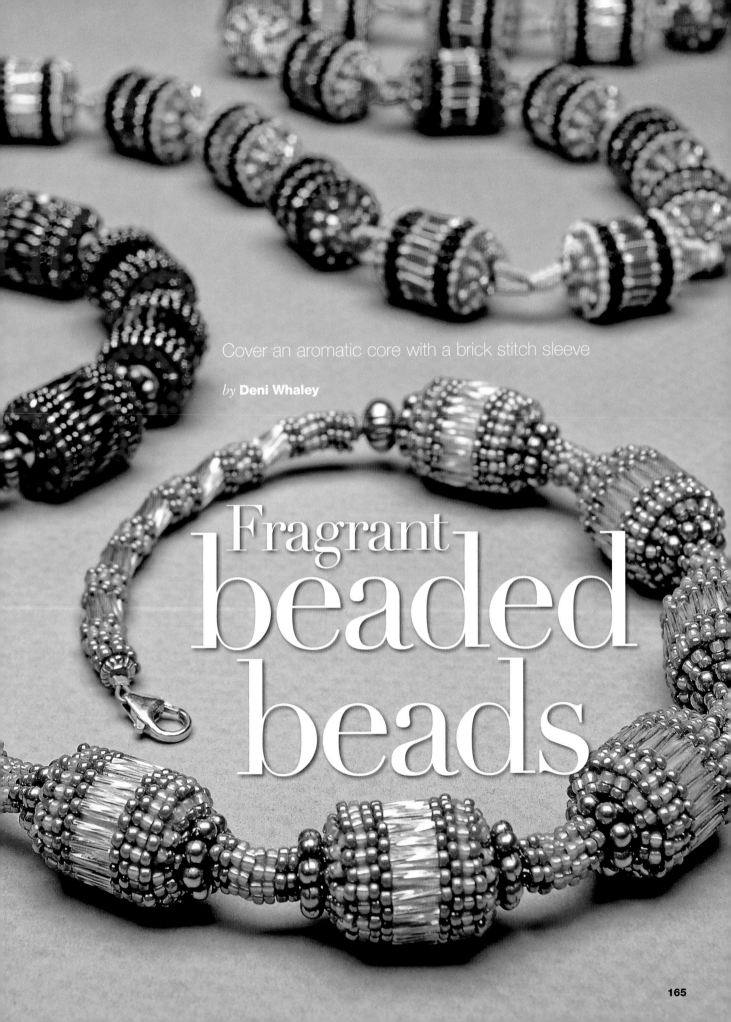

Cover an aromatic core with a brick stitch sleeve

by **Deni Whaley**

Fragrant
beaded
beads

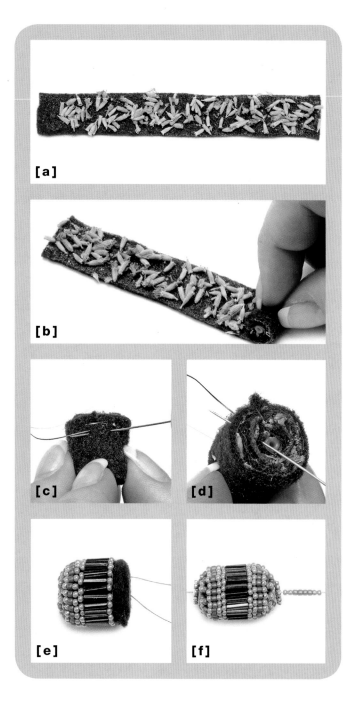

[a]

[b]

[c]

[d]

[e]

[f]

Beaded beads take on a new dimension when infused with aroma. This versatile project demonstrates several ways to add a favorite scent to a customizable necklace.

step*by*step

Green necklace (p. 165, front) – soft-centered beads

Preparing the form

[1] Cut a 5 x ¾-in. (13 x 1.9cm) strip of felt.

[2] Coat one side of the felt with rubber cement, and sprinkle dried lavender or other herbs over it (photo a). Place a ¾-in. tube bead or piece of a coffee stirrer at one end of the felt, and roll it up tightly (photo b) until it is ⅝ in. (1.6cm) in diameter. Cut off any excess felt, and tuck in or brush off any loose lavender.

[3] Thread a needle with 18 in. (46cm) of Nymo or Fireline, and make a large overhand knot (see Basics, p. 10) at the end. Stitch the end of the felt down to close the form (photo c).

[4] When you reach the end of the form, sew into the form from the center, go through all the layers of felt, and exit through the outer layer (photo d). Repeat around to tack the entire edge. Sew through to the other end, and tack it in the same manner.

[5] Repeat steps 1–4 to make a total of seven soft forms.

Beaded cover

The following is one of many patterns you can use to make these beads. Try this pattern first, then change the colors, sizes, or shapes of the beads to make your own design.

[1] Thread a needle on 4 ft. (1.2m) of Nymo or Fireline, and, leaving a 6-in. (15cm) tail, pick up a color A 11º seed bead, a bugle bead, two As, a bugle, and an A. Sew back through all six beads again, and pull them snug so you have two columns sitting side by side (figure 1, a–b). Pick up an A, a bugle, and an A, go through the last three beads again, and continue through the three new beads (b–c). Repeat this bead pattern, and continue working in ladder stitch (Basics) until you have 24 bugles. Test that the ladder will fit around your form, and add or remove beads if necessary.

[2] To form the ladder into a ring, sew through the first three ladder beads, the last three ladder beads, and the first three ladder beads again.

[3] Pick up an A, a color B 11º, two As, a B, and an A. Working in modified brick stitch (Basics), go under the thread bridge between the first and second ladder beads and back through the last three beads picked up (figure 2, a–b). Pick up an A, a B, and an A. Go under the next thread bridge, and come back through the last three beads (b–c). Repeat around for a total of 24 stitches.

[4] After you've added your final stitch on this round (figure 3, a–b), sew down through the first three beads of this round, under the thread bridge, and back up through the same beads (b–c).

[5] Pick up a B, an A, two Bs, an A, and a B. Skip a thread bridge on the row below, go under the next one, and sew back up through the last three beads (c–d). Pick up a B, an A, and a B, skip a thread bridge, go under the next bridge, and come back up through the last three beads (d–e). Repeat around for a total of 12 stitches. Repeat step 4 to finish the row.

[6] Pick up two As. Skip a thread bridge, go under the next thread bridge on the row below, and go back up through the second A just picked up (figure 4, a–b). Pick up an A, skip a thread bridge, go under the next bridge, and come back up through the A just picked up (b–c). Repeat for a total of six stitches. Repeat step 4 to finish the row.

[7] Sew through the beadwork to exit the other edge of the ladder. Slide the soft center into the beaded cover (photo e), and repeat steps 3–6 to complete the other side. Secure the tails with a few half-hitch knots (Basics) between beads, and trim.

[8] Repeat steps 1–7 to cover the remaining six forms.

Peyote spacers

[1] On 2 ft. (61cm) of thread, pick up a stop bead (Basics), two As, four Bs, and two As (figure 5, a–b).

[2] Pick up two As, and go through the last two Bs in the opposite direction (b–c). Pick up two Bs, and go through the first two As (c–d).

[3] Repeat step 2 to continue working in two-drop peyote (Basics) for a total of 14 rows. You should have seven As on each straight edge of the strip.

[4] Join the strip into a tube by zipping up (Basics) the edges. Secure the tails with half-hitch knots, and trim.

[5] Repeat steps 1–4 to make a total of six peyote spacers.

Peyote neck tube

[1] On 4 ft. of thread, pick up a stop bead, two As, two Bs, two As, and a bugle. Repeat this pattern four times, then pick up two As, four Bs, and two As (figure 6, a–b).

[2] Pick up two As, and sew through the last two Bs in the opposite direction (b–c). Treating the bugles as though they were pairs of 11°s, work 11 two-drop peyote stitches across the row, alternating a stitch of two Bs with a stitch of one bugle (c–d).

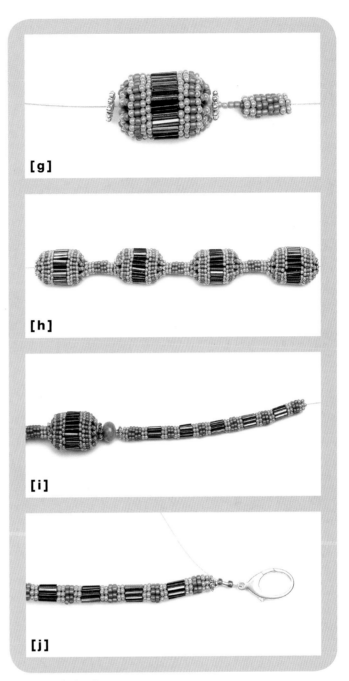

[g]

[h]

[i]

[j]

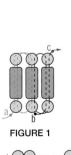

FIGURE 1

FIGURE 2

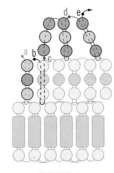

FIGURE 3

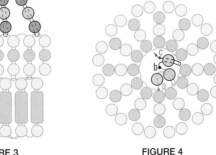
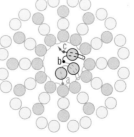

FIGURE 4

FIGURE 5

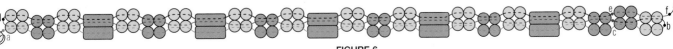

FIGURE 6

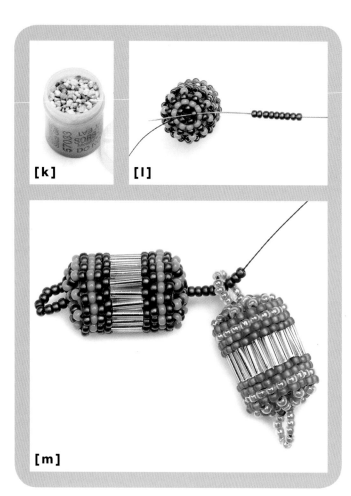

[k] [l]

[m]

[3] Continuing in two-drop peyote, work 11 stitches of As (d–e), then one stitch of Bs (e–f) to complete the row.
[4] Repeat steps 2 and 3 five times for a total of 14 rows.
[5] Zip up the tube, finish the tails, and trim.

Necklace assembly
[1] Determine the desired length of your necklace (this one is 19 in./48cm), add 6 in., and cut a piece of beading wire to that length. Center an 11mm spacer, a scented bead, and an 11mm.
[2] On one end, string the bead sequence used to begin the small peyote spacers, omitting the stop bead (photo f), and then slide a peyote spacer over these beads (photo g). String an 11mm, a scented bead, and an 11mm.
[3] Repeat step 2 twice (photo h).
[4] String a 9mm rondelle and a 3mm spacer. String the bead sequence used to begin the peyote neck tube, omitting the stop bead. Slide one peyote tube over these beads (photo i).
[5] String a 3mm, an 8º, a crimp bead, an 8º, and one clasp half. Go back through the last three beads (photo j).
[6] Repeat steps 2–5 on the other end. Test the fit, and add or remove beads if necessary. Crimp the crimp beads (Basics), and trim the wire.

Purple necklace (p. 165, left) – hard-centered beads
[1] Discard the contents of the desiccant canisters, and fill them with drawer sachet pellets (photo k) or small pieces of cotton infused with a few drops of essential oil. Close the canisters, and

puncture the center of each end with a T-pin or awl to make a stringing hole.
[2] Make seven beaded covers as in the green necklace, but substitute a desiccant canister for the soft-centered form.
[3] On 17 in. (43cm) of necklace-diameter memory wire, string an 8mm disk bead, an 11mm spacer, an 8mm, and a scented bead. Repeat six times, then string an 8mm, an 11mm, and an 8mm.
[4] On each end, string 4 in. (10cm) of 8–12mm beads as desired.
[5] Test the fit, and add or remove beads if necessary.
[6] Make a simple loop on each end.
[7] Open one loop (Basics), and attach one half of a magnetic clasp. Close the loop. Repeat on the other end.

Multicolored necklace (p. 165, top) – hard-centered beads
This necklace consists of 18 beads. You'll choose six colors, C–H, and make three beads in each color. Colors A and B will remain the same for all beads.
[1] Prepare the desiccant canisters as in the purple necklace, but do not puncture the ends.
[2] Make 18 beaded covers as in the green necklace with the colors described above, but make the following changes: In step 3, begin by picking up two Bs, two color C 11ºs, and two Bs. For each remaining stitch, pick up a C and two Bs. In step 5, begin by picking up an A, a C, two As, a C, and an A. For each remaining stitch, pick up an A, a C, and an A. Test the fit once the ladder is 23 beads long. Substitute a desiccant

[n] **[o]** **[p]**

EDITOR'S NOTE: If you can't find desiccant canisters, try an empty bead tube for the hard-centered beads. With a permanent marker, mark the tube 11/16 in. (1.7cm) from the bottom (**photo n**). Cut off the portion above the mark, and, with a T-pin or awl, puncture the remaining portion many times (**photo o**). Fill the tube with fragrance, and replace the cap (**photo p**). Depending upon the diameter of the tube, you may need to adjust the number of beads in your ladder.

canister for the soft-centered form. Do not trim the tails.

[3] With the thread exiting an A in the final row, pick up nine or ten As, and sew into the opposite A on the final row (**photo l**). Retrace the thread path a few times, and sew through the beadwork to exit an A on the other end. On the first bead only, repeat to make a second loop.

[4] Repeat step 3 on the remaining beads, but don't make the second loop.

[5] Thread a needle on the tail of a bead with only one loop. Pick up nine or ten As, and go through the finished loop of a bead with two finished loops (**photo m**). Connect the new loop as above, retrace the thread path, and secure the tail. Repeat to connect all your beaded beads into a chain.

[6] If you don't want to use a clasp, simply connect the first bead to the last to make a continuous strand. To attach a clasp, pick up ten

11°s and one clasp half on 1 ft. (30cm) of thread. Go through the available loop on an end bead, and tie the ends together with a surgeon's knot (Basics). Retrace the thread path a few times, and finish the tails. Repeat on the other end with the other clasp half.

MATERIALS

all projects
- Nymo D conditioned with beeswax or Thread Heaven, or Fireline 8 lb. test
- beading needles, #10 or #12

green necklace (soft-centered beads) 19 in. (48cm)
- 2 9mm rondelles
- 7g Czech size 3 (7mm) or Japanese size 2 (6mm) bugle beads
- 4 size 8° seed beads
- 8g size 11° Japanese seed beads in each of **2** colors: A and B
- 14 11mm daisy spacers
- 4 3mm spacers
- clasp
- 2 crimp beads
- flexible beading wire, .019
- craft felt
- dried herbs
- 7 ¾-in. (1.9cm) 3mm-diameter ceramic tube beads or pieces of hollow coffee stirrers
- rubber cement
- crimping pliers
- wire cutters

purple necklace (hard-centered beads) 17 in. (43cm)
- assorted 8–12mm beads
- 14 8mm disk beads
- 7g 6–7mm bugle beads
- 8g size 11° Japanese seed beads in each of **2** colors: A and B
- 7 11mm daisy spacers
- magnetic clasp
- necklace-diameter memory wire
- 7 14 x 18mm-diameter desiccant canisters (from a pharmacy)
- drawer sachet pellets or cotton infused with essential oil
- roundnose pliers
- spring wire cutters
- T-pin or awl

multicolored necklace (hard-centered beads) 27 in. (69cm)
- 3g 6–7mm bugle beads in each of **6** colors: C–H
- size 11° Japanese seed beads
  10g color A
  10g color B
  3g each of **6** colors: C–H
- clasp or button (optional)
- 18 14 x 18mm-diameter desiccant canisters (from a pharmacy)
- drawer sachet pellets or cotton infused with essential oil

EDITOR'S NOTE: Another option for making the necklace is to string a soft-centered bead on a 2-in. (5cm) piece of wire, and make a plain loop (Basics) at each end. Repeat with the remaining beads, and connect the loops to form a chain.

Checkered panel bracelet

Pave the way for Cupid with a bold square stitch bracelet

by **Barbara Klann**

Stitch cube beads into checkered panels, then string them between heart-shaped beads and bicone crystals. Go vintage '60s with black, white, and red beads, or playful with a mix of pink, purple, and fuchsia.

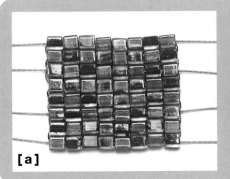

[a]

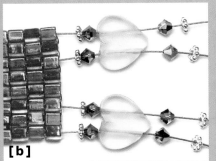

[b]

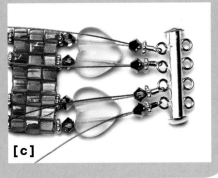

[c]

step*by*step

Checkerboard panels

[1] On 1 yd. (.9m) of Nymo or Fireline, string a stop bead (see Basics, p. 10) 6 in. (15cm) from the end. String a repeating pattern of cube beads, one color A and one color B, four times.

[2] Working in square stitch (Basics), pick up an A, and sew through the last B picked up in step 1 **(figure 1, a–b)**. Go back through the bead just added **(b–c)**.

[3] Referring to **figure 2**, work eight rows of square stitch. This is the center panel. Remove the stop bead, secure the tails in the beadwork with a few half-hitch knots (Basics) between beads, and trim the tails.

[4] Make two square stitch panels four beads across by eight rows and two panels three beads across by eight rows. End the threads as before.

Assembly

[1] Cut four 13-in. (33cm) pieces of beading wire. Go through an edge row of the center panel with one of the wires. With the other wires, go through the third, sixth, and eighth rows. Center the panel on the wires **(photo a)**. Tape one end of the wires to your work surface temporarily to hold them in place.

[2] On each of the unsecured ends, string a spacer, a crystal, one hole of a heart-shaped bead (wide end first), a crystal, and a spacer **(photo b)**.

[3] String a four-bead panel on all four wires, going through the corresponding first, third, sixth, and eighth rows.

[4] Repeat step 2, but string the heart-shaped beads narrow-end first so they're facing the other direction. Repeat step 3 with a three-bead panel.

[5] Repeat step 2. String a crimp bead on each wire. Go through a loop on the clasp and back through each crimp bead, spacer, and crystal **(photo c)**. Do not crimp the crimp beads yet.

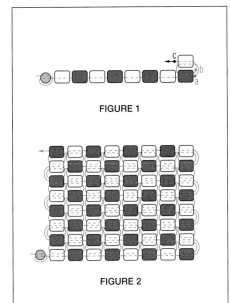

FIGURE 1

FIGURE 2

[6] Remove the tape from the other side. Repeat steps 2–5.

[7] Check the fit. Add or remove beads if necessary.

[8] Making sure the bracelet isn't twisted and the clasp is correctly oriented, crimp the crimp beads (Basics) on one side. Snug up the beads, and crimp the crimp beads on the other end. Trim the excess wire.

MATERIALS

bracelet 8½ in. (21.6cm)

- **12** 12mm two-hole heart-shaped beads (Pam's Bead Garden, 734-451-7410, pamsbeadgarden.com)
- **48** 4mm bicone crystals
- 4mm cube beads
  88 color A
  88 color B
- **48** 4mm daisy spacers
- Four-strand clasp
- 8 crimp beads
- Nymo B, or Fireline 6 lb. test
- flexible beading wire, .014–.015
- beading needles, #12
- crimping pliers
- wire cutters

EDITOR'S NOTE:
To make this bracelet about 1 in. (2.5cm) shorter, omit the row of hearts on each end. Another option: Adjust the number of beads on the square stitch panels.

Tile

bracelet

Bezeled glass tiles make fabulous focal pieces in a square stitch bracelet

by **Susan Frommer**

Using unusual materials in your jewelry can produce inspired results. Here, decorative mosaic tiles get a new look in these terrific beaded bracelets.

[a]

step*by*step

Peyote bezel

[1] Cut three pieces of Lacy's Stiff Stuff slightly larger than your tiles. Glue a tile to the center of each piece, and let them dry completely.

[2] Using a comfortable length of Nymo, backstitch (see Basics, p. 10) a row of color A 15º seed beads around the tile **(photo a)**. This row must have an even number of beads.

Condition the remaining thread (Basics).

[3] Using As, work in tubular, even-count peyote (Basics) for five rounds, or until the tile is securely surrounded **(photo b)**. Secure the thread, and trim the tail.

[4] Make two more bezeled tiles.

Square stitch

[1] Using a comfortable length of Nymo, backstitch eight 8º hex-cut

172

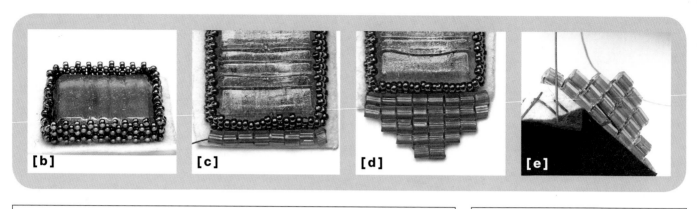

[b]   [c]   [d]   [e]

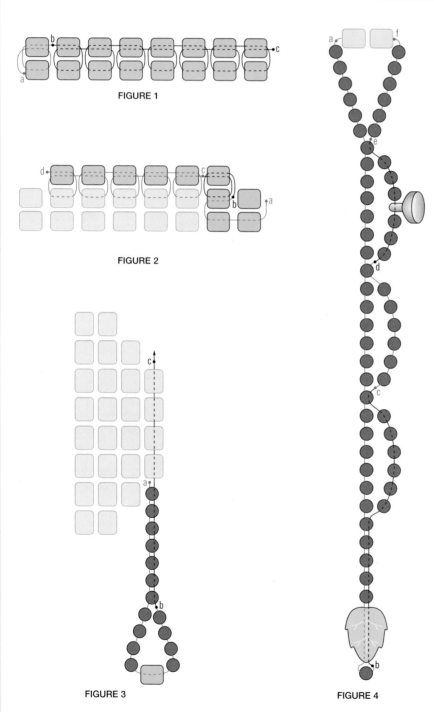

FIGURE 1

FIGURE 2

FIGURE 3

FIGURE 4

MATERIALS

bracelet 7–9 in. (18–23cm)

- **3** ¾-in. (1.9cm) square glass tiles (Michaels, michaels.com)
- **2** top-to-bottom-drilled glass leaves (Fire Mountain Gems, 800-355-2137, firemountain.com)
- 10g size 8º hex-cut beads, color to match tiles
- size 15º seed beads
  5g bronze mix, color A
  5g green mix, color B
- magnetic clasp (ez2clasp, 877-421-8722, ez2clasp.com)
- 4mm jump ring
- Nymo D conditioned with beeswax or Thread Heaven
- beading needles, #12
- E6000 adhesive
- Lacy's Stiff Stuff (Designer's Findings, 262-574-1324)
- Ultrasuede or other fabric, color to match tiles
- chainnose pliers

beads along one edge of the exposed Lacy's **(photo c)**. Condition the remaining thread.

[2] Pick up an 8º, go through the last backstitched 8º and the 8º just added **(figure 1, a–b)**. Work across the row in square stitch (Basics) to **point c.**

[3] Go through the first two back-stitched 8ºs and the next-to-last 8º in row 2 **(figure 2, a–b)**.

[4] To start row 3, pick up an 8º. Go through the previous 8º and the new 8º again **(b–c)**. Work across the row in square stitch for a total of six beads **(c–d)**.

[5] Continue working in square stitch for a total of five rows. Row 4 has four

[f]

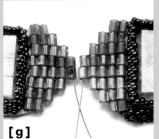

[g]

[h]

[i]

8°s; row 5 has two 8°s (photo d). Secure the thread, and trim the tail.

[6] Repeat steps 1–5 on the opposite edge of the tile. Complete the other two tiles identically.

Connecting the tiles

[1] Glue a piece of Ultrasuede or other fabric to the back of the Lacy's, and let them dry. Carefully trim the fabric and Lacy's as necessary.

[2] Start a new length of thread, and knot the end. Go through the fabric, exiting away from the tile (photo e). Pick up three color B 15° seed beads, and go through the Lacy's and the fabric (photo f). Using Bs, continue around the tile, including the underside of the square stitch elements, until the edges are covered with beads. Finish the other tiles.

[3] To join the tiles, secure a thread within a square stitch section, and weave through the beads until you exit either of the end two 8°s (photo g). Sew through the end two 8°s of another tile.

Weave through the beads, then retrace the thread path to secure the join. Repeat to connect the third tile.

[4] To make the optional fringe, secure a new thread, and exit the last 8° in row 4 of the square stitch section. Pick up 11 As, an 8°, and four As (figure 3, a–b). Starting with the seventh bead, go back through the fringe, and exit the last 8° in row 4 (b–c). Make an identical fringe on the other side, and exit either bead in row 5.

[5] Pick up 14 color As, an 8°, and four As. Starting with the tenth bead, go back through the fringe, and exit the other 8° in row 5. Make an identical fringe, and exit either bead in row 5 of the adjoining tile.

[6] Fringe rows 5 and 4 of the adjoining tile to mirror the first (photo h). Fringe an identical connection between the other two tiles.

Adjustable beaded chain

[1] Secure a new thread on one end of the bracelet, and exit a bead on the end row.

[2] Pick up 32 As, a leaf bead, and an A (figure 4, a–b). Go back through the leaf and the next five As.

[3] Pick up six As, and go through the 21st bead (b–c). Pick up six As, and go through the 14th bead (c–d).

[4] Pick up three As, one half of the magnetic clasp, and three As. Go through the seventh bead (d–e).

[5] Pick up six As, and connect the chain to the adjacent 8° on the end row (e–f). Weave through the square stitch section, secure the thread, and trim the tail.

[6] Repeat on the other end of the bracelet without adding the clasp half. Open the jump ring (Basics), and slide the clasp half onto the ring (photo i). Close the jump ring through the desired link in the chain.

Woven bands bracelet

Frame a peyote bracelet band with square stitch windows

by **Susan Frommer**

Stitch a series of framed window openings to create a bracelet that lets you weave in a peyote band. Make the windows using triangles or hex cuts, then work the band using seed beads in a contrasting finish or color.

step*by*step

Window panels

This portion of the bracelet should measure at least ½ in. (1.3cm) shorter than your wrist measurement. To estimate the number of windows to stitch, figure that 16 windows (eight on each side of the center bar) equal approximately 8 in. (20cm), and 14 windows (seven on each side) equal approximately 6½ in. (16.5cm).

[1] Center a stop bead (see Basics, p. 10) on 4 yd. (3.7m) of conditioned Nymo (Basics). Thread a needle on one end, and wind the other end onto a bobbin to keep it out of the way. Pick up nine triangle beads or hex cuts, and work in square stitch (Basics) for a total of three rows **(figure 1, a–b)**. This becomes the bracelet's central horizontal bar. (You can add more rows here, but always stitch an odd number of rows.)

[2] Work four rows of square stitch across the two end beads **(figure 2, a–b)** to form the right edge

of the window. Set the thread aside.

[3] Remove the stop bead, and thread a needle on the tail. Weave up to the top row of the bar. Work five rows of square stitch across the two end beads to form the left edge of the window **(figure 3, a–b)**.

[4] Using the same thread, pick up six triangles. Square stitch the sixth triangle to the first triangle on the right edge. Pick up another triangle and work one more square stitch to complete the horizontal bar **(b–c)**.

[5] Work another row of square stitch across all nine triangles **(figure 4, a–b)**. This completes one window.

[6] Using the same thread, work four rows of square stitch two beads wide, as in step 2.

[7] Pick up the thread on the opposite side, and weave it up to the top row. Work five rows of square stitch two beads wide, as in step 3.

[8] Using the same thread, connect the beads with a horizontal bar, as in step 4. Work another horizontal

row of square stitch across all nine triangles.

[9] Repeat steps 6–8 to make the desired number of window panels for the first half of the bracelet. Secure and cut one of the threads, leaving one to use later for adjustments.

[10] Begin the second half of the bracelet by securing 4 yd. of conditioned thread through the bar stitched in step 1. Center the thread, and thread a needle on each end.

[11] Make the second half of the bracelet to match the first.

[12] Secure and trim one thread. If necessary, use the threads remaining at each end to add rows of square stitch to increase the overall length. Do not cut these threads.

Peyote strip

[1] On 2 yd. (1.8m) of conditioned Nymo, string a stop bead, leaving a 24-in.

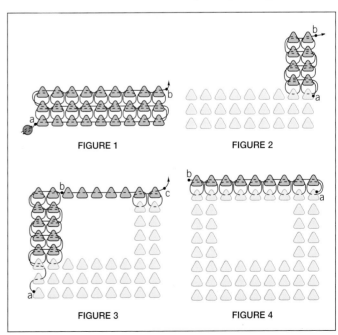

FIGURE 1

FIGURE 2

FIGURE 3

FIGURE 4

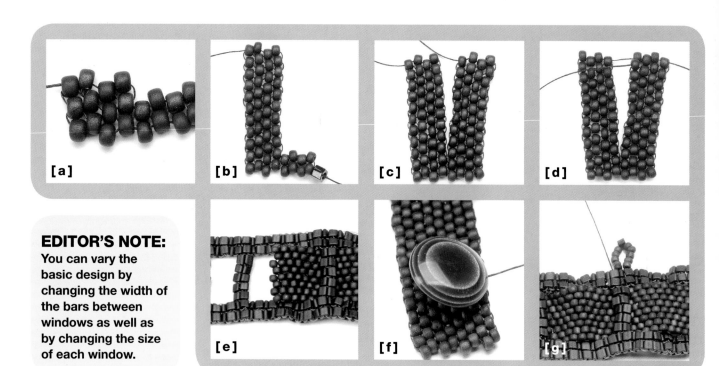

[a]

[b]

[c]

[d]

EDITOR'S NOTE:
You can vary the basic design by changing the width of the bars between windows as well as by changing the size of each window.

[e]

[f]

[g]

(61cm) tail. Pick up eight 11º seed beads, and work two rows of flat, even-count peyote (Basics). Each flat edge will have two beads. Turn your work so that the stop bead is on the right and the working thread is on the left.

[2] To start the buttonhole, work in peyote halfway across the strip. Turn, and work back to the edge (photo a). Work back and forth across the same beads for a total of 18 rows. End with the thread at the top left edge of the row (photo b).

[3] To stitch the second half of the buttonhole, remove the stop bead, and thread a needle on the tail. Go through four beads to the left so that you are at the center. Work in peyote for 18 rows. End with the thread at the top left of the row (photo c).

[4] Pick up the thread on the left outer edge, and work one peyote row across to connect the two strips (photo d). This forms the buttonhole.

[5] Make sure the button fits through the hole before proceeding. If you need

a larger hole, remove the connecting row, and add an equal number of rows to each half of the strip. Reconnect the buttonhole.

[6] Continue to work in peyote across all eight beads until the strip measures 1 in. (2.5cm) longer than your wrist measurement. Don't cut the thread.

[7] Use the tail near the buttonhole to reinforce the buttonhole's connection with a few thread passes. Secure the thread, and cut.

[8] Weave the peyote strip through the window panels. Go over the first horizontal bar and under the next (photo e). Adjust the strip so the ends extend an equal distance on either side of the end window panel. Check the fit.

[9] Use one of the remaining threads from the window panel to stitch the peyote strip to the horizontal end bar to hold it in place. Repeat on the opposite end. Secure the thread, and cut.

[10] Use the remaining thread to add the button.

Weave through the beads until you are about nine rows from the end opposite the buttonhole, and exit a center bead on the strip. Sew through the button, then check the fit before reinforcing the button several times (photo f). Secure the thread, and cut.

Adding fringe

[1] Secure a comfortable length of thread in the triangle beads over the fourth bar from either end. Pick up five 11ºs, a triangle, and five 11ºs. Go through the adjacent triangle, and exit the next one to form a fringe loop (photo g).

[2] Continue making loops along the edge, ending at the fourth bar from the opposite end. Secure the thread in the beadwork, and trim the tail.

[3] Repeat on the other edge.

MATERIALS
bracelet 6½ in. (16.5cm)
- 20g size 11º triangles or size 10º hex cuts
- 20g size 11º seed beads
- ½–⅝-in. (1.3–1.6cm) button with shank
- Nymo B conditioned with beeswax
- beading needles, #10 or #12

Right-angle weave on the diagonal

Turn this favorite stitch on its side to produce a flexible necklace you can embellish with pearls

by **Beth Stone**

Beaders who love right-angle weave, this one's for you. Challenge your skills with a sophisticated necklace in which modified right-angle weave is complemented with top-drilled pearls. Then create a peyote toggle clasp that blends seamlessly into the ends of the band.

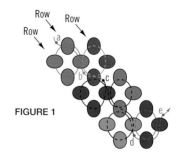

FIGURE 1

step*by*step

Necklace band

[1] On 2 yd. (1.8m) of thread, pick up four 15º seed beads. Leaving an 8-in. (20cm) tail, sew back through the first two beads again, and pull the beads into a ring **(figure 1, a–b)**. (The beads are shown in different colors to help clarify which beads to add in each step.)

[2] Pick up three beads, sew back through the bead the thread is exiting, and continue on through the next new bead **(b–c)**.

[3] Repeat step 2 three times **(c–d)**.

[4] Pick up three beads, and sew through the bead the thread is exiting and the next two beads **(d–e)**. This completes the first three diagonal rows, but they won't take shape until you add the next three sets of beads.

[5] Pick up three beads, and sew back through three beads in the previous row, starting with the bead the thread is exiting **(figure 2, a–b)**.

[6] Pick up two beads, and sew back through four beads in the previous row **(b–c)**.

[7] Pick up two beads, sew through two beads in the previous row, and continue on through three beads in the new row **(c–d)**.

[8] Pick up two beads, and sew back through four beads in the previous row **(d–e)**.

[9] Pick up two beads, and sew back through three beads in the previous row **(e–f)**.

[10] Pick up three beads, and sew back through the bead the thread is exiting and on through the first new bead **(f–g)**.

[11] Pick up two beads, a pearl, and two beads. Sew back through the bead the thread is exiting and on through the next bead **(g–h)**.

[12] Repeat steps 5–10, but in step 10, sew through the first two beads **(h–i)**. Repeat steps 5–11.

[13] Continue stitching as in step 12 to the desired length, adding a pearl to every fourth row. If your thread is at least 24 in. (61cm) long, set it aside to use later. If it is shorter, weave it in the beadwork for about an inch (2.5cm). Tie a few half-hitch knots (see Basics, p. 10) between beads, and trim the tail.

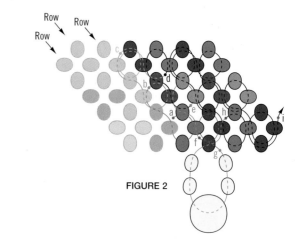

FIGURE 2

MATERIALS

necklace 18 in. (46cm)
- **45** 6mm top-drilled pearls
- 10g size 15º or 11º Japanese seed beads
- Nymo D or Fireline 6 lb. test
- beading needles, #12 or #13

FIGURE 3

Toggle

[1] On 1 yd. (.9m) of thread, pick up 16 15º seed beads. Stitch a flat peyote strip (Basics) 16 beads long for 14 rows. Zip up the ends (Basics) to form a tube.

[2] Exiting a bead on one end of the tube, pick up a pearl, and sew into a bead on the opposite side of the tube **(photo)**. Repeat on the other end. Secure the tails.

[3] Using the tail at the start of the necklace, pick up three beads, and sew through two beads at the center of the toggle. Sew back through the three beads and into the adjacent bead on the end of the necklace **(figure 3, a–b)**. Retrace the thread path a few times. Secure the tails, and trim.

Loop

[1] Use the working thread to make a loop at the other end of the necklace, or secure a new 1-yd. length of thread, exiting at **figure 4, point a**.

[2] Pick up 37 beads, and sew into the adjacent bead on the necklace **(a–b)**. Weave through the last two diagonal rows of the necklace and through the first bead in the loop **(b–c)**.

[3] Pick up one bead, and sew through the third bead in the loop **(c–d)**. Continue in peyote around the loop, and secure the thread in the end of the necklace.

EDITOR'S NOTE:
If 15º seed beads intimidate you, try this project with 11ºs or larger beads until you get comfortable with the stitch.

FIGURE 4

Flower vine

The simplicity of this bracelet heightens its appeal

by **Donna Graves**

bracelet

Drops of color blossom on this delicate vine bracelet. After stitching the vine, space your flowers evenly along its length.

step*by*step

Vine

[1] Using a comfortable length of Fireline, attach a stop bead (see Basics, p. 10) 8 in. (20cm) from the tail.

[2] Pick up three color A 11º seed beads and five color B 11º seed beads.

[3] Sew back through the As (figure 1, a–b). Skip the last bead, and sew through the As again (b–c).

[4] Pick up three As and five Bs. Sew through the As and the last B from step 2 (c–d).

[5] Pick up three As and five Bs. Sew through the As (figure 2, a–b) and the first B from the previous leaf (b–c).

[6] Continue stitching the vine by alternating steps 4 and 5 until your bracelet is the desired length. This bracelet is 7 in. (18cm) long without the clasp. Don't cut the Fireline.

[7] Pick up four As, the split ring, and three As. Sew through the first A and into several nearby beads (photo). Retrace the thread path, secure the thread, and trim the tail.

[8] Remove the stop bead, and thread a needle on the tail. Pick up three As, the lobster claw clasp, and three As. Sew through the first A on the vine and into several nearby beads. Retrace the thread path, secure the thread, and trim the tail.

Flowers

[1] Secure a new thread, and exit the last B of the first leaf (figure 3, point a).

[2] Refer to figure 4 as you stitch the flowers. Pick up a color C 11º seed bead, and sew back through the B (a–b).

[3] Pick up three Cs, and sew back through the B (b–c).

[4] Repeat with four Cs (c–d).

[5] Sew through the vine and exit the first B of the fourth leaf (figure 3, point b). Repeat steps 2–4 to make another flower.

[6] Continue stitching a flower on every third leaf at the point where the leaf meets the vine. When you have finished the flowers, sew into several nearby beads, secure the thread, and trim the tail.

MATERIALS

bracelet 7 in. (18cm)

- size 11º seed beads
  10g copper-lined clear, color A
  10g silver-lined green, color B
  10g purple, color C
- gold-filled lobster claw clasp
- 6mm gold-filled split ring
- Fireline 8 lb. test
- beading needles, #12

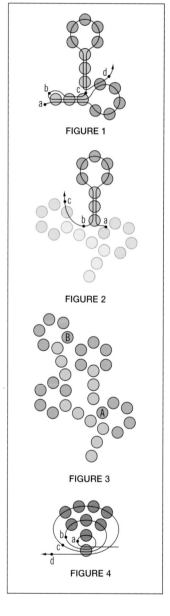

FIGURE 1

FIGURE 2

FIGURE 3

FIGURE 4

Arabesque bracelet

Crystals and seed beads team up
for a bracelet with grace and charm

by **Joanie Jenniges**

Layers of beads stitched with an easy cross-needle technique make a bracelet that looks more intricate than it really is. Once you discover how easy it is, you'll want to make several.

step*by*step

Base

[1] Cut 2 yd. (1.8m) of Fireline. Thread a needle on both ends.

[2] Center ten 15º seed beads on the Fireline. Pick up an 11º, a 4mm color A bicone crystal, and an 11º on the first needle. Cross the second needle through the 11º, the A, and the 11º in the opposite direction (**figure 1**).

[3] On each needle, pick up an 11º, a 4mm color B bicone crystal, and an 11º. On the first needle, pick up an 11º, a 6mm color C bicone crystal, and an 11º. Cross the second needle through the 11º, the C, and the 11º in the opposite direction (**figure 2, a–b** and **g–h**).

[4] On each needle, pick up an 11º, a C, and an 11º. On the first needle, pick up an 11º, a C, and an 11º. Cross the second needle through the 11º, the C, and the 11º in the opposite direction (**b–c** and **h–i**).

[5] On each needle, pick up an 11º, a B, and an 11º. On the first needle, pick up an 11º, an A, and an 11º. Cross the second needle through the 11º, the A, and the 11º in the opposite direction (**c–d** and **i–j**).

[6] Repeat steps 3–5 six times or to the desired length, ending with step 5.

[7] Pick up ten 15ºs on the first needle. Cross the second needle through the ten 15ºs. Cross both through the 11º, A, and 11º from step 5.

[8] Secure the tails in the loop of 15ºs using half-hitch knots (see Basics, p. 10).

Embellishment

[1] Thread a needle on both ends of a new length of Fireline. Center it in the 11º, C, and 11º on one end of the bracelet (**figure 3, a–g**).

[2] On each needle, pick up an 11º and a 4mm color D bicone crystal. Sew through an 11º with both needles (**a–b** and **h–i**).

MATERIALS

bracelet 7¼ in. (18.4cm)
- bicone crystals
  24 6mm, color C
  12 4mm, color A
  34 4mm, color B
  24 4mm, color D
- Japanese seed beads
  3g size 11º
  3g size 15º
- toggle clasp
- **2** 4mm jump rings
- Fireline 6 lb. test
- beading needles, #12

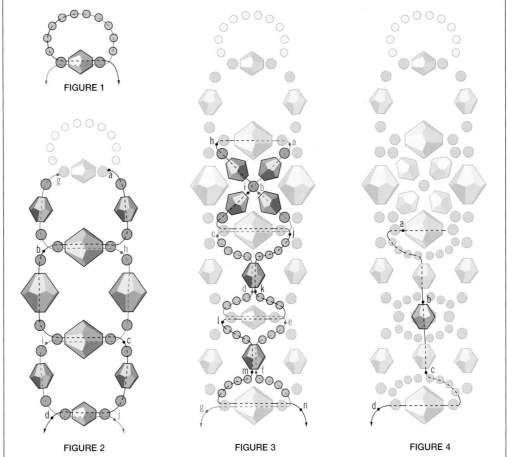

FIGURE 1

FIGURE 2

FIGURE 3

FIGURE 4

[3] On each needle, pick up a D and an 11º. Cross both needles through the next 11º, C, and 11º on the base (**b–c** and **i–j**).

[4] On each needle, pick up four 15ºs. Pick up a B with the first needle, and sew through it in the same direction with the second needle (**c–d** and **j–k**). On each needle, pick up three 15ºs. Cross both needles through the next 11º, A, and 11º on the base (**d–e** and **k–l**).

[5] On each needle, pick up three 15ºs. Pick up a B with the first needle, and sew through it in the same direction with the second needle (**e–f** and **l–m**). On each needle, pick up four 15ºs, and cross both of the

needles through the next 11º, C, and 11º on the base (**f–g** and **m–n**).

[6] Repeat steps 2–5 over the length of the bracelet, ending with step 3.

[7] Secure the tails in the loop of 15ºs.

[8] Start a new thread, and secure one end in the beadwork, exiting at **figure 4, point a**.

[9] Sew through the 11º, the four existing 15ºs, and the B (**a–b**).

[10] Pick up an A, and sew through the next B (**b–c**). Continue to sew through the existing beads, exiting at **point d**.

[11] Sew through to the next section to repeat steps 8–10. Secure the tails.

[12] Open a jump ring (Basics), and attach half of the clasp to either of the 15º loops on the ends of the bracelet. Close the jump ring. Repeat on the other end.

Ruffled rondelles

Stitch a bracelet using a new netting technique

by **Maiko Kage**

This bracelet showcases an innovative technique for making netted circles, and once you try it, you'll be tempted to design a few variations of your own. The project uses netted loops worked from a simple eight-bead base to build a rondelle of ruffles. You can wear one individually as a small brooch, or link several to make a bracelet or necklace. In floral colors, it's easy to see these as flowers; in bold colors, they have a more contemporary appeal.

stepbystep

Making the rings
[1] On 1½ yd. (1.4m) of thread, attach a stop bead (see Basics, p. 10) 6 in. (15cm) from the end.
[2] Pick up two color A 11º seed beads, a color B 11º, a color C 11º, a 4mm bead, a C, a B, and an A. Sew through the first A **(figure 1, a–b).**
[3] Pick up six color D 11ºs, two As, and a B. Sew through the second C **(b–c).**
[4] Pick up a 4mm bead, a C, a B, and an A. Sew through the first A from the previous step **(figure 2, a–b).** Pick up six Ds, two As, and a B. Sew through the C **(b–c).**
[5] Repeat step 4 five more times.
[6] Pick up a 4mm bead, and sew through the C on the left of the first 4mm bead **(figure 3, a–b).** Pick up a B and an A, and sew through the A from the previous stitch **(b–c).**
[7] Pick up six Ds, and sew through the beads from step 2 **(c–d).** Sew through the first four Ds from step 3 **(d–e).**

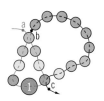

FIGURE 1

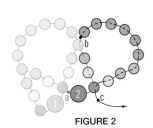

FIGURE 2

MATERIALS
bracelet 7½ in. (19.1cm)
- **48** 4mm Czech round or fire-polished glass beads
- 8g size 11º Japanese seed beads, in each of **4** colors
- clasp
- Nymo B conditioned with beeswax, or SoNo beading thread
- beading needles, #12 or #13

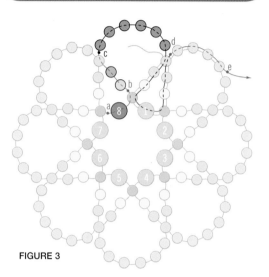

FIGURE 3

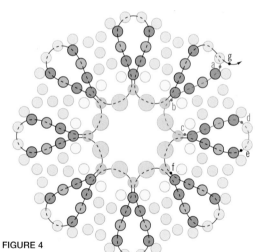

FIGURE 4

[8] Pick up a D, an A, a D, and a C (**figure 4, a–b**). Sew through the C, the 4mm bead, and the next C in the inner ring (**b–c**).

[9] Pick up a C, a D, an A, and a D (**c–d**). Sew through the third and fourth Ds on the next set of six Ds (**d–e**).

[10] Pick up a D, an A, and a D. Sew through the two Cs, the 4mm bead, and the next C on the bottom of the petal (**e–f**).

[11] Repeat steps 9–10 around the ring, ending where you began step 8 (**f–g**).

[12] Turn the beadwork over and repeat steps 8–11 on the other side of the ring. Secure the threads, and trim.

[13] Make five more rondelles, changing the color placement of the 11ᵒs for each one.

Assembling the bracelet

[1] Arrange the rondelles on your work surface in the order they will be sewn. Secure a new 1½ yd. thread in the first one, leave a 12-in. (30cm) tail, and exit at **point a** on figure 5.

[2] Sew up through the corresponding two beads on the next rondelle, and stitch them together as shown (**a–b**). Sew through the second rondelle, and exit at **point c**.

[3] Continue connecting the remaining rings as in step 2.

[4] To attach a clasp half to the last rondelle, pick up three Bs, sew through the loop on the clasp, and pick up three Bs (**figure 6, a–b**). Sew through the two edge beads (**b–c**). Retrace the thread path a few times to secure the clasp (**c–d**). Secure the thread, and trim.

[5] Thread a needle on the tail, weave through the rondelle, and exit at **point c** as in step 2. Repeat step 4 to attach the remaining clasp half. Secure the thread, and trim.

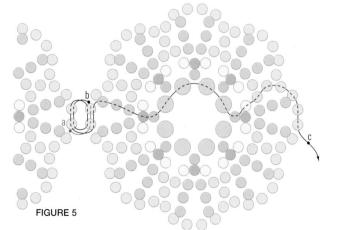

FIGURE 5

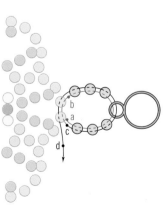

FIGURE 6

Ice
crystals

Add glamour to the holidays with crystal-laden ornaments

by **Diane Jolie**

If you enjoy creating handmade ornaments, you'll love our netted snowflakes. They work up quickly in 11º seed beads, so there's time to make several, even during the busiest holiday season. There's no need to put them in storage when the holidays are over. These ornaments will look wonderful hanging in a sunny window all winter long.

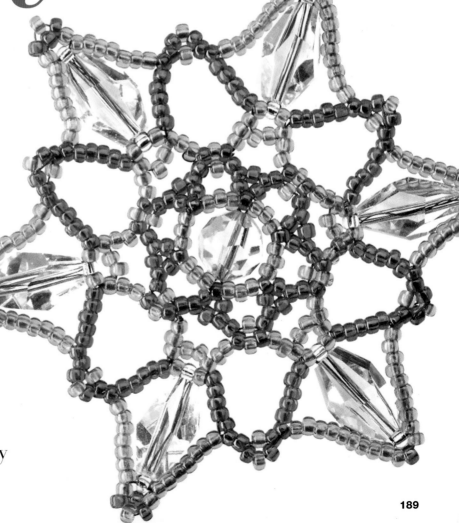

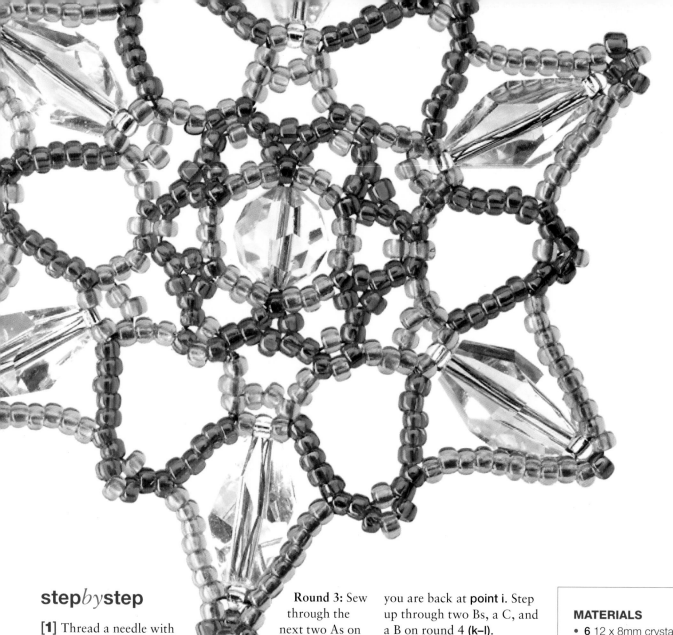

step*by*step

[1] Thread a needle with 7 ft. (2.1m) of Fireline, SoNo, or conditioned Nymo (see Basics, p. 10).
Round 1: Pick up one color A 11º seed bead and three color B 11ºs. Repeat this four-bead sequence five times for a total of 24 beads. Tie the beads in a ring with a square knot (Basics), leaving a 6-in. (15cm) tail. Sew through the first A **(figure 1, a–b)**.
Round 2: Pick up four As, a B, and four As. Sew through the second A in the ring **(b–c)**. Repeat until you have picked up a total of six groups of nine beads. Step up through the first A in this round **(c–d)**.

Round 3: Sew through the next two As on round 2, and pick up a B **(d–e)**. Sew through two As on round 2, and pick up an A **(e–f)**. Repeat until you are back at **point d**. Sew through three As, a B, and an A on round 2 **(f–g)**.
Round 4: Pick up four Bs, a color C 11º, and four Bs. Sew through an A, a B, and an A from round 2 **(g–h)**. Repeat until you are back at **point g**. Step up through two Bs from round 4 **(h–i)**.
Round 5: Pick up two Bs. Sew through two Bs on round 4 **(i–j)**. Sew through an A, a B, and an A on round 2, and through two Bs on round 4 **(j–k)**. Repeat until

you are back at **point i**. Step up through two Bs, a C, and a B on round 4 **(k–l)**.
Round 6: Pick up eight As, a B, and eight As. Sew through a B, a C, and a B from round 4 **(l–m)**. Repeat until you are back at **point l**. Sew through seven As on round 6 **(m–n)**.
Round 7: Pick up one B **(n–o)**. Sew through seven As, a B, a C, and a B (end at **point m**). Repeat until you are back at **point l**. Sew through eight As, a B, and three As **(o–p)**.
Round 8: Pick up eight Bs, an A, a B, an A, and eight Bs **(p–q)**. Sew through three As, a B, and three As **(q–r)**. Pick up ten Bs, an A, and ten Bs. Sew through three As, a B, and three As **(r–s)**. Repeat until you are back at **point p**.

MATERIALS

- **6** 12 x 8mm crystals
- 8mm crystal
- Japanese seed beads, size 11º
  2g color A
  2g color B
  1g color C
- Fireline 8 lb. test, SoNo, or Nymo B conditioned with beeswax
- beading needles, #12
- small paintbrush
- varnish or floor wax

Round 9: Sew through eight Bs **(s–t)**. Pick up an A and go through a B. Pick up a C, sew back through the B, the A, and the B, and go through seven Bs (end at **point q**). Sew through three As, a B, and three As on round 6 (end at **point r**). Sew through nine Bs on round 8 (**t–u**). Pick up a C, and sew through nine Bs on round 8. Sew through three As, a B, and three As on round 6 (end at **point s**). Repeat until you are back at **point p**.

[2] Sew through seven Bs on round 8 and a C on round 9 (**figure 2, a–b**). Pick up a 12 x 8mm crystal (**b–c**). Sew through a C on round 4 and go back through the crystal (**c–d**). Sew through the C on round 9. Go through seven Bs on round 8 (**d–e**). Sew through three As, a B, and three As on round 6 (**e–f**).

[3] Sew through nine Bs on round 8 and a C on round 9 (**f–g**). Pick up a 12 x 8mm crystal (**g–h**). Sew through a C on round 4, and go back through the crystal (**h–i**). Sew through the C on round 9. Go through nine Bs on round 8 (**i–j**). Sew through three As, a B, and three As on round 6 (**j–k**).

[4] Repeat steps 2–3 twice. Tie a half-hitch knot (Basics), sew through three beads, and cut the thread.

[5] With the 6-in. tail, pick up the 8mm crystal, and go through the opposite A on the first round (**figure 3, a–b**). Sew through the 8mm crystal and the first A. Retrace the thread path, tie a half-hitch knot, go through the next few beads, and trim the tail.

[6] With a paintbrush, coat the seed beads, not the crystals, with varnish or floor wax to stiffen them. Let dry, then coat the other side.

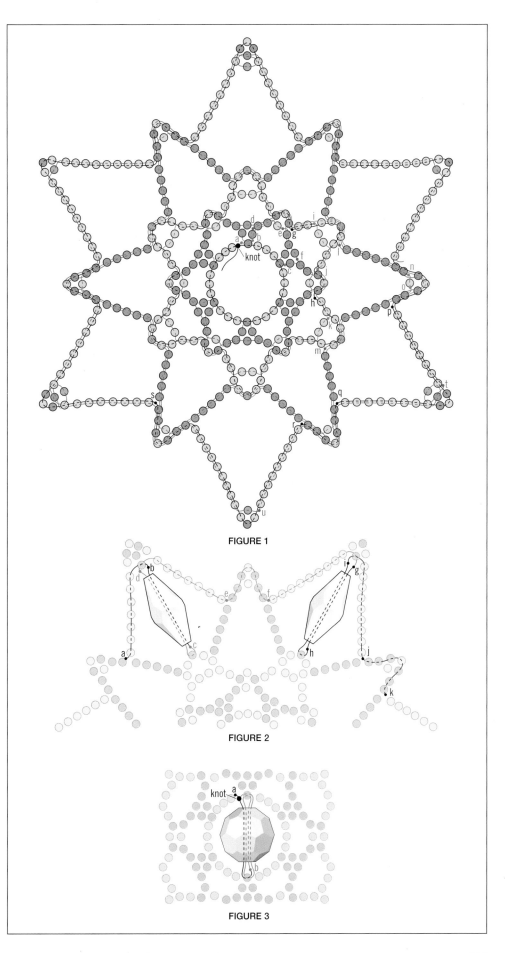

FIGURE 1

FIGURE 2

FIGURE 3

Netted lace necklace

Make rectangles and diamonds
with an angular netting technique

by **Rebecca Peapples**

Basic shapes come together seamlessly in an unusual
necklace. This easy netting technique will have you covering
all the angles as well as creating a few of your own.

stepbystep

Center rectangle

[1] On 4 ft. (1.2m) of conditioned thread (see Basics, p. 10), pick up a color A 15º seed bead, leaving an 8-in. (20cm) tail. Sew through the A again in the same direction. Pick up 22 As, a color C 15º seed bead, a 2mm round bead, and a C (**figure 1, a–b**).

[2] Skip the last C, and sew through the 2mm (**b–c**). Pick up a C and two As. Skip three beads on the previous row, and sew through the fourth bead (**c–d**).

[3] Pick up three As, skip the next three beads on the previous row, and sew through the next bead (**d–e**). Repeat four more times (**e–f**).

[4] Pick up a C, a 2mm, and a C. Repeat steps 2–3 (**f–g**).

[5] Repeat step 4 (**g–h**) until you have a netted strip with 19 2mms along the top edge and 20 2mms along the bottom. End at **figure 2, point a**.

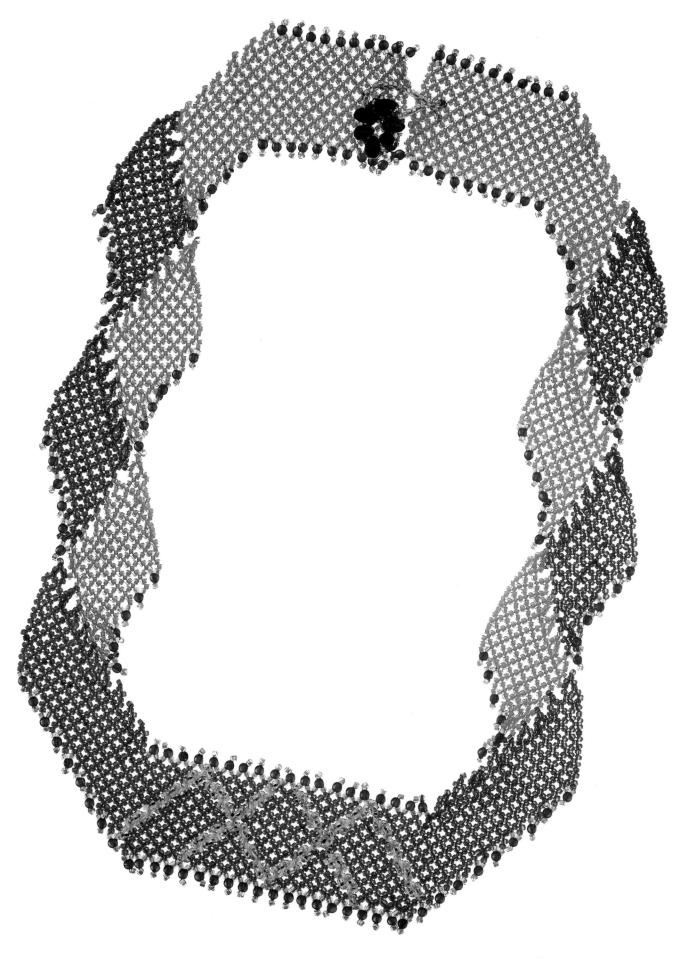

Angular netting

[1] Pick up seven As, skip the last A, and sew back through the sixth A **(figure 2, a–b)**.

[2] Pick up three As, skip the next three beads on the previous row, and sew through the next bead **(b–c)**. Repeat five more times **(c–d)**.

[3] Pick up a C, a 2mm, and a C. Skip the last C and sew through the 2mm. Pick up a C and two As. Skip the next three beads on the previous row, and sew through the fourth bead **(d–e)**. Pick up three As, skip the next three beads on the previous row, and sew through the next bead **(e–f)**. Repeat four more times **(f–g)**.

[4] Repeat steps 1–3 **(g–h)** until there are nine seven-bead points on the top edge and nine 2mms along the bottom edge.

Diamonds

[1] Flip your beadwork over and weave through the last seven-bead point as shown in **figure 3, a–b**.

[2] Pick up seven color B 15º seed beads, skip the last B, and sew back through the sixth B **(b–c)**. Pick up three Bs, and sew through the second B picked up **(c–d)**.

[3] Pick up three Bs, and sew through the A at the tip of the next seven-bead point **(d–e)**. Repeat four more times **(e–f)**.

[4] Pick up a C, a 2mm, and a C. Skip the last C, and sew through the 2mm. Pick up a C and two Bs. Skip the next

MATERIALS
necklace 18 in. (46cm)
- **200** 2mm round glass or stone beads
- size 15º Japanese seed beads
  10g color A
  10g color B
  5g color C
- 8–12mm bead for clasp
- Nymo D conditioned with beeswax
- beading needles, #13
- Liquid Paper

three beads on the previous row, and sew through the fourth bead **(f–g)**.

[5] Pick up three Bs, skip the next three beads on the previous row, and sew through the next bead **(g–h)**. Repeat four more times **(h–i)**.

[6] Repeat step 2 **(i–j)**. Continue using Bs, and complete the row **(j–k)**. Repeat steps 4 and 5 **(k–l)**.

[7] Repeat step 6 until this section has six seven-bead points along the top and six 2mms along the bottom to complete the first diamond shape.

[8] Repeat steps 1–7 using As for your main color to complete the second diamond.

[9] Repeat steps 1–8 to make the second A and B diamonds.

[10] Repeat steps 1–7 to make the third A diamond.

Finishing

[1] Using Bs, repeat steps 4 and 5 of the center rectangle until you have a straight strip with ten 2mms along the top and bottom. Secure the threads by weaving them into the beadwork, and trim.

[2] Secure a new thread in the center rectangle, and exit at **figure 1, point a**. Follow the directions for the angular netting and diamonds to complete the left side of the necklace.

[3] Repeat step 1.

[4] To attach the clasp bead, secure 12 in. (30cm) of thread in the small rectangle at one end of the necklace. Exit at **figure 4, point a**. Pick up a B, a 2mm, three Bs, a 2mm, the clasp bead, a 2mm, and a C **(a–b)**. Skip the C, and sew back through the 2mm, the clasp bead, and the second 2mm **(b–c)**. Pick up two Bs, and sew through the first three beads **(c–d)**. Retrace the thread path, sew into the netting, and secure the tails.

[5] To make the loop closure, secure 12 in. of thread in the small rectangle at the other end of the necklace. Exit at **figure 5, point a**. Pick up five Bs plus enough Bs to make a loop around the clasp bead **(a–b)**. Sew

through beads five and four, and pick up three Bs **(b–c)**. Sew into the netting, retrace the loop's thread path, secure the threads, and trim.

Center embellishment

[1] Using the Liquid Paper, refer to **figure 6** and make a small mark on the fourth, tenth, and 15th 2mms along the top edge of the center rectangle. On the bottom edge, mark the fifth, tenth, and 16th 2mms. Then, mark the first and last diagonal 2mms. The marked 2mms are only a guide – don't sew through them.

[2] Secure a comfortable length of thread in the beadwork, and exit the vertical A bead above the 2mm starting point **(figure 6, point a)**.

[3] Pick up three Cs, follow the beads outlined in red on the diagonal, skip a vertical bead, and sew into the next vertical bead. Repeat four more times to reach the top of the rectangle.

[4] Weave through the beadwork to the first outlined bead on the next diagonal and repeat step 3 until you reach **point b**.

[5] Weave through the netting to the vertical bead at **point c**, and repeat step 3 until you reach **point d**.

[6] Weave through the netting to the vertical bead at **point e**, above where you started. Repeat steps 3–5, sewing through the skipped vertical beads to add a second row. Secure the thread in the beadwork, and trim. Use your fingernail to remove the Liquid Paper from the 2mms.

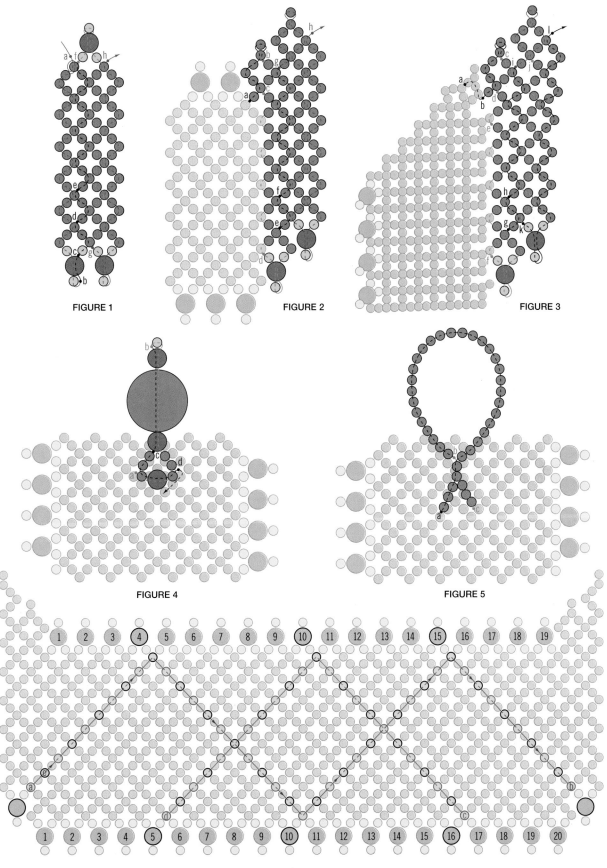

FIGURE 1

FIGURE 2

FIGURE 3

FIGURE 4

FIGURE 5

FIGURE 6

Loomwoven bracelets

Bracelets work up quickly using basic patterns and 11º seed beads

*by **Virginia Jensen***

Embellishing these bracelets while they are still attached to the loom creates an easy, semi-hands-free way to work. It's also a great opportunity to experiment with different embellishment techniques. When you finish the band, stitch a few rows of two-drop peyote, sew them around a piece of plastic tubing, and you will have created a cool, custom clasp.

step*by*step

Woven band

[1] Choose one of the patterns (right) and refer to Basics, p. 10, to set up the loom and review loom-weaving techniques. The checkerboard pattern uses 22 warp threads; the diagonal pattern uses 21 warp threads. Both bands use 11º seed beads in two colors.

[2] Thread a needle with 2 yd. (1.8m) of Nymo, and begin weaving as shown in Basics. When about 8 in. (20cm) of thread remains, make a few half-hitch knots (Basics) between the beads, and trim.

[3] Weave a 7-in. (18cm) band or to the desired length. When you finish the band, secure the working thread, and trim the tail, but don't take the beadwork off the loom. Secure a new thread, and exit the last row on either end of the band **(figure 1, point a)**.

Loops

Embellish your band with jagged or straight loops.

Jagged loops

[1] Pick up a color A 11º, three color B 11ºs, and one color C 8º **(figure 1, a–b)**. Sew through the first three beads in the next row **(b–c)**.

[2] Pick up an A, four Bs, and a C. Sew back through the first four beads in the next row. Make two more loops, adding one more B per loop. The number of beads you sew through in each row is determined by the number of Bs in each loop. When you've made the loop with six Bs, work back down to three Bs. Continue along one edge of the bracelet. Secure the thread as before.

[3] Start a new thread, and exit the other edge bead on the end where you started. Make loops along this edge, but start with an A, six Bs, and a C. Finish the embellishment on this edge, and secure the thread as before.

[4] Cut the work from the loom, and weave the warp threads into the beadwork. Don't tie off the threads in the first two rows on the short edges. You will need these rows to be free of knots in order to add the beaded clasp and loop.

Straight loops

[1] Pick up six color A 11ºs, and sew back through the first four beads in the next row **(figure 2, a–b)**.

[2] Repeat step 1 along the length of the band on both edges.

[3] Finish as in step 4 of the jagged loops.

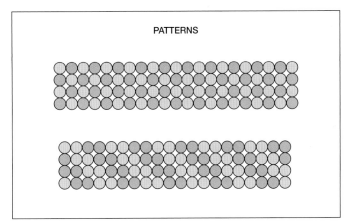

PATTERNS

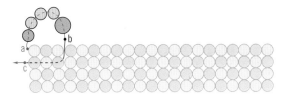

FIGURE 1

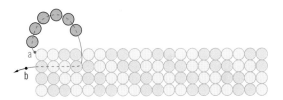

FIGURE 2

MATERIALS

bracelet 7½ in. (19.1cm)

- 5g size 8º seed beads, color C
- 30g size 11º Japanese seed beads, in each of **2** colors: A and B
- Nymo B or D
- beading needle, #12
- beading loom
- plastic tubing, ¼-in. (6mm) outside diameter

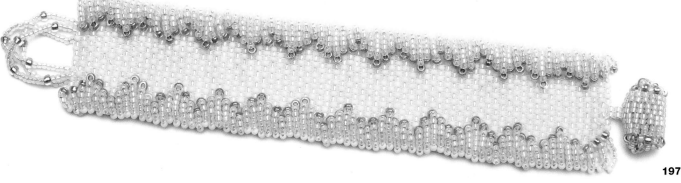

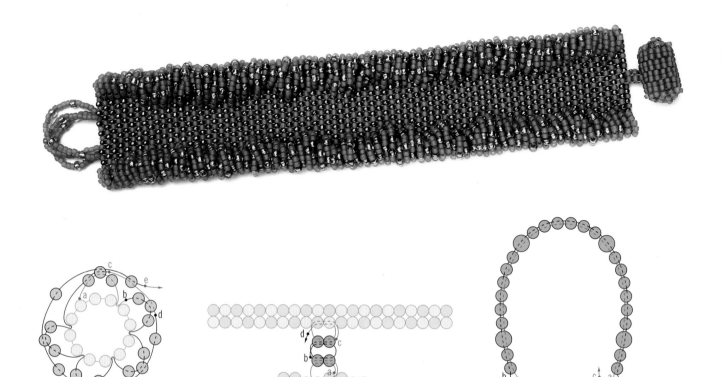

FIGURE 3

FIGURE 4

FIGURE 5

Beaded clasp

[1] Cut a piece of plastic tubing ⅞ in. (2.2cm) long, and set it aside.

[2] Using As, make a two-drop peyote strip (Basics) eight beads wide (four stitches) and 12 rows long.

[3] Wrap the strip around the tubing (add or subtract a row of peyote if necessary), and zip up (Basics) the first and last rows.

[4] Exit at the edge of the tube, **figure 3, point a**. Pick up three As, skip the next thread bridge, and sew under the next one **(a–b)**. Repeat around the edge. When you reach the first three beads added, sew through the first two **(b–c)**.

[5] Pick up an A, and sew through the second bead in the next set of three As **(c–d)**. Repeat to complete the round **(d–e)**. Pull this round tightly to bring the beads into a ring. Sew through the last round again. Repeat on the other edge of the bead.

[6] Bring the working thread to the middle of the beaded clasp, and exit at **figure 4, point a**. Use this thread to attach the toggle clasp to one end of the band. To make a bead ladder (Basics), pick up two As, and sew back through two

As in the toggle. Sew through the new As **(a–b)**. Make one more stitch **(b–c)**, and then connect the last stitch to the middle two beads on one end of the band **(c–d)**. Retrace the thread path, and secure the tails.

[7] Secure 1 yd. (.9m) of thread in the last few rows at the other end of the band, and exit at **figure 5, point a**. Pick up enough As and Cs to fit around the beaded clasp. Skip eight beads along the end row, and sew through the ninth **(a–b)**. Then sew back through the bead loop, and exit at **point c**. Make two more loops in the same manner, anchoring them to different beads in the end row so you have three offset loops. Secure the threads.

Woven wonders

Adorn loomed pendants with cabochons and fringe

by **Heidi Kummli**

Loomwork needn't be a long-term, large-scale undertaking, as these fabulous embellished pendants prove. These creative designs offer attractive options whether your taste runs to the traditional or the contemporary.

step*by*step

The pattern

Review loomweaving techniques (see Basics, p. 10), before you start.
[1] Set up the loom with 26 warp threads, which is one more warp thread than the number of beads across the width of the pattern.
[2] Start a 2-yd. (1.8m) weaving thread, or weft, and leave an 18 in. (46cm) tail. Weave part 1 of the pattern.
[3] You need to decrease two times within part 2. To decrease, sew back through the beads you need to skip on

the next row, and exit at **point a.** Wrap the weft around the warp thread as shown in **figure 1.** Now you are in position to start the next row. Repeat to make the second decrease at **point b.**
[4] End the weft by tying it to the warp thread next to the last bead on the last row. Then weave through a few beads, and trim the excess thread. Seal the knot with G-S Hypo Cement.
[5] To weave the bail (part 3 of the geometric pattern), thread a needle on the tail, and sew through the beads on row 1 to exit at **point c.** Wrap the weaving thread around the warp as you

did in step 3, and weave the bail from the bottom up. For the flower pattern, exit at **point c,** weave the right strip, and end the thread. Start a new thread,

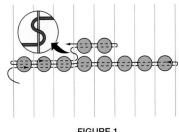

FIGURE 1

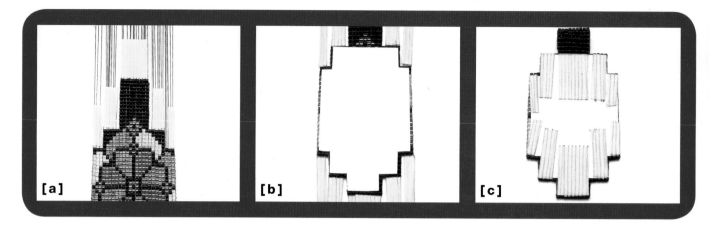

[a]   [b]   [c]

exit at **point d**, and work the left section of the bail.

[6] Secure the weaving thread, and trim.

Finish the warp threads

[1] While your piece is on the loom, tape the warp threads as shown (**photo a**). Don't tape the warp threads too close to the loomwork or the tape will show along the edges.

[2] Trim the warp threads just past the tape. Place the loomwork on a flat surface. Flatten the tape with the edge of a ruler to secure the threads.

[3] Trace the shape of the pendant, but not the bail, on poster board. Then cut out the shape, making it slightly smaller than the actual loomwork.

[4] Glue the poster board cutout to the back of the loomwork with tacky glue

MATERIALS

one pendant

- 6 x 8–10 x 14mm cabochon
- 1–2g size 11º Japanese seed beads, in **6–15** colors
- 2–3g seed beads, size 15º (edging for pendant and cabochons)
- assorted accent beads and charms for fringe (optional)
- Ultrasuede
- Nymo B or Fireline 6–8 lb. test
- beading needles, #12 and #12 sharps
- beading loom
- G-S Hypo Cement
- Aleene's Tacky Glue
- E6000 adhesive
- clear nail polish
- ¾ in. (1.9cm) masking tape
- poster board

(**photo b**). Fold the warp threads over the poster board, and glue the tape to the board. Let it dry under a heavy, flat object like a thick book to keep it flat.

[5] Fold the bail over, so it forms a loop above the pendant, and glue the tape to the board (**photo c**). Allow the glue to dry, as before.

Attach the cabochons

[1] Apply E6000 to the loomwork where you want to set the cabochon. Work the glue into the spaces between the beads with a toothpick. Apply glue to the back of the cab, set it in place on the loomwork, and let it dry.

[2] With a #12 sharp, make a hole in the board just above the cab.

[3] Thread the sharp with 2 ft. (61cm) of Nymo or Fireline, and knot the end. Sew through the hole from the back to the front of the loomwork.

[4] Pick up six 15º seed beads, and position them along the edge of the cab. Sew through the loomwork and board next to the sixth 15º (**photo d**).

[5] Position the needle between the third and fourth 15º, and make a hole in the board, as in step 3. Sew through the board from the back to the front, and sew back through the last three 15ºs.

[6] Continue working in beaded backstitch (Basics) around the cab. Then sew through all the 15ºs again, and pull them snug against the cab. Work a second row if desired. Secure the thread, and trim.

Finishing

[1] Cut a piece of Ultrasuede slightly larger than the loomwork.

[2] Glue the Ultrasuede to the board on the back of the loomwork with Aleene's

Tacky Glue. Press the loomwork flat against the Ultrasuede to smooth out the glue.

[3] After the glue is dry, carefully trim the Ultrasuede around the loomwork.

[4] Using the #12 sharp and 1 yd. (.9cm) of thread, knot one end of the thread. Position your needle at **point d** on the pattern, between the loomwork and the Ultrasuede. Sew through the Ultrasuede near the edge to hide the knot, and go under the thread bridge in the corner of the loomwork.

[5] Pick up four 15ºs, and sew under the thread bridge between the third and fourth beads on the loomwork. Sew through the Ultrasuede and up through the fourth 15º (**photo e**).

[6] Repeat step 5 around the pendant. As you work, adjust the number of 15ºs to follow the shape of the pendant.

Fringe

[1] Secure 1 yd. of thread in the Ultrasuede, as in step 4 of "Finishing," where you will place the first strand of fringe.

[2] Pick up three to five 15ºs or 11ºs, accent beads, and three to five 15ºs or 11ºs. If adding a charm, sew through the loop on a charm and pick up the same number of 15ºs or 11ºs. Sew through the accent beads (**photo f**). Pick up three to five 15ºs or 11ºs, and sew through the loomwork to the back of the pendant (**photo g**).

[3] Continue adding fringe as desired. Secure the thread, and trim.

200

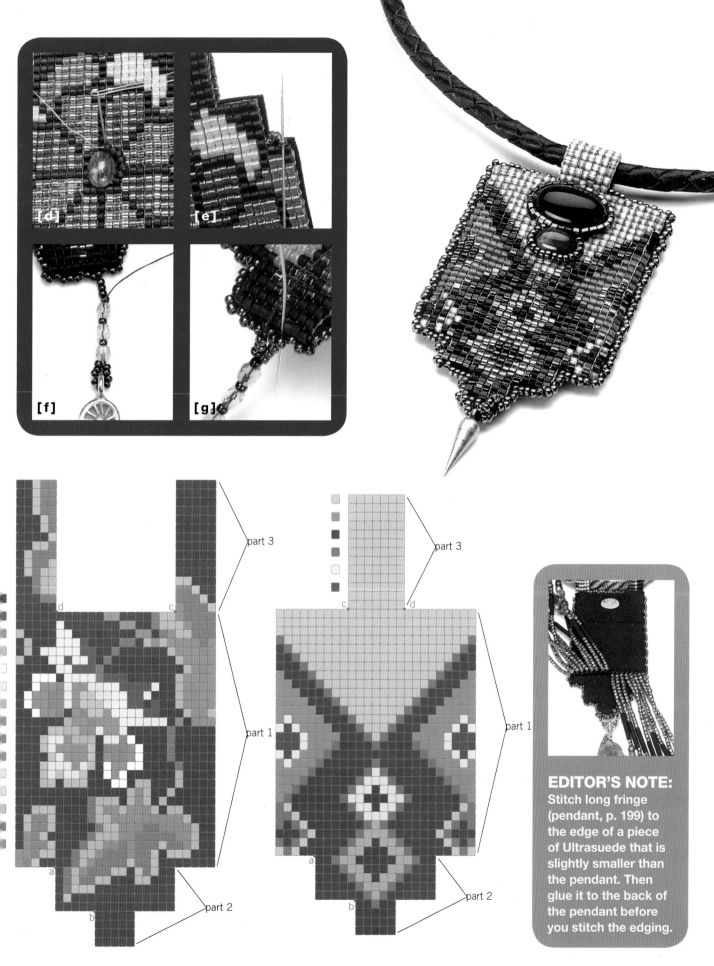

[d]

[e]

[f]

[g]

part 3

part 3

part 1

part 1

part 2

part 2

d

c

c

d

a

a

b

b

EDITOR'S NOTE:
Stitch long fringe
(pendant, p. 199) to
the edge of a piece
of Ultrasuede that is
slightly smaller than
the pendant. Then
glue it to the back of
the pendant before
you stitch the edging.

Bands
color

Weave strips of matte cylinder beads
to create an impressive container

by **Cindy Kinerson** *and* **Anna Elizabeth Draeger**

Cindy Kinerson's woven basket (previous page) boasts an intriguing combination of loomwork and basketweaving. This uncommon pairing provides significant potential for creating the sturdy forms found in the basket maker's repertoire.

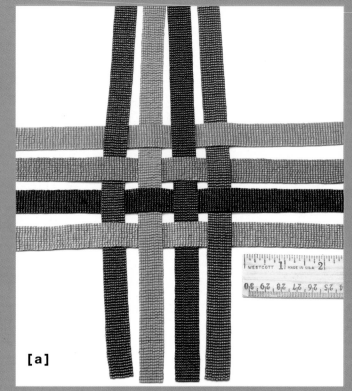

[a]

step*by*step

Review loomweaving techniques (see Basics, p. 10) before you start.

[1] Using 12 warp threads, weave eight strips of beadwork 13 in. (33cm) long and four strips 10¼ in. (26cm) long. Secure all the tails in the beadwork, weaving them in away from the end rows. You will be sewing through the end rows again to assemble the basket. Sew the first and last rows together on each of the shorter strips to make four joined bands.

[2] Weave all eight 13-in. strips together to make the bottom of the basket. Measure the strips to make sure the bottom of the basket is centered (photo a).

[3] Fold every other strip over the bottom of the basket (photo b). These strips are group A. The remaining strips are group B.

[4] Place one of the four joined bands around the outer edge of the bottom of the basket. Bring group A over the joined band (photo c).

[5] Fold group B over the band and toward the bottom of the basket (photo d).

[6] Place the second band on top of the first one, and bring group B back out over the band. Fold group A in toward the middle of the basket (photo e).

[7] Repeat with the third band (photo f).

MATERIALS
one basket
- Japanese cylinder beads 10g each of **12** colors
- Fireline 6 lb. test
- beading needles, #12
- beading loom
- clothespins
- chainnose pliers
- furniture polish (optional)

[d]

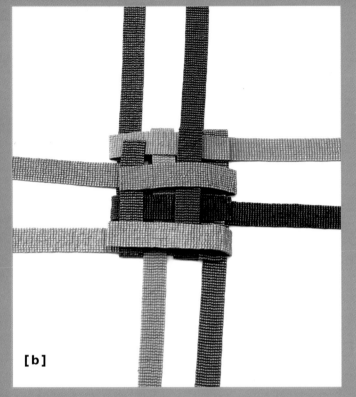

[b]

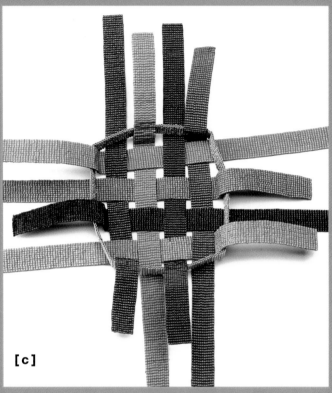

[c]

[e]

[f]

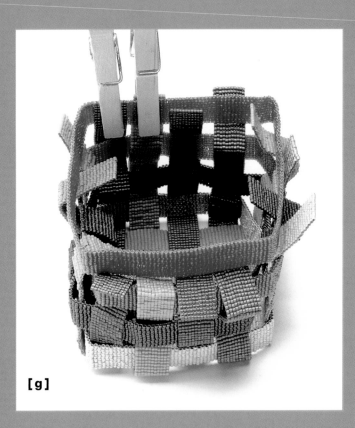

[g]

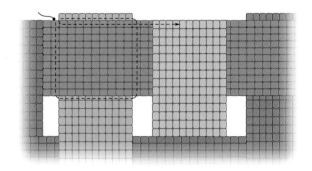

FIGURE 1

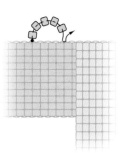

FIGURE 2

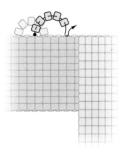

FIGURE 3

[8] Repeat with the fourth band. Hold the ends in place with clothespins while you adjust the strips and make the spacing between the rows equal **(photo g)**. Sew through the rows of loomwork **(figure 1)** at each intersection to reinforce the basket. Start a new 1-yd. (.9m) length of Fireline, and secure it under one of the thread bridges along the basket's rim. Pick up five cylinders, skip two thread bridges, and sew under the next one **(figure 2)**. Pick up five cylinders of another color, and repeat **(figure 3)**. Continue around the rim, using all 12 bead colors. Secure the tail, and trim.

EDITOR'S NOTE: You can easily change the dimensions of the basket. Lay out a pattern using construction paper before starting the woven strips. String some cylinders and lay them across the width of your paper to determine the number of warps you will need. Weave the strips to the desired length. Depending on your tension, you may need to coat the inside of the basket with furniture polish to add stiffness.

Tips & Techniques

Separate components

One of the best beading tips I ever received was from a beading instructor who does restoration and repair work. She recommended that I use a separate piece of thread for each component of my work. For example, if making a bracelet, use one thread to make the base, a second thread for embellishments, a third for one clasp half, and a fourth for the other clasp half. If any of these components break, the break is confined to that segment and is easy to repair.
– *S.J. Sanchez, Albuquerque, N.M.*

Thread on the go

To make my thread collection quickly accessible and portable, I string my spools, sorted by size, onto 8-in. (20cm) ball chains. Then, I string an alphabet bead to indicate the thread size. This handy method allows me to cut the desired length of thread off the spool without removing it from the chain. If you can't find 8-in. chains, connect two 4-in. (10cm) chains.
– *Rhonda M. Guy, Lexington, Ky.*

Fringe benefit

To plan fringe, use a piece of wide-wale corduroy with grooves wide enough to hold your beads. Lay the fringe beads out in rows so you can easily make design or bead changes as you see the pattern unfold. Stringing becomes very easy, since all you have to do is go down one groove to the end bead, turn around, and go back up again. This works especially well for geometric patterns.
– *Marilyn Peters, Vallejo, Calif.*

Alternate peyote start

When I start a flat peyote project, I turn my pattern on its side, and bead up the first four rows in brick stitch. Then I turn it back, and proceed in peyote. I find this much easier than the conventional approach.
– *Jean Watkins, Aberdeen, Wash.*

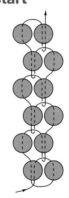

Magic with markers

I used to have trouble getting light-colored thread through the eye of a needle. The thread would "disappear" between my fingers. Now, I color the thread's end with a black marker. No more vanishing threads!
– *Barbara Toomey, Gainesville, Fla.*

Peyote aid

When working in flat peyote with 11º seed beads, I slip a quilter's pin through the first row after completing the third row. This maintains the project's shape and makes it easy to hold. Cover the pin's tip with tape to protect against scratches.
– *Pat Harter, Cary, N.C.*

Pattern markers

I love beading with a charted pattern, but I've never been crazy about using a ruler to mark my progress. While doing a square stitch pattern at work one day, I stumbled upon the answer – sticky notes. They are inexpensive and easy to move, they keep their stickiness for a long time, they don't leave any residue on the page, and you can make notes to yourself right on them about any changes you want to make to the pattern. The best part is that they stay in place when you have to pack up your project. So, when you open your pattern book again, your place is still marked.
– *Jennifer Howe, Carson City, Nev.*

Other
techniq

ues

by **Mary Hettmansperger**

String dangles on snap swivels
for easy charm bracelets

Fishing
tackle bracelet

These lively bracelets feature snap swivels, a component that's more at home in a tackle box than on a beading table. The easy-to-use connectors create an unexpected background for all kinds of beads, like the brightly colored monochromatic palettes shown here. One thing that's certain – you won't end up fishing for compliments.

[a]

[b]

[c]

[d]

[e]

[f]

MATERIALS

bracelet 7½ in. (19.1cm)

- **50** 10–20mm glass beads (Fire Mountain Gems, 800-355-2137, firemountaingems.com)
- 4g size 6º or 8º seed beads
- toggle clasp
- **50** head pins
- **17** snap swivels (available in fishing supply departments)
- chainnose pliers
- roundnose pliers
- wire cutters

step*by*step

[1] On a head pin, string a seed bead, a 10–20mm bead, and a seed bead **(photo a)**. Make a wrapped loop (see Basics, p. 10), and trim the excess wire **(photo b)**. Make a total of 50 bead units.
[2] Arrange the bead units on your work surface as desired **(photo c)**.

[3] Open a snap swivel using chainnose pliers. String a bead unit, the loop of the toggle bar, and a bead unit. Close the swivel **(photo d)**.
[4] Open another swivel. String a bead unit, the soldered end of the snap swivel (not the swivel section) from the previous step, and two bead units. Close the swivel **(photo e)**.

[5] Repeat step 4, connecting a total of 16 swivels.
[6] Open one more swivel. String a bead unit, the remaining clasp half, and a bead unit. String the soldered end of the last swivel from the previous step and a bead unit. Close the swivel **(photo f)**.
[7] Check the fit, and add or remove swivels if necessary.

EDITOR'S NOTE:
To vary the bracelet's appearance, try using wood, ceramic, or shell beads. String crystals or pairs of seed beads next to the larger beads for more variation among the dangles.

Crystal-and-

Glue-on crystals provide plenty of sparkle in a flash

by **Anna Elizabeth Draeger**

Looking for instant gratification? Try your hand at applying crystals with a heat-set adhesive. Embellish your work with a picot edge.

step*by*step

Embellish the band

[1] Cut your Ultrasuede to the desired length and width, making sure the ends overlap ½ in. (1.3cm) to accommodate the snap closure. Or, make the band the exact length and use a crimp-style clasp. (This band is 7 x 1 in. /18 x 2.5cm).

[2] At one end, sew the female snaps to the underside of the Ultrasuede **(photo a)**.

[3] Using a permanent marker, draw or stencil a design on the underside of the Ultrasuede **(photo b)**. Cut out the design with a utility knife **(photo c)**.

[4] Lay out about 1 in. of your crystal design **(photo d)**.

[5] Prepare the BeJeweler with the correct metal tip for the size of the crystal you will adhere. Use the solid metal tip for the smaller crystals **(photo e)**.

[6] Preheat the BeJeweler.

For the larger crystals, pick up the crystal with the tip, and watch the bottom of the crystal until the heat melts the adhesive. Place the crystal on the desired location. It is not necessary to press hard, and don't let the metal tip touch your Ultrasuede. For the smaller crystals, place the crystal where you want it, put the tip on top of the crystal for several seconds using gentle pressure **(photo f)**, and then lift the tip off. (Before changing tips, unplug the tool and wait until the tip cools.)

[7] Continue to adhere the crystals to the Ultrasuede,

MATERIALS

bracelet 7 in. (18cm)

- Swarovski Hot Fix crystals (bejeweler.com)
  30 30ss (6mm)
  30 20ss (5mm)
  30 16ss (4mm)
- 10g size 15º seed beads
- **2** snaps, size 4/0, or crimp clasp bars with lobster claw clasp

- Nymo B or Fireline 6 lb. test for picot edge
- thread for sewing snap
- beading needles, #12
- sewing needles
- BeJeweler Stone Styler (bejeweler.com)
- permanent marker
- tweezers or chainnose pliers
- Ultrasuede
- utility knife

suede cuff

FIGURE

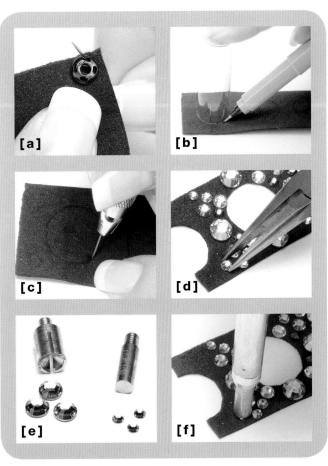

stopping to lay out more crystals as you go.

[8] Sew the male half of the snaps to the top of the Ultrasuede, or crimp the clasp bars to the ends of the band.

Picot edge

[1] Using 1 yd. (.9m) of thread, sew through the end of the Ultrasuede along one side of the band.
[2] Pick up three 15º seed beads, and sew through the Ultrasuede, two beads' width from where the thread is exiting (figure, a–b). Sew through the third bead just added (b–c).

[3] Pick up two 15ºs, sew through the Ultrasuede one bead's width from the last bead, and sew through the second bead just added (c–d).
[4] Repeat step 3 along the side edge of the band. Secure the tails in the beadwork with half-hitch knots (see Basics, p. 10), and trim the tail.
[5] Repeat the picot edge along the other side, and repeat inside the cut-out designs, if desired.

Dazzling beaded brooc

beaded brooc

Surround crystals with bead embroidery for brooches that are sure to get noticed

by **Janet-Beth McCann Flynn**

Brooches of all sizes, shapes, and styles are everywhere lately. Here's a quick way to make your own using fun and easy-to-find crystal sliders. These components are so light, the brooches can sparkle on spring linens or winter wools.

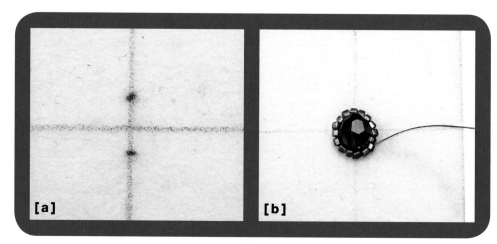

[a] [b]

hes

step*by*step

Bead embroidery

[1] Cut a 2-in. (5cm) square piece of Lacy's Stiff Stuff. Divide the square into quarters by drawing a cross through the center. Center the crystal, and make a small mark on the square at each hole (**photo a**).

[2] Thread a needle on comfortable length of Nymo, and knot the end. Come up through the Lacy's at one of the marked points. Pick up the crystal, and slide it to the square. Go down through the square at the second marked point. Repeat until the crystal is secure.

[3] Come up adjacent to the crystal, and backstitch (see Basics, p. 10) a row of cylinder beads around the crystal (**photo b**). When backstitching around design components, using fewer beads at a time results in a more fluid curve.

[4] Line up a metal slider along the cross. Attach the slider as you did the crystal, taking care to keep it aligned. Repeat with three more sliders (**photo c**).

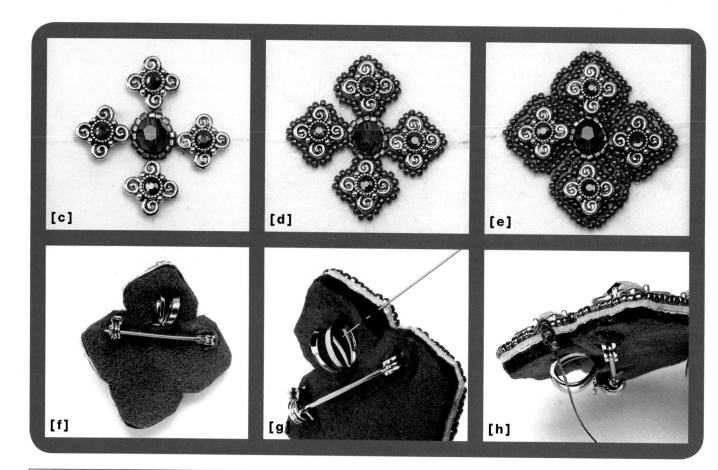

[c]

[d]

[e]

[f]

[g]

[h]

MATERIALS

brooch approximately 1¼ in. (3.2cm) square

- **4** Crystal Innovations designer metal sliders with Swarovski crystals (Michaels, michaels.com)
- 8mm faceted round crystal, amethyst
- 10g size 11º seed beads, purple
- 3g Japanese cylinder beads, lavender
- pin finding with pendant bail (Michaels)
- Nymo D, purple
- beading needles, #12
- E6000 adhesive
- G-S Hypo Cement
- Lacy's Stiff Stuff (Designer's Findings, 262-574-1324)
- Ultrasuede
- permanent marker to match Ultrasuede (optional)

[5] Using 11º seed beads, complete a row of backstitch around all four sliders (photo d).

[6] Fill in the remaining space with another row of 11ºs (photo e) or other beads as desired.

Finishing

We've chosen a pin finding that doubles as a pendant bail. You may use a plain pin finding just as successfully.

[1] Carefully trim the Lacy's close to the beadwork.

[2] Place the piece bead side up on a piece of Ultrasuede, and use it as a template to cut the Ultrasuede to match.

[3] Center the pin finding on the Ultrasuede, and make an incision that will allow the finding to poke through.

[4] Center the finding on the back of the Lacy's. Using E6000, glue the Ultrasuede to the back of the Lacy's, allowing the finding to emerge (photo f). Let the piece dry completely.

[5] If you prefer a crisp edge, use a marker that matches the Ultrasuede to camouflage the Lacy's. For a beaded edging, start a comfortable length of thread, and knot the end. Pierce the inside edge of the Ultrasuede, and exit away from the beadwork (photo g).

[6] Pick up three 11ºs (or other beads as desired), and go through the Lacy's and the Ultrasuede (photo h). Repeat until the edges are covered. Secure the thread, and trim the tail. Dot the knot with G-S Hypo Cement.

EDITOR'S NOTE: Have fun experimenting with a variety of bead and slider choices. Some seed beads can give this piece an antique silver or marcasite effect. The gold brooch on p. 215 uses bugle beads to mimic baguette-cut gemstones. The brooch above it surrounds one slider with crystals. For a more organic look, mix bead colors and sizes, and edge the brooch.

Beaded
butterfly
bag

Embroider butterflies and flowers
on a simple drawstring bag

by **Myra B. Kurtz**

Add a personal touch to a special occasion handbag with bead embroidery. Whether you make your own bags or want to embellish a pre-made bag or fabric panel, you can turn a few simple stitches into a glittering accessory for all your holiday outings.

step*by*step

[1] Make a copy of the butterfly pattern (figure 1). You can either use it at 100 percent, or size it according to your needs.

[2] Put the pattern on a Styrofoam board, and place a piece of vellum over it. Use the tapestry needle to punch holes along the entire pattern (photo a).

[3] Position the perforated vellum on the velvet. Follow the pattern with the chalk pen to transfer the image (photo b). When you lift the vellum, a pale image of the design will remain (photo c). This chalk comes off quite easily without smearing, so just brush away the excess.

[4] Using a comfortable length of Fireline (or embroidery floss if you desire additional color), make a double overhand knot (see Basics, p. 10) at the end of the thread. Come up through the fabric where you want to start beading.

[5] Use beaded backstitch (figure 2) to embroider the fabric (photo d). Pick up three beads according to the color chart (figure 3), and slide them down to the fabric. Place them along the pattern, and sew through the fabric after the last bead. Come up through the fabric between the second and third beads. Go through the third bead, pick up three beads, and repeat.

[6] When you have beaded the entire pattern, add the butterflies' antennae and legs with embroidery floss by using small, running stitches. Come up through the fabric where you want to begin. Following the pattern, go down through the fabric, making approximately a ¼-in. (6mm) stitch. Come up through the fabric just beyond the last stitch, and continue stitching the pattern.

[7] When finished, sew through the fabric, and turn the bag inside out. If beading on a panel, turn it over. Secure the thread, and trim the tail. Wherever you've used embroidery floss, dot the knots with glue, and let them dry. Turn your panel into a bag, or turn your bag right side out, and you've got butterflies to go.

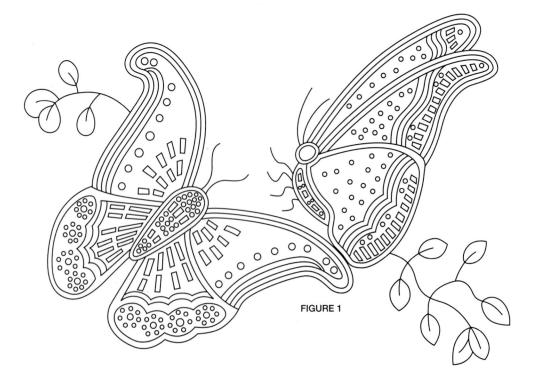

FIGURE 1

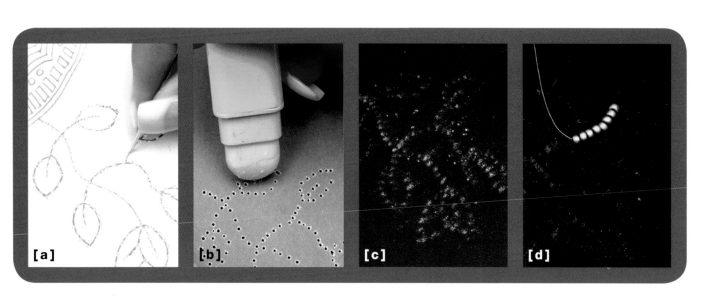

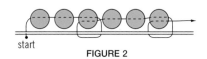

start

FIGURE 2

MATERIALS
butterfly pattern 5 x 5 in.
(13 x 13cm)
- bugle beads, 10g each
  7mm, purple iris twist (G)
  5mm, gold twist (F)
  5mm, gold (J)
  4mm, purple iris matte
  twist (H)
- seed beads, 15g each
  size 6º, gold (E)
  size 11º, transparent
  yellow (A)
  size 11º, orange (B)
  size 11º, iridescent
  blue (C)

size 11º, light blue (D)
size 11º, gold (K)
size 11º, cobalt (I)
size 15º, brown (L)
size 15º, green (M)
- Fireline 8 lb. test
- velvet or other fabric bag
  or panel
- embroidery floss, gold
- beading needles, #12
- tapestry needle
- chalk pen (Jo-Ann
  Stores, joann.com)
- G-S Hypo Cement
- Styrofoam board
- vellum (Jo-Ann Stores)

A ☐ transparent yellow 11º
B ☐ orange 11º
C ☐ iridescent blue 11º
D ☐ light blue 11º
E ☐ gold 6º
F ☐ 5mm gold twist bugle
G ☐ 7mm purple iris twist bugle
H ☐ 4mm purple iris matte twist bugle
I ☐ cobalt 11º
J ☐ 5mm gold bugle
K ☐ gold 11º
L ☐ brown 15º
M ☐ green 15º

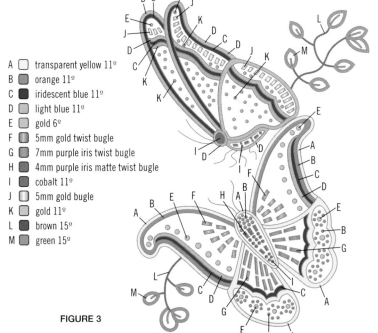

FIGURE 3

Macramé choker

Knotted leather cord and beads team up in a versatile choker

by **Miachelle DePiano**

Dress up leather cord with large beads and a glass pendant in this fast and easy choker. By using just two knots – the square and the overhand – even those who have never done macramé can complete this piece with confidence. The zigzagging knotwork provides a chic setting that can go dressy or casual, and an asymmetrical finish lends a playful attitude.

step*by*step

[1] Cut the leather cord into three 3-yd. (2.7m) lengths. Gather them so the ends are even with each other, and fold them in half. Make an overhand knot (see Basics, p. 10) near the fold, leaving an opening large enough for the tip of your index finger to fit through (photo a).

[2] String a 6mm bead over all six cords (photo b).

[3] Pin the knot to the macramé board, and spread out the cords. Number them 1–6 from left to right. Make a square knot (figures 1 and 2) around cord 2 with cords 1 and 3 (photo c).

[4] Renumber the cords 1–6. Make a square knot around cord 3 with cords 2 and 4 (photo d).

[5] Repeat across, each time setting aside the left-hand cord, picking up the next cord on the right, and making a square knot around the middle cord of the three-cord group.

[6] After you've made a knot with cords 4 and 6, work the pattern in reverse. Begin by making a square knot with cords 5 and 3 (photo e). Continue tying knots to the left. Before making the knot with cords 3 and 1, string a 14mm bead (photo f).

[7] Tie the knot (photo g), and work the pattern to the right. Again, before knotting with the final three cords, string a 14mm.

[8] Continue working this pattern until you're preparing to string the 12th bead. Instead of stringing a 14mm, string a 6mm, the pendant, and a 6mm. Tie the knot as usual (photo h).

Macramé square knot

[1] Cross the right-hand cord over the core and the left-hand cord under the core. This creates a loop between each cord and the core. Pass the right-hand cord through the loop on the left from front to back and the left-hand cord through the other loop from back to front (figure 1).

[2] Cross the left-hand cord over and the right-hand cord under the core. Pass the cords through the loops (figure 2), and tighten.

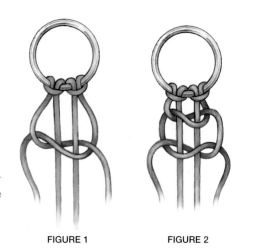

FIGURE 1   FIGURE 2

[9] Continue working the pattern until you've strung 22 14mms. String a 6mm over all six strands (photo i).

[10] Tie two square knots, using cords 1 and 2 and 5 and 6 to knot around cords 3 and 4 (photo j).

[11] String a 6mm over the two middle strands, and tie a square knot after it as in step 10 (photo k).

[12] Separate the cords into two groups of three. Make a square knot around cord 2 with cords 1 and 3 and around cord 5 with cords 4 and 6 (photo l).

[13] Tie a square knot around cords 3 and 4 with cords 2 and 5 (photo m).

[14] String a 6mm on cord 2, and tie a square knot with cords 1 and 3. String a 6mm on cord 5, and tie a square knot with cords 4 and 6 (photo n).

[15] Repeat step 13.

[16] Repeat step 10.

[17] Repeat steps 12–14.

[18] Repeat step 13.

[19] Tie three square knots, using cords 1 and 2 and 5 and 6 to knot around cords 3 and 4. Test for fit. Make more or fewer knots as needed.

[20] String a 6mm, and tie an overhand knot against it. Slip the knot through the loop you made in step 1 to make sure it won't slip out. If it's too small, make another knot over the first. Test again, and make any necessary adjustments. Trim the cords evenly about ¼ in. (6mm) after the knot. **Photo o** shows this end of the necklace.

MATERIALS

necklace 14½ in. (36.8cm)

- glass pendant
- **22** 14mm beads
- **10** 6mm large-hole beads (holes must be able to accommodate six strands of 1mm leather cord)
- 9 yd. (8.2m) 1mm leather cord
- macramé board or self-healing Styrofoam pad
- T-pins

EDITOR'S NOTE: Leather cord can be as much as 25 percent thicker than its labeled diameter. Try to find cord that is as close to 1mm as possible, as using cord that is even a bit thicker will alter your results. Furthermore, leather cord is relatively weak and is easier to break or tear than you may expect. If, as you're knotting, you see a crack forming in your cord, grasp the cord above the crack, and proceed. As long as you're careful, you should be able to get past the crack without breaking the cord. The structure of the macramé should support the cracked cord and prevent further damage.

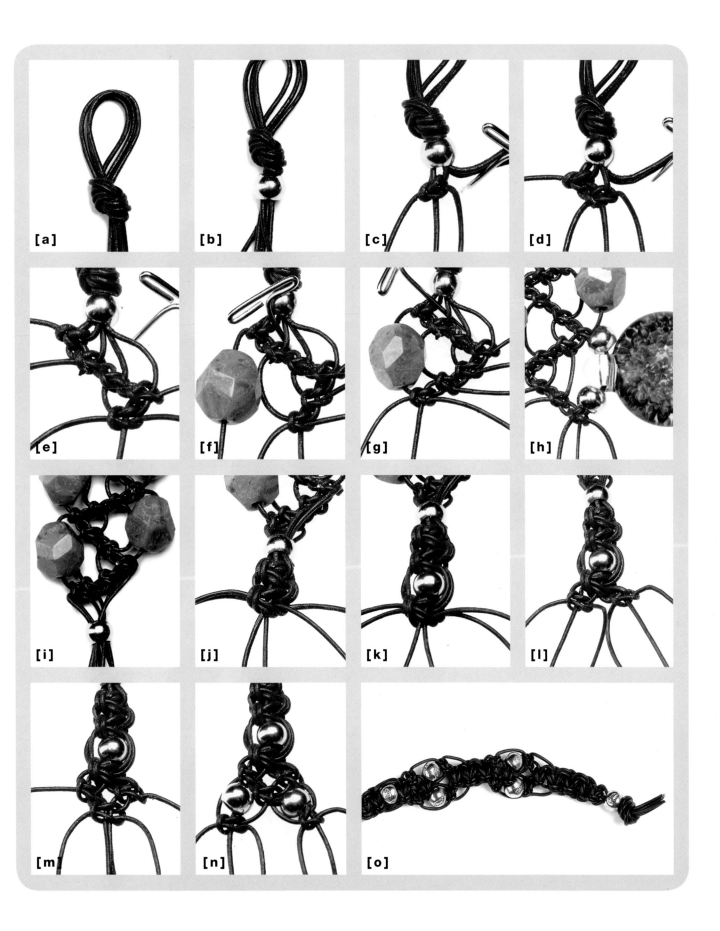

[a]

[b]

[c]

[d]

[e]

[f]

[g]

[h]

[i]

[j]

[k]

[l]

[m]

[n]

[o]

ASIAN

Embellish a jade medallion with delicate knots

by **Irina Serbina**

accents

If you're looking for an unusual tassel, consider adding macramé embellishment to a stone medallion. The project calls for three knots, but the leaf-shaped central design is worked solely in clove hitch, making this a perfect piece for beginners. Attach your finished tassel to a purse, as on page 227, or display it on a lampshade or drapery tieback.

step*by*step

[1] Pin your medallion to the macramé board. Cut eight 5-ft. (1.5m) pieces of knotting cord.

[2] Attach one piece of cord to the medallion with a lark's head knot (see Basics, p. 10, figure 1, and photo a). Attach a second cord to a second hole in the same manner. Fold a third cord in half, and pin it to the board between the first two cords.

[3] Fold the fourth cord in half, and pin it to the left of the first cord. Bring the right half of the cord over the other cords (photo b). This is the anchor cord.

[4] Working from left to right, tie each vertical cord around the anchor cord with a clove-hitch knot (figure 2). Remove the pin holding the anchor cord (photo c).

[5] Fold the fifth cord in half, pin it to the left of the first cord, and bring the right half of the cord over the other cords. Repeat step 4, using the new cord as the anchor.

[6] Repeat step 5 with the sixth cord (photo d). You now have 12 working cord ends. Number them from left to right: cord 1 through cord 12.

[7] Tie cords 3 and 6 in a square knot (figures 3 and 4) around cords 4 and 5. Then tie cords 7 and 10 in a square knot around cords 8 and 9 (photo e).

[8] Bring cord 12 diagonally to the left across the top of the cords. Working right to left, use cord 12 as the anchor and tie clove-hitch knots with cords 11–7 (photo f).

[9] Using cord 1 as the anchor, work from left to right, and make clove-hitch knots with cords 2–6.

[10] Repeat step 8, using the far right cord – the new cord 12 – as the anchor (photo g).

[11] Repeat step 9, using the far left cord – the new cord 1 – as the anchor.

[12] Turn your board and position the macramé as shown in photo h. Using cord 8 as the anchor, work from left to right, tying clove-hitch knots with cords 9–12.

[13] Repeat step 12 three more times. Then bring cord 12 to the left across the top of the cords and pin it to the board (photo i).

[14] Using cord 12 as the anchor, work from right to left, tying clove-hitch knots with cords 11–8 (photo j).

[15] Repeat step 14 four more times. On the fifth row, tie clove-hitch knots with cords 11–7. As you make the last knot, pull tight to create a symmetrical fold that resembles the shape of a leaf (photo k).

[16] Turn your board and position the macramé as shown in photo l. Using cord 5 as the anchor, work from right to left, tying clove-hitch knots with cords 4–1 (photo m).

MACRAMÉ KNOTS

lark's head knot

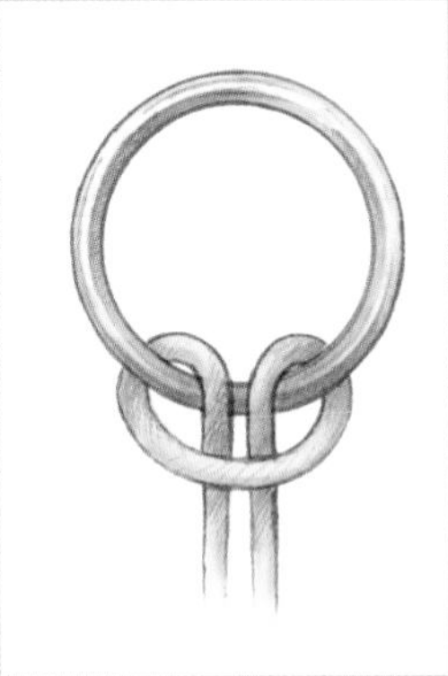

FIGURE 1

clove-hitch knot

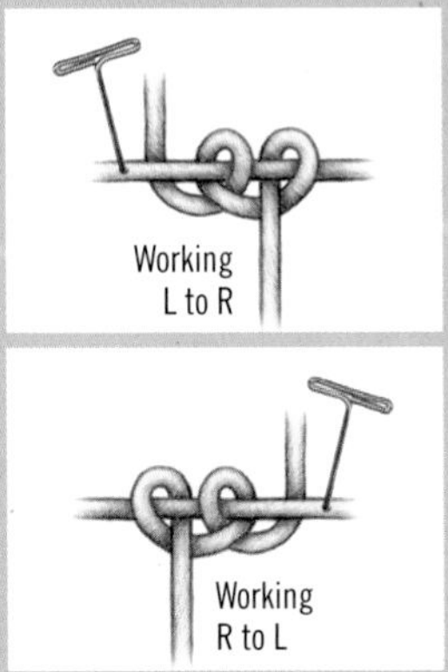

Working L to R

Working R to L

FIGURE 2

MATERIALS

macramé tassel

• Chinese jade medallion (Macramé Boutique, 415-449-3508, macrameboutique.com)
• 40–80 ft. (12.2–24.4m) 1.2mm knotting cord
• 12 in. (30cm) knotting cord, contrasting color
• quilter's pins
• macramé board or self-healing polyfoam
• glue

macramé square knot

FIGURE 3

FIGURE 4

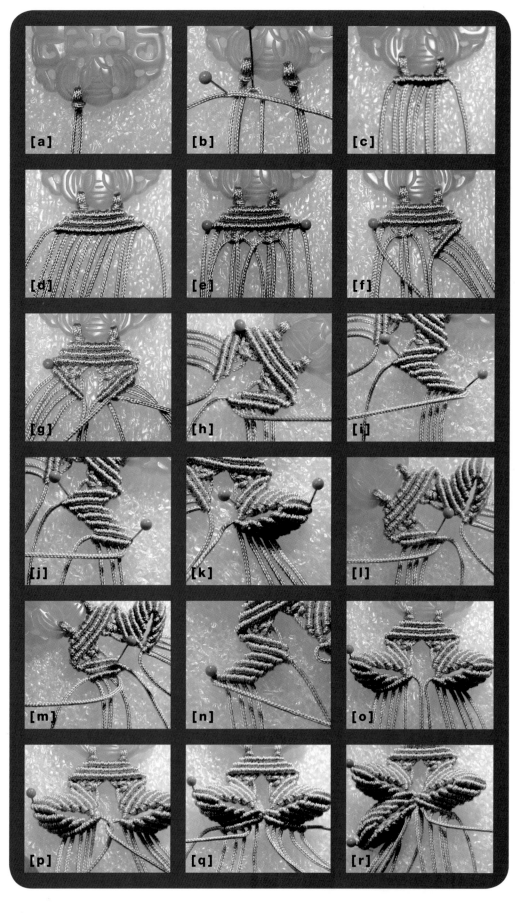

[a] [b] [c]
[d] [e] [f]
[g] [h] [i]
[j] [k] [l]
[m] [n] [o]
[p] [q] [r]

[17] Repeat step 16 four more times. After the last knot, pin the anchor cord – the new cord 1 – to the board, and bring it to the right across the top of the cords (photo n).

[18] Using cord 1 as the anchor, work from left to right, tying clove-hitch knots with cords 2–5.

[19] Repeat step 18 four more times. On the fifth row, tie clove-hitch knots with cords 2–6. Pull the last knot tight (photo o).

[20] Cross cords 6 and 7 as shown in **photo p**. Using cord 6 as the anchor, work from right to left, tying clove-hitch knots with cords 5–1. Using cord 7 as the anchor, work from left to right, tying clove-hitch knots with cords 8–12 (photo q).

[21] Repeat steps 16–19 to make a third leaf shape (photo r).

[22] Repeat steps 12–15 to make a fourth leaf shape.

[23] Repeat step 20.

[24] Bring cord 7 to the left across the top of the cords, and tie clove-hitch knots with cords 6–2, skipping the anchor cord from the previous row – new cord 1. Bring the new cord 7 to the right across the top of the cords, and tie clove-hitch knots with cords 8–11, skipping the anchor cord from the previous row – cord 12.

[25] Bring the new cord 7 to the left across the top of the cords, and tie clove-hitch knots with cords 6–3, skipping the anchor cords – cords 1 and 2 (photo s).

[26] Continue alternating sides, working from the center out, until you only have one knot to tie in the center to create a diamond shape (photo t).

[27] Cut a 12-in. (30cm) cord of a contrasting color. Fold the cord in half, and hold it next to the other cards, with the loop hanging down with the tassel as shown in **photo u**.

[28] Wrap cord 1 around all the cords, including the contrasting cord. Cord 1 will wrap over itself on the first wrap. Continue wrapping cord 1 around the other cords for six to eight wraps, forming a tassel (**photo v**).

[29] Hold the wraps in place with your fingers, and bring cord 1 halfway through the contrasting cord's loop (**photo w**). Pull the tails of the contrasting cord to bring cord 1 up under the wraps (**photo x**).

[30] Secure the cords by adding glue to the center of the wrap on both ends. Once the glue is dry, trim cord 1 as close to the wraps as possible, and cut the tassel to the desired length.

[31] Repeat steps 1–30 on the other side of the medallion, if desired.

EDITOR'S NOTE:
The medallion can be any shape as long as it has a pair of holes drilled on one or both sides for attaching the cords.

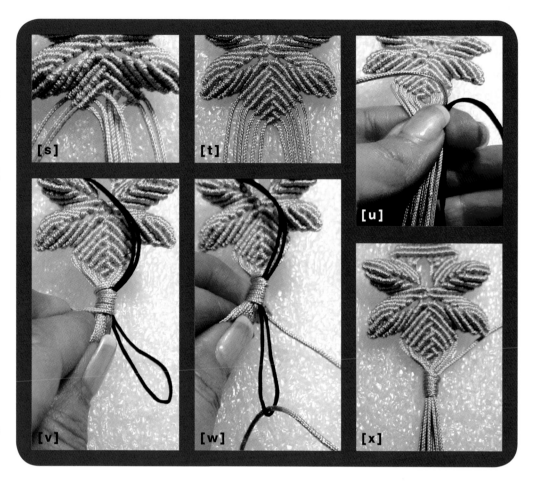

Infinity bangles

Discover how to make an invisible crochet join

by Linda Lehman

Hand your friends a beautiful conundrum with these seemingly seamless crocheted bangles. Use this technique to create a secure and imperceptible join for any crocheted bangle, but follow the pattern to make a bracelet with a beguiling twirl of colorful beads.

stepbystep

Crochet the tube

[1] Measure the largest part of your hand to determine how long your crocheted rope should be. There are approximately 16 rows per inch (2.5cm).

[2] Using a Big Eye needle on crochet cotton, string the following:

Round 1: three color As, two Bs, one D, one C, one D.

Round 2: three As, two Bs, three Cs.

Continue stringing, alternating rounds 1 and 2, until you use all the beads. End with round 2.

[3] Slide the beads down on the spool to give yourself about 20 in. (51cm) of working thread. As you crochet, adjust the beads so you don't run out of working thread.

[4] Work eight beaded-chain stitches (see Basics, p. 10), leaving a 12-in. (30cm) tail (photo a).

[5] Connect the chain stitches into a tube by inserting the crochet hook under and to the left of the first bead, and working a beaded slip-stitch (Basics and photo b). The new bead becomes the first bead in the second round.

[6] Insert the crochet hook to the left of the second bead in the first round, push this bead over to the right, slide a new bead down to the hook, and work a beaded slip-stitch.

[7] Continue to work in bead crochet, counter-clockwise, until the tube is long enough to slip over the largest part of your hand when the ends are connected. End with the bead pattern for round 2.

[8] Work a slip-stitch without a bead, and pull the working thread through until you have a 12-in. tail. Cut the thread from the spool.

[9] Block the crochet tube by pinning the ends to a terry cloth towel and spraying it with water. Let it dry overnight. This process will stretch the tube, so you may have to remove a few rows of stitches to adjust the fit.

Connect the ends

[1] Thread a tapestry needle onto the tail coming out of the first round. Sew up through the middle of the tube, and exit between two beads. Sew back into the tube close to where the thread exited, and make a small half-hitch knot (Basics). Repeat a few times to secure the tail, then trim.

[2] Thread the tapestry needle on the working thread. Align the first and last rounds, keeping the pattern intact (photo c).

[3] Starting with the first bead chain, sew under the thread that is exiting the first bead (photo d). Sew under the thread to the left of the next bead on the first round, pushing the bead to the right as you pull the first and last rounds together so you don't see the join (photo e). Repeat around the first and last rounds to secure the join, and tighten the stitches.

[4] Secure the working thread in the same manner as the tail.

EDITOR'S NOTE:
Use a safety pin to hold your stitches in place when you set your work down (photo f).

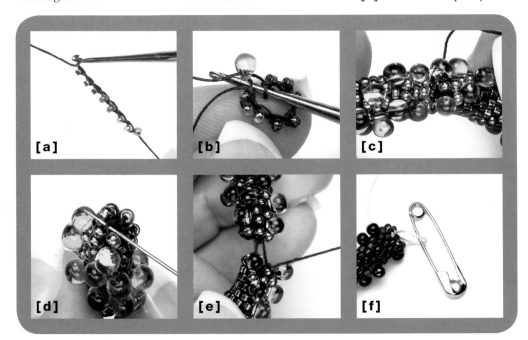

[a]
[b]
[c]
[d]
[e]
[f]

MATERIALS
bracelet 7 in. (18cm)
- 3g Japanese cylinder beads, color A
- Japanese seed beads 8g size 11º, color B 8g size 11º, color C
- 8g 4mm drops, color D
- Flora crochet cotton #20 (or Opera #20, Cebelia #20, Finca Perle cotton #8)
- Big Eye needle
- thin tapestry needle
- steel crochet hook, #8
- safety pins
- terry cloth towel

Memory
wire

Enhance bead-crochet ropes
with memory-wire slides

by **Gloria Farver**

EDITOR'S NOTE:
Don't cut memory wire with
your wire cutters or you'll
ruin them. Use memory-wire
shears, or bend the wire back
and forth with chainnose pliers
until it snaps off.

Dress up a plain bead-crochet rope with
complementary beaded slides. Ring-sized memory
wire travels smoothly over the crochet and can
accommodate an unlimited variety of beads.
Dangle some sparkling crystals from a few inches
of chain, and you're ready to hit the town.

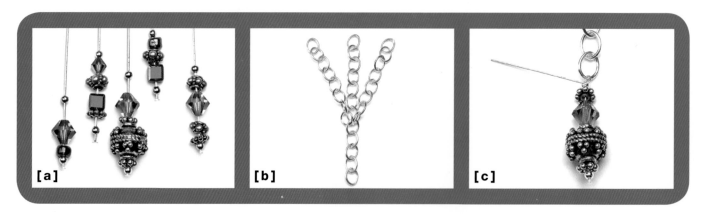

[a] [b] [c]

slides

step*by*step

Dangles

[**1**] Stack any combination of crystals, beads, charms, and spacers on head pins (**photo a**) until you have the desired number of dangles. This slide has 19 dangles, but make your piece as full as you'd like.

[**2**] Cut one 2½-in. (6.4cm) piece of chain and two 1½-in. (3.8cm) pieces. With the 2½-in. chain in the middle, line up the top links of all three chains. Use jump rings (see Basics, p. 10) to connect the shorter chains to one link on the 2½-in. chain as shown in **photo b**. Keep the top links aligned.

[**3**] Make the first half of a wrapped loop (Basics) on your largest dangle. Attach the dangle to the bottom link on the center chain (**photo c**), and finish the

[d]

[e]

[f]

[g]

FIGURE

wraps. Working from the bottom up, add dangles to the links on all three chains. Make sure to attach a dangle to the top link of each chain.

Slide
[1] Cut a piece of memory wire to the desired length. This one is four loops wide and, with beads, measures ¾ in. (1.9cm). Cut the wire so both ends line up with each other (figure).
[2] Using roundnose pliers, start a small loop at one end of the wire. String enough color A, B, C, or D 6º seed beads (photo d) to cover half the coil.
[3] Slide the top link of the 2½-in. chain to the middle of the coil (photo e). Continue stringing the same color 6ºs to the end of the wire. Start another loop at the end of the coil.
[4] Slide the top link of a 1½-in. chain onto an end loop. Roll the loop closed with roundnose pliers (photo f). Repeat at the other end of the coil with the remaining 1½-in. chain.

Crochet rope
[1] Determine the number of beads you need to string based on the desired length of your rope. This rope is 24 in. (61cm) long and used approximately 54 beads per inch (2.5cm).
[2] Leaving the cord attached to the spool, thread a needle, and pick up the following seed beads: a color A, a color B, a color C, and a color D. Repeat this pattern, loading approximately 14 ft. (4.3m) of beads onto the cord. Do not cut the cord.
[3] Crochet six chain stitches (Basics), and join the end to the beginning with a slip stitch to form a ring (Basics).
[4] Position the hook so it goes through the two loops on the first stitch from the inside of the ring (photo g).
[5] Slide the first bead down the cord to the ring. Make a

beaded slip stitch (Basics). One loop remains on the hook **(photo h)**.

[6] Working counterclockwise, insert the hook through the two loops of the next stitch. Slide a bead down the cord as before, and make a slip stitch. Repeat until you have stitched six beads on the ring **(photo i)**.

[7] To start the second row, insert the hook under the next bead **(photo j)**. Push the bead over the hook to the right. Position the cord between the bead and the ring. Slide a new bead into place, and make a slip stitch. Repeat until the rope is the desired length.

[8] To end the rope, work a slip stitch without a bead, and pull the working thread through until you have an 8-in. (20cm) tail. Cut the cord from the spool.

Finishing

[1] Make a wrapped loop at one end of a 3-in. piece of 20-gauge wire. String the wrapped loop on the end of the crochet cord **(photo k)**.

[2] Make two overhand knots (Basics) around the loop in the wire. Rethread the needle, and go through several nearby beads to reinforce the connection. Secure the cord, and trim the tail.

[3] On the wire, string a cone, a 6mm silver accent bead, and a 6mm bicone crystal. Pull the rope into the cone **(photo l)**.

[4] Make the first half of a wrapped loop, slide half the clasp into the loop, and finish the wraps **(photo m)**.

[5] Secure an 8-in. cord at the other end of the rope. Repeat steps 1–4 to finish the necklace. String the slide onto the rope. Your slide will fit easily over many sizes of cones and findings, so you can wear it with a variety of necklaces.

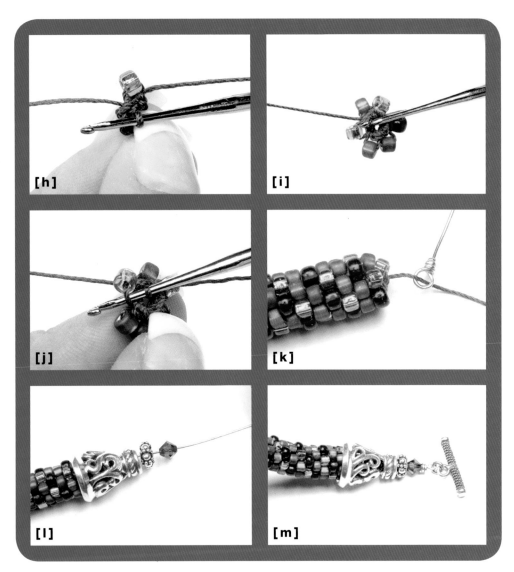

[h] [i] [j] [k] [l] [m]

MATERIALS

both projects
- chainnose pliers
- roundnose pliers
- wire cutters

slide ¾ in. (1.9cm)
- assortment of accent beads, spacers, bicone crystals, and charms for dangles
- 10g size 6º seed beads to match any color in the crochet rope
- memory wire, ¾-in. (1.9cm) diameter
- 5½ in. (14cm) sterling silver link chain
- 2 6mm silver jump rings
- head pins for dangles
- memory-wire shears (optional, Fire Mountain Gems, 800-355-2137, firemountaingems.com)

crochet rope 24 in. (61cm)
- 2 6mm silver accent beads
- 2 6mm bicone crystals
- seed beads, size 6º
  30g royal blue luster, color A
  30g royal blue matte, color B
  30g lime luster, color C
  30g olive green matte, color D
- toggle clasp
- 2 silver cones with the wide opening at least ½ in. (1.3cm) diameter
- 6 in. (15cm) of 20-gauge sterling silver wire, half-hard
- Mastex or Conso cord, navy
- Big Eye needle
- crochet hook, size 7

Crochet 2 ways

Create totally different looks using the same mix of beads

by **Anna Elizabeth Draeger**

Here are two novel ideas for making jewelry from crocheted tubes. Because they're small, these earrings are a great way to play with the assortment of beads in your stash. Although both pairs start with short tubes, that's where the similarity ends.

step*by*step

Fringed earrings
Tube

[1] On silk thread, string the following pattern 15 times: two cylinder beads, two 11º seed beads, two 2mm silver beads, and an 8º. Slide the beads down on the silk so that you have about 24 in. (61cm) of working thread.

[2] Leaving an 8-in. (20cm) tail, make a slip stitch (see Basics, p. 10). Then make seven beaded chain stitches (Basics and **photo a**).

[3] Connect the last bead chain stitch to the first by inserting the crochet hook to the left of the first bead **(photo b)**. Push the bead over to the right **(photo c)**, bring the working thread over the previous bead, and slide the next bead down **(photo d)**. Make a beaded slip stitch **(photo e)**.

[4] Continue working in beaded slip stitch until all the beads are used. Work the last row in slip stitch. Cut the thread about 8 in. from the work, and

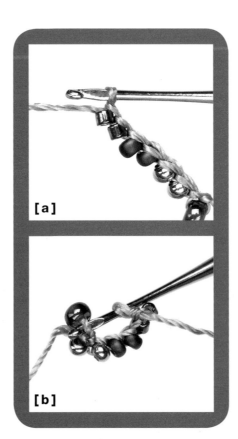

[a]

[b]

MATERIALS
both projects
- Gudebrod silk thread, size E
- crochet hook, size 8 (1.4mm)
- thin tapestry needle
- chainnose pliers
- roundnose pliers
- wire cutters

one pair of fringed earrings
- **14** 4mm bicone crystals
- **2** 4mm silver beads
- **4g** 2mm silver-plated beads
- **4g** each Japanese beads
  cylinder beads
  size 8º seed beads
  size 11º seed beads
- **2** 4mm daisy spacers
- **2** bead caps
- **2** 2-in. (5cm) head pins
- pair of earring findings

one pair of hoop earrings
- **4** 4mm bicone crystals
- **3g** 2mm silver-plated beads
- **3g** each Japanese beads
  cylinder beads
  size 8º seed beads
  size 11º seed beads
- **4** bead caps
- **10** in. (25cm) 20-gauge wire, half-hard

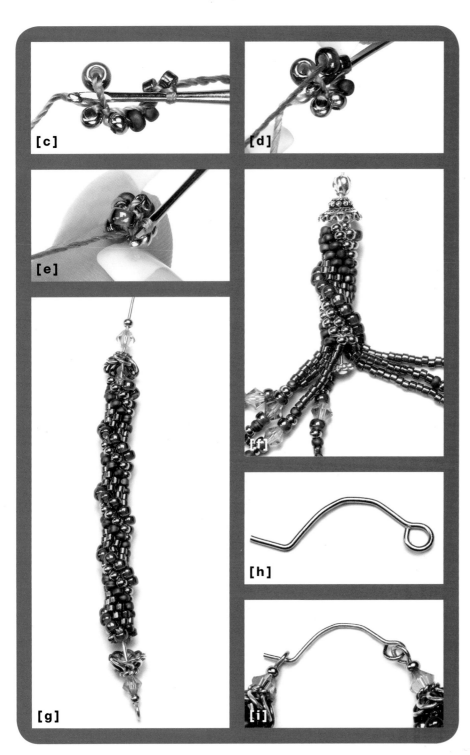

[c]

[d]

[e]

[g]

[f]

[h]

[i]

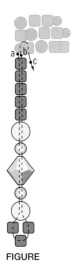

FIGURE

pull the working thread through the loop on your hook.

[5] Thread a needle on the tail, and secure it using half-hitch knots (Basics) between the 8°s. Pull the tail into the next 8°, and trim it next to the bead. Repeat with the working thread.

Fringe

[1] Secure 1 yd. (.9m) of thread in the beadwork, and exit any bead in the end

round. Pick up five cylinders, an 8°, a 2mm silver bead, a 4mm bicone crystal, a 2mm silver bead, an 8°, and three cylinders. Skip the cylinders, and sew back through the beads to the crocheted tube (figure, a–b).

[2] Sew back through the bead the thread was exiting and through the next bead in the end round (b–c).

[3] Continue making fringe, adding two more cylinders each time, until

you have a total of seven fringes. Secure the tails in the beadwork.

Assembly

[1] On a head pin, string a daisy spacer, the crocheted tube (fringe-side first), a bead cap, and a 4mm silver bead (photo f).

[2] Make a plain loop (Basics) above the last bead. Open the loop and attach the earring finding. Close the loop.

[3] Make a second earring to match the first.

Hoop earrings

[1] On silk thread, string the following pattern 37 times: two cylinders, an 11° seed bead, a 2mm silver bead, and an 8°.

[2] Leaving an 8-in. tail, make a slip stitch and five bead chain stitches.

[3] Repeat steps 3–5 of the fringed earring tube.

[4] Make a plain loop on one end of the wire. String a silver bead, a 4mm bicone crystal, a bead cap, the crocheted tube, a bead cap, a crystal, and a silver bead (photo g). Trim the wire 3/8 in. (1cm) longer than the tube, and make a plain loop. Set the remaining wire aside.

[5] Bend the tube into a hoop with about 1/2 in. (1.3cm) between the loops.

[6] Cut about 1 in. (2.5cm) off the remaining wire, leaving the rest for the second earring. On the 1-in. piece, make a loop at one end and a 45-degree bend at the other. Curve the wire slightly (photo h). Open the loop and connect it to the hoop (photo i). Close the loop.

[7] Make a second earring to match the first.

Lacy
wire crochet
necklace

A brooch becomes a removable centerpiece

by **Shirley Ciacci**

If you've never tried wire crochet, you might be surprised by the way wire responds to being wrapped, looped, hooked, and pulled. The wire is stiff, so expect some resistance, and it will kink if you're not careful with the coils. But once you've gotten a feel for it, we think you'll enjoy making elegant jewelry with substance and plenty of style.

step*by*step

[1] Using craft wire and the size G crochet hook, chain stitch (see Basics, p. 10 and **photo a**) a strip long enough to fit around your neck. The first row of this necklace measures 16 in. (41cm).
[2] Work back across the chain in single crochet (Basics and **photo b**).
[3] Grab the ends of the chain, and pull outward slightly to straighten the piece. Use roundnose pliers to open and reshape the single-crochet stitches, if necessary.
[4] Work the next two rows with the size H crochet hook.
[5] Work the next two rows with the size I crochet hook. Pull the ends slightly to straighten the piece as before **(photo c)**. Cut the working wire, leaving a 3-in. (7.6cm) tail. Secure the wire by weaving it into the nearby stitches.
[6] Cut a 3-in. piece of craft wire. Fasten one end of the wire to the edge stitch on the first crocheted row (or use the wire tail at the start of the chain stitch row). String six 6mm fire-polished beads. Fasten the wire's other end to the edge stitch on the last row **(photo d)**. Repeat on the other end of the necklace.

[7] To make the clasp connector, cut 1 in. (2.5cm) of 20-gauge wire. Make a plain loop (Basics) on one end. String a 6mm, and make another loop **(photo e)**. Make three more connectors.
[8] Attach one connector to the wire between the third and fourth 6mms added in step 6. Attach a second connector to the first. Attach half the clasp to the available loop on the second connector **(photo f)**. Repeat on the other end of the necklace.
[9] Center the brooch on the crocheted wire, and pin the brooch into place **(photo g)**. If you're using a broken brooch or a button, secure it with a piece of craft wire.
[10] Adjust the shape of the necklace to fit your neck.

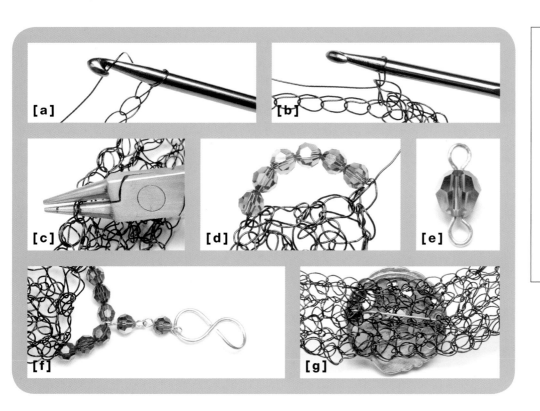

MATERIALS

necklace 20 in. (51cm)

- Victorian-style brooch
- **16** 6mm crystals or fire-polished beads
- clasp
- 26-gauge craft wire
- 4 in. (10cm) 20-gauge wire
- crochet hooks, sizes G, H, I
- chainnose pliers
- roundnose pliers
- wire cutters

Beaded
wire choker

Crochet a sparkling choker with wire and beads

by **Shirley Ciacci**

Add a little heat to an easy wire-crochet necklace with chaton montees, a crystal more at home in sewing projects than in jewelry. The montees are easy to use – simply string them through a pair of holes in their metal base. They'll lend a splash of color to any outfit as they dangle gracefully along your neckline.

step*by*step

[1] On 3 yd. (2.7m) of wire, string all the chaton montees or 4mm beads.
[2] Leaving a short tail, chain stitch (see Basics, p. 10) the first row until you reach your desired length.
[3] Turn and work a single crochet (Basics) in each chain stitch. Carefully straighten the first two rows by pulling gently on the ends.
[4] Work the final row along the other edge of the chain stitch as follows: Make four single crochet stitches.

Then alternate between single crochet and beaded single crochet (Basics). Work the last four stitches in single crochet.
[5] Trim the wire on both ends, leaving about ¼-in. (6mm) tails. Using chainnose pliers, secure the short wire tail by wrapping the tails around the end stitches **(photo a)**.
[6] Connect the clasp to the end link of one length of chain. Open a jump ring (Basics), and connect the other end of the chain to the last stitch on the necklace **(photo b)**. Close the jump ring.

[7] Open a jump ring, and slip it into the first stitch on the other end of the necklace. Slide the first link of the other length of chain into the same jump ring **(photo c)**. Close the jump ring.
[8] Shape the necklace by pulling and flattening it to lie comfortably around your neck.
[9] Add a dangle to the end link of the chain by stringing a montee or bead on a head pin. Make a plain loop above the bead (Basics). Open the loop, and connect it to the end link of the chain. Close the loop **(photo d)**.

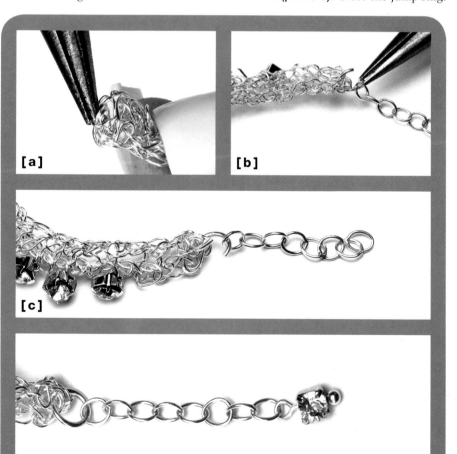

[a]

[b]

[c]

[d]

MATERIALS
necklace 14 in. (36cm)
- **40** 4mm chaton montees (thatbeadlady.com) or any 4mm beads
- hook or lobster claw clasp
- approximately 8 ft. (2.4m) 26-gauge sterling silver wire
- **2** 2-in. (5cm) lengths of chain, links large enough to accommodate clasp
- head pin
- **2** jump rings
- crochet hook, size 2–3mm
- chainnose pliers
- roundnose pliers
- wire cutters

EDITOR'S NOTE: If you can't find chaton montees, you can buy rhinestone chain from a fabric store and cut it apart.

Beaded scarf

Beads add pizzazz to a hand-crafted accessory

by **Linda Lehman**

Knit a scarf adorned with beads. Then add the finishing touches: a bead-crochet edging and fringe.

step*by*step

As you work, refer to the knitting and crochet instructions in Basics (p. 10).

[1] Using a Big Eye needle, string 12–15g of 8º Japanese seed beads onto a skein of sock yarn. Don't cut the yarn from the skein.

[2] Cast on 29 stitches, and knit the first row.

[3] Work the remaining rows as follows:

Row 2: Knit 1, bead knit 1. Repeat across the row, end with knit 1.

Row 3: Knit 29. Push the beads on the previous row to the front with the index finger of your nondominant hand as you work each stitch.

Row 4: Knit 1. Repeat knit 1, bead knit 1 across the row, end with knit 2.

Row 5: Repeat row 3.

Row 6: Knit 1, yarn over three times, knit 1. Repeat across the row, end with knit 1.

Row 7: Knit 1, drop the yarn overs. Repeat across the row, end with knit 1.

[4] Repeat rows 2–7 until you reach the desired length. This scarf is 5 ft. (1.5m) long.

[5] Bind off, and weave in the tails.

[6] To block the scarf, pin it to a large bath towel with T-pins. Keeping it flat on the floor, spray it with cold water, and let it dry. This will set the stitches.

[7] Continue working with the sock yarn and attach it to one corner, with the beaded side of the scarf facing you. Single crochet (Basics) around the edge of the scarf, making five single crochets in each six-row repeat and three in each corner.

[8] Transfer the cylinder beads onto the silk thread.

[9] With the wrong side of the scarf facing you, secure the silk in one corner.

Round 2: Make a beaded single crochet (Basics) in each single crochet stitch on the previous round, increasing by one beaded single crochet in every fourth stitch. Make three single crochets in each corner stitch.

Round 3: Make a beaded single crochet in each stitch on the previous round. Make three single crochets in each corner stitch, as before.

Round 4: Crab stitch (right) around.

[10] Repeat step 6.

[11] Using a tapestry needle, weave in the tails.

[12] Wrap the sock yarn around a 9-in. (23cm) book 20 times. Cut the yarn along the page indentations on one side of the book.

[13] Take four strands, and fold them in half over the index finger of your nondominant hand. Working on the back of the scarf, push the crochet hook between stitches on a short edge of the scarf, close to the corner. Grab the center of the two strands with the hook, and pull them through until you have a 1-in. (2.5cm) loop.

[14] Pull the ends of the yarn through the loop, and tighten the knot next to the edge of the scarf.

[15] Repeat steps 13 and 14 along both short edges of the scarf, positioning one fringe every ¾ in. (1.9cm). When you run out of strands for the fringe, repeat step 12.

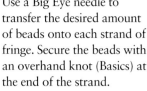

Use a Big Eye needle to transfer the desired amount of beads onto each strand of fringe. Secure the beads with an overhand knot (Basics) at the end of the strand.

Crab stitch

Crab stitch is worked from left to right.

1 With the work at your right, enter the first stitch, yarn over, and pull through the stitch.

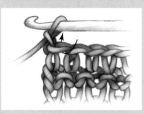

2 Yarn over, and pull through both the remaining loops.

MATERIALS

scarf 5 ft. (1.5m) long, 4¾ in. (12.1cm) wide

- 65g size 8º Japanese seed beads
- 8g size 11º Japanese cylinder beads, hex cut
- 2 skeins (200 yds./ 183m) sock yarn
- spool Gudebrod silk, size FFF (.0165 in./ .42mm diameter)
- Big Eye needle
- tapestry needle
- pair of knitting needles, U.S. size #3 (3.25mm)
- crochet hook, U.S. size C (2.75mm)
- spray bottle
- T-pins
- large bath towel

Reversible knitted bracelets

by **Mary Libby Neiman**

Knitting every row creates colorful two-sided bands

If you're comfortable working with ultrathin knitting needles and fine yarn or thread, you'll enjoy making these versatile bracelets. Start by prestringing beads in your choice of colors and patterns, then simply knit every row. The bracelets work up quickly and are a delight to wear.

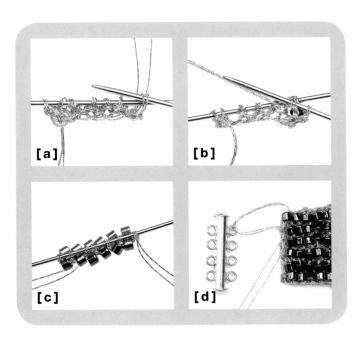

[a]

[b]

[c]

[d]

MATERIALS
bracelet 7 in. (18cm)
- 14g size 8º cylinder or seed beads, in each of **2** colors: A and B
- 1-in. (2.5cm) slide clasp
- 24 yd. (22m) New Metallics two-ply thread, or E- or F-weight buttonhole-twist silk
- twisted-wire or Big Eye needles
- tapestry needle, #24
- pair of steel knitting needles, size 0000
- charms (optional)
- bobbin (optional)

Bead-Knitting Tips

- Before taking on a bead-knitting project, it's a good idea to be comfortable with basic knitting techniques. For this bracelet, you need to know how to cast on, cast off, slip a stitch purlwise, and work in knit stitch.
- To check the accuracy of your pattern when stringing beads for a knitting (or crochet) project, string several pattern repeats, and make a color copy of the beads. Then, as you string the entire length of beads for the project, compare the bead placement to the pattern on your copy. You should be able to spot and correct any errors before your project gets underway.
- In bead knitting, the thread will show between beads and along the edges, so choose a hard-twisted thread or yarn in a color that complements your beads.

step*by*step

[1] Center a twisted-wire or Big Eye needle on 24 yd. (22m) of thread. Line up the tails so they are even, and wind 10 yd. (9m) of the doubled thread onto a bobbin (reuse an empty thread package if available).

[2] String a repeating pattern of six color A and six color B 8º cylinder or seed beads 60 times (720 beads total), releasing thread from the bobbin as needed. Distribute the beads along the length of the thread, and rewind the bobbin.

[3] Leaving a 1-ft. (30cm) tail, cast on (see Basics, p. 10) seven stitches, keeping the tension loose.

[4] Knit (Basics) across the row.

[5] Slip the first stitch as if to purl, but keep the thread back in the knit position (**photo a**). Slide a B against the needle, and knit one stitch, keeping the bead on the back of the knitting (**photo b**). Make sure your tension is tight enough to prevent the bead from coming through to the front. Repeat across the row.

[6] Repeat step 5. The first row of beads will face you; the second row will be on the back (**photo c**). Continue until your bracelet is about ½ in. (1.3cm) short of the desired length.

[7] Cast off (Basics), keeping the tension loose, as at the start. Cut the thread, leaving a 1-ft. tail.

[8] Thread a tapestry needle on one of the tails. Sew the clasp to the bracelet by stitching through a clasp loop and through the nearest stitch (**photo d**). Sew through every stitch for a firm, even connection. Repeat on the other end. Add small charms to the clasp loops if desired.

The *enduring*
iris

Enjoy splendid
beaded blooms
that never fade

by **Andrea Alyse**

Flowers lend an elegant touch to any room, and when the flowers are made from glass beads, you have an arrangement that will last for many years. This iris combines classic French beaded-flower techniques with several innovations to create a frilly, lifelike blossom.

stepbystep

Lower petals

[1] Cut 1 yd. (.9m) of 24-gauge purple wire. Make a temporary loop on one end to keep the beads from sliding off.

[2] Pick up the following 11º seed beads and bugle beads:
  one yellow 11º
  eight light purple 11ºs
  five medium purple 11ºs
  one bugle
  three medium purple 11ºs
  three white 11ºs
  three clear 11ºs
  three white 11ºs
  three medium purple 11ºs
  one bugle
  five medium purple 11ºs
  eight light purple 11ºs
  one yellow 11º

[3] Slide the beads to 6 in. (15cm) from the loop end of the wire. Fold the wire so the clear beads are at the petal's top. Twist the long wire around the short one (figure, a–b).

[4] On the long wire, pick up the bead pattern in step 2, but use two yellow 11ºs instead of one at the start and end. Slide the beads close to the first petal. Twist the wires as shown (b–c).

[5] Repeat step 4, but use three yellow 11ºs to start and end the pattern (c–d).

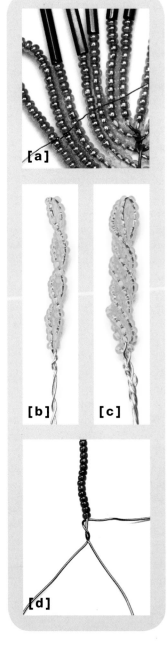

[a]

[b]   [c]

[d]

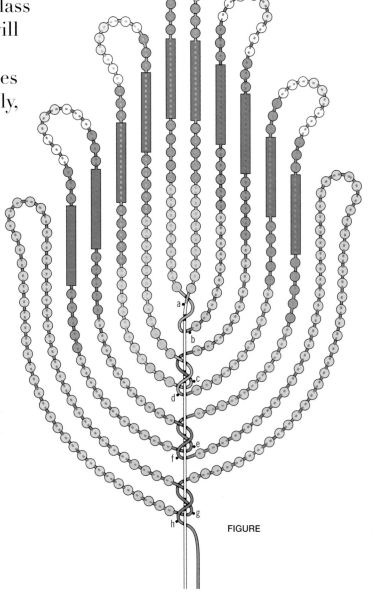

FIGURE

MATERIALS

one iris

- 50 ½-in. (1.3cm) dark purple bugle beads
- size 11º seed beads
  20g light purple
  20g medium purple
  10g dark purple
  5g yellow
  5g white
  5g silver-lined clear

hank of light green
hank of dark green

- craft wire
  24-gauge in green, purple, and yellow (or gold)
  34-gauge in green and purple
- 3 16-gauge floral stem wires
- green floral tape
- wire cutters

247

[e]   [f]   [g]   [h]   [i]   [j]

[6] Repeat step 5 (d–e).

[7] Repeat step 5 again (e–f).

[8] Make one outer loop on each side of the center petals. Use four yellow 11ºs, 50 medium purple 11ºs, and four yellow 11ºs (f–g and g–h). Twist the two wires tightly together below the beads.

[9] Make two more lower petals.

[10] To lace the petal loops together, cut an 8-in. (20cm) piece of 34-gauge purple wire. Wrap one end of the wire around the outside loop twice, working between beads about halfway down the side of the loop. Go around the next wire so the two sides of the loop are pulled tightly together (photo a). Repeat across the row. Wrap the wire around the outer loop several times to secure it. Trim the excess lacing wire. Repeat with the remaining lower petals.

Upper petals

Make the upper petals following the steps for the lower petals. Make two petals using the bead sequence below (for the third, substitute ten dark purple 11ºs for the bugles, if desired):

    five light purple 11ºs
    three medium purple 11ºs
    five light purple 11ºs

    one bugle
    three medium purple 11ºs
    three white 11ºs
    three clear 11ºs
    three white 11ºs
    three medium purple 11ºs
    one bugle
    five light purple 11ºs
    three medium purple 11ºs
    five light purple 11ºs

Stamens

[1] Cut three 5-in. (13cm) pieces of yellow wire. Center 2½ in. (6.4cm) of yellow 11ºs on one wire. Make a narrow loop, and twist the wire below the beads. Then twist the beads to form a spiral (photo b). Repeat with the remaining two wires.

[2] Twist two of the spirals together (photo c).

Small leaves

[1] Transfer 24 in. (61cm) of dark green 11ºs onto the 24-gauge green wire, but don't cut the wire off the spool. Make a temporary loop at the end of the wire to keep the beads from falling off.

[2] Slide all but 2 in. (5cm) of beads away from the cut end, leaving about 8 in. of bare wire. Make a loop below the beads using the bare wire, and twist it closed (photo d). These beads become the first row of the

leaf and are referred to as the base row.

[3] Working on a flat surface, slide enough beads next to the base row so they extend slightly past it. Wrap the working wire around the wire, coming out the top of the base row. These leaves are pointed at the top and bottom, so wrap the wire at an angle to form the points (photo e).

[4] Repeat step 3 on the other side of the base row, adding a bead or two as necessary to create the oval shape. Work a total of nine rows, counting across the leaf.

[5] Cut the wire from the spool, leaving a 2-in. tail. Twist the tail and loop wires tightly to secure the beads (photo f). Trim the wire above the leaf to ⅜ in. (1cm), and fold it against the back of the leaf (photo g).

[6] Lace the rows together as in step 10 of the lower petals.

[7] To make a second small leaf, transfer 28 in. (71cm) of dark green 11ºs to the wire, and work 11 rows across.

Large leaves

[1] Transfer 64 in. (1.6m) of dark green 11ºs to the spool of green wire. Start with an 11-in. (28cm) base row.

[2] To keep the rows in place, lace them as you

work. Start a 6-in. piece of 34-gauge green wire, fold it in half to find the center, and secure it with several wraps between beads at the center of the base row (photo h). Attach a second and third lacing wire close to each end of the base row.

[3] Make four more rows as in steps 3 and 4 of the small leaves. Lace the wire across the rows (photo i). Don't cut off the lacing wires yet.

[4] To make rows 6–9, slide any remaining beads toward the leaf, allow 1½ yd. (1.4m) of wire from the leaf to the spool, and cut the wire at the spool.

[5] String dark green and light green 11ºs for each of the next four rows. Use light green 11ºs to accent the leaf tips and outer rows (photo j). Finish lacing these rows, and secure the wires around the end rows with a few wraps. Add one or two more rows of lacing to the leaf, if desired.

[6] Make a second large leaf, starting with a base row approximately 2 in. shorter than the first.

Assembly

[1] Determine the finished length of your flower stem. These irises range from 8–12 in. (20–30cm) tall. Cut the three stem wires to that length.

248

[2] Cut an 18-in. (46cm) piece of floral tape in half lengthwise. Hold the tape at an angle, and wrap the three stem wires together with one thin layer (photo k).

[3] Wrap the exposed wire on each petal, stamen, and leaf with a thin layer of floral tape (photo l).

[4] Using a 1-yd. piece of green lacing wire, bind the stamens to the stem by wrapping them together (photo m). Make several passes to hold them securely. Don't cut the wire.

[5] Place a lower petal under the single stamen, wrong side down. Bind the petal to the stem with the lacing wire (photo n). Position the remaining two lower petals on each side of the first so the three are close together. Bend the petals so they point down (photo o).

[6] Bind the upper petal opposite the first lower petal, wrong side toward the inside. Position the remaining two upper petals on each side of the first so the three are close

together. These petals point up. Bend the single spiral stamen down (photo p).

[7] Wrap the lacing wire around the stem several times, and cut it. Wrap the upper section of the stem with another thin layer of floral tape (photo q).

[8] Attach a new piece of lacing wire approximately 3 in. (7.6cm) below the flower, and bind the nine-row small leaf to the back of the stem. The tip of the leaf should extend slightly above the stem. Attach the other small leaf to the front of the stem, about ½ in. (1.3cm) below the first leaf (photo r).

[9] Transfer 2½ yd. (2.3m) of dark green beads to the spool, and wrap the beaded wire around the spool to keep it from getting tangled. Secure the bare end of this wire around the top of the stem with several wraps, then wrap the stem with an even layer of beads (photo s), leaving the bottom ½ in. exposed. Secure the beads with several wraps of bare wire. Cut the wire.

Cover the bare wire at the bottom of the stem with a thin layer of floral tape.

[10] To keep the small leaves close to the stem, attach a 6-in. piece of lacing wire near the center of a leaf's edge row. Go behind the leaf, and attach the wire to the other edge row. Then go around the stem and connect the wire at the starting point (photo t). Make a second pass a few beads above or below the laced beads. Repeat with the other leaf. Trim the wire.

[11] Attach a new piece of lacing wire near the bottom of the stem. Bind a large leaf to each side of the stem ½ in. above the bottom. Lace the bottom 4 in. (10cm) of one leaf and 6 in. of the other to the stem (photo u). Bend the unattached portions into a natural arching shape.

[12] Gently shape the petals and leaves as shown on p. 246. Use floral clay to anchor the stem in a vase or cachepot. Cover the floral clay with Spanish moss or decorative stones.

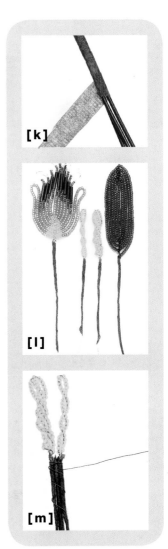

[k]

[l]

[m]

[n]

[o]

[p]

[q]

[r]

[s]

[t]

[u]

Felted rose lariat

Create a fashion accessory with the magic of beads and felted flowers

by **Carol Cypher**

Felting, like beadwork, involves intoxicating colors and an engaging process. The sharp definition of brilliant glass beads against the matte, light-absorbing surface of felted wool makes an intriguing combination. To get started, try this simple felted rose with a herringbone stitch calyx.

step*by*step

Calyx

[1] Using a comfortable length of Fireline, pick up 16 8º seed beads, and slide them to 6 in. (15cm) from the end. Go through the beads again to form a ring. Keep the tension tight, and tie the tail and working thread together with a surgeon's knot (see Basics, p. 10). Go through the next bead after the knot (figure, a–b).

[2] To work in tubular Ndebele herringbone (Basics), pick up two 8º's and go through the next two beads. Repeat, picking up eight pairs of beads in this round (b–c). Step up through the first bead in this round (c–d).

Rounds 3–7: Continue working in tubular herringbone (d–e).

Round 8: Increase, adding a bead between each pair of beads in the previous round (e–f).

Round 9: Increase, adding two beads between each pair (f–g).

Rounds 10–13: Work in tubular herringbone, which now has 16 pairs of beads (g–h).

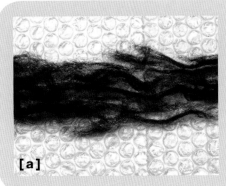

[a]

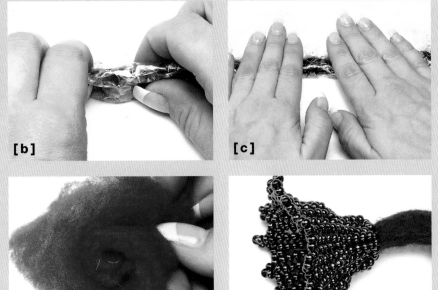

[b]

[c]

[d]

[e]

Round 14: Increase, adding one bead between each pair (h–i).

Round 15: Increase, adding two beads between each pair (i–j).

Round 16: Work in tubular herringbone, but don't add beads to the increase, sew through them (j–k).

Round 17: Pick up one bead per stitch (k–l), sewing through the increase beads, as in the last step.

[3] Sew through several nearby beads, secure the Fireline, and trim the tails.

Rope

Felting is a two-phase process. The first involves opening the fiber's cuticle and pressing the fibers together. The second, called fulling, mats the fibers by agitation and pressure, producing a hardened and denser material.

[1] Pull wisps of green wool from the end of the roving, and lay them on bubble wrap in a row about 2 ft. (61cm) long **(photo a)**.

[2] Continue to pull more fibers, placing them on, and perpendicular to, the wisps in the first row. Continue building layers until all the fiber is used. Approximately 1½ oz. of wool produces a rope that can exceed 2 yd. (1.8m) in length, depending on how thick you make it.

EDITOR'S NOTE: After you get the hang of felting, you'll want to try color blending. Wool roving comes in a variety of delicious colors, and Carol Cypher often achieves a painterly effect by layering wisps of different colors over each other. Don't be afraid to get in there and mix it up!

[3] Starting at one end, tightly roll up the fiber lengthwise. Fold the bubble wrap over the fiber so it sits in the crease **(photo b)**. Gently roll the fiber back and forth for two minutes **(photo c)**.

[4] To lengthen the rope, open the bubble wrap, and grab the fibers with your hands about 8 in. (20cm) apart. Pull evenly, working your way along the entire length of the rope.

[5] Dribble a few drops of hot, soapy water along the rope. Starting at one end, roll the wool back and forth for 30 seconds. Repeat to the end of the rope.

[6] After rolling the rope, increase the pressure and work from end to end until you reach the desired diameter. The rope should feel solid yet flexible. You should not be able to remove any of the fibers when you pinch the surface.

[7] Rinse the rope in hot, then cold water. Place it between two towels on the floor, and walk on it to extract the excess water. Hang vertically to dry. Felt retains water when held horizontally, and sheds water when held vertically. To achieve a branched or crooked appearance, bunch it up and let it dry. Similarly, if you want it to spiral, coil it before drying.

Rose

[1] Work on a piece of bubble wrap with the bubble side down. Pull wisps from the red roving, as in steps 1 and 2 of "Rope." Arrange them in a rectangle approximately 5 x 18 in. (13 x 46cm).

[2] Sprinkle the fiber with ½ cup of hot, soapy water.

[3] Cut the plastic bag into one large sheet, and cover the fiber with it. Flatten the plastic, pressing out any air bubbles and spreading the water throughout the fiber without disturbing it. Rub the plastic for several minutes without agitating the fiber, then remove the plastic.

[4] Place the roller at the edge of the fiber, and roll it into a tube. Secure it with a tie at each end. Roll it gently in the same direction for 5 minutes.

[5] Untie the fiber and place the roller at the opposite edge. Repeat step 4. Unwrap and pinch the fibers of the felt. If the fibers come loose, re-roll for another 5 minutes.

[6] Leaving the felt uncovered, lay it across a new piece of bubble wrap with the bubble side up. Without using the roller or ties, roll the felt into a tube, and roll it over the bubble wrap. Unroll the tube, and re-roll it into another tube, starting from the opposite edge. Roll the felt across the bubble wrap. Repeat 12 times to complete the fulling process.

[7] Rinse the felt under hot, then cold, water. Squeeze out the excess water, place the felt between two towels, and stand on it to remove any remaining moisture.

[8] Create the rose by rolling the felt into the desired shape (photo d). Manipulate the felt to form simple buds or full flowers with the petals curled over. Stitch the flower together loosely at the bottom to hold its shape.

Assembly

[1] To attach the end of the felted rope to the small opening of the calyx (photo e), secure a comfortable length of Fireline in the first several rows of the calyx. Sew through the felt, then through several nearby beads. Repeat until the rope is firmly attached. Secure the thread, but don't cut it.

[2] Use the existing thread to secure the rose inside the calyx. Sew through the flower and nearby beads in the calyx until the rose is secure. Weave in the thread, and trim the tail.

[3] Embellish the petals, rope, or any portion of the felt with beads as desired.

[4] Drape the rope around your neck or shoulders with the rose in front. The felt can be further secured by a pin once you have it just right.

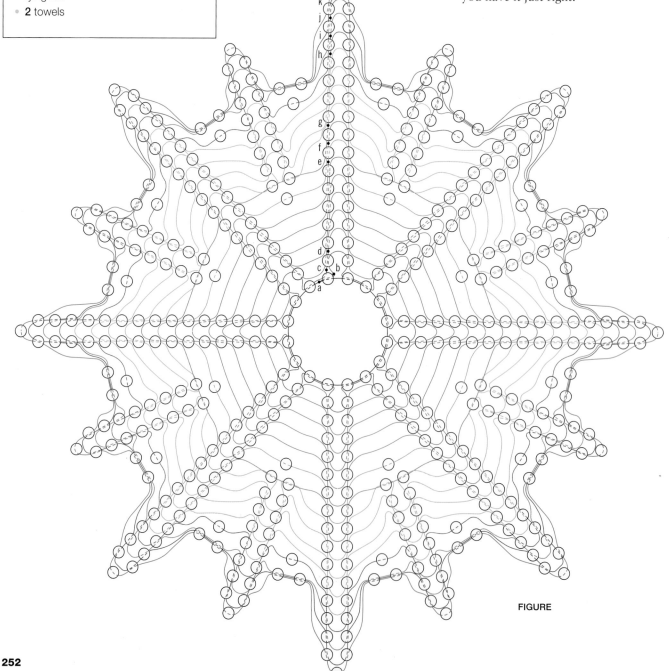

FIGURE

Tips & Techniques

Tangle prevention

If you are working on a project with embellishments and your thread keeps getting tangled in the project, simply put the completed portion in a plastic bag. Small bead bags work great!
– *Judy Glover, via e-mail*

Finger protection

Since I don't like to wear a thimble but occasionally need some protection from the needle, I wrap an adhesive bandage or a piece of masking tape around the tip of my finger. It seems to do the job and is easily removed and discarded.
– *Nancy Zellers, Aurora, Colo.*

All wound up

As an avid bead crocheter, I used to struggle with keeping the extremely long strand of strung beads on a bobbin. Now I use Bryson E-Z Bobs. These are round, plastic, donutlike bobbins with a curved top that flips down. Simply string your beads, wind the thread onto the bobbin, then flip the top down. Your project will be easy to transport, the strung beads won't fall off, and the thread stays clean. E-Z Bobs are available in three sizes and can be found in your local yarn shop.
– *Susan Helmer, Newark, Calif.*

Get the kinks out

Here's a quick and easy way to remove kinks and curls from leather cord. Cut a piece of cord 1 in. (2.5cm) longer than the desired length of your finished piece. Thoroughly soak the cord in water. Attach a heavy C-clamp on both ends of the cord, and hang it on a clothes hanger so one of the clamps hangs freely. Once the cord is completely dry, remove the clamps, and you will have a nice, flat piece of leather cord.
– *Sandy Bowlin, Twin Falls, Idaho*

Easier stringing for bead crochet or knitting

Several years ago, I made a small knitted bag with beads, and I developed a good method for stringing beads onto the thread used in the project.

The knitted bag was made with perle cotton, but this tip would work with all cotton threads. I threaded my long beading needle with Nymo, then used Aleene's Tacky Glue to glue the two ends of the Nymo to the end of the perle cotton, overlapping both. After it dried for an hour or so, I picked up the beads with the needle, and they glided easily over the join. I found I was able to string about 1,000 beads onto the perle cotton before the join broke. I repeated the gluing process with fresh pieces of Nymo and perle cotton and kept on stringing.
– *Althea Church, via e-mail*

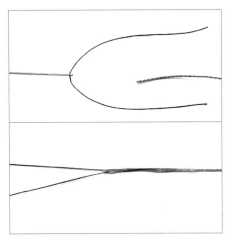

Contributors

Andrea Alyse
Contact Andrea via e-mail at andreaalyse@comcast.net.

Perie Brown
Visit Perie's Web site, thebrownpear.com.

Shirley Ciacci
Contact Shirley via e-mail at shirleyanne@snet.net, or visit her Web site, stores.ebay.com/thebeadsstophere.

Julia Coale
Contact Julia via e-mail at glassgurl@charter.net, or visit her Web site, galswithglass.com.

Jennifer Cook
Contact Jennifer via e-mail at jmc-lampwork@charter.net, or visit her Web site, jmcglassart.com.

Jennifer Creasey
Contact Jennifer by phone at (907) 842-2266, via e-mail at creasey@starband.net, or visit her Web site, polarbeads.com.

Carol Cypher
Contact Carol via e-mail at carol@carolcypher.com. Carol showcases her hand-felted jewelry and beads on her Web site, carolcypher.com.

Miachelle DePiano
Contact Miachelle via e-mail at cosmoaccessories@cox.net, or visit her Web site, cosmopolitanaccessories.net.

Anna Elizabeth Draeger
Anna is an associate editor at *Bead&Button* magazine. Contact her in care of *Bead&Button*.

Wendy Ellsworth
Contact Wendy via e-mail at wendy@ellsworthstudios.com, or visit her Web site, ellsworthstudios.com.

Gloria Farver
Contact Gloria via e-mail at rfarver@wi.rr.com.

Janet Beth McCann Flynn
Janet teaches beading classes nationwide. Contact her via e-mail at janet@janetflynn.com or visit her Web site, janetflynn.com.

Susan Frommer
Contact Susan via e-mail at firstwaterlady@verizon.net, or visit her Web site, pamperedpeacock.com.

Julia Gerlach
Julia is an associate editor at *Bead&Button* magazine. Contact her in care of *Bead&Button*.

Donna Graves
Contact Donna at Planet Bead, 244 E. Main St., Hillsboro, OR 97123, by phone at (503) 615-8509, or by e-mail at kissmybead@planetbeadllc.com. View Donna's work at planetbeadllc.com.

Sandra D. Halpenny
Visit Sandra's Web site, sandradhalpenny.com.

Aasia Hamid
Aasia teaches beading in Arizona. Contact her by phone at (480) 722-9198 or via e-mail at massa00@cox.net. You can see her work on her Web site, elegantartjewelry.com.

Mary Hettmansperger
Mary is a fiber and jewelry artist who teaches and exhibits her work throughout the United States. Visit her Web site, maryhetts.com.

Joanie Jenniges
Contact Joanie via e-mail at joanie@beadworkdesigns.com, or visit her Web site, beadworkdesigns.com.

Virginia Jensen
Contact Virginia via e-mail at virg@leafmedia.com, or visit her Web site, virjenmettle.com.

Jacqueline Johnson
Contact Jacqueline via e-mail at jackie@jjattic.com.

Diane Jolie
Contact Diane in care of *Bead&Button* magazine.

Julz
Contact Julz in care of Busy Beads at (951) 695-3338.

Maiko Kage
Visit Maiko's Web site, happybeading.net.

Marcia Katz
Marcia is the author of two books, *Sculptural Flowers I: The Trumpet Flower* and *Adorned Wrists*. Contact her by phone at (706) 425-1859 or via e-mail at mkatz@gate.net, or visit her Web site, festoonery.com.

Zurina Ketola
Contact Zurina via e-mail at zurina@zurinaketola.com, or visit her Web site, zurinaketola.com.

Cindy Kinerson
Contact Cindy via e-mail at renobeadshop@aol.com.

Barbara Klann
Contact Barbara in care of *Bead&Button* magazine.

Heidi Kummli
Heidi is a bead embroidery artist. Contact her via e-mail at heidik@starband.net, or visit her Web site, freespiritcollection.com.

Myra B. Kurtz
Myra was an avid beader and bag maker from Martinsville, New Jersey.

Linda Lehman
Contact Linda via e-mail at lehman_linda@hotmail.com, or visit her Web site, emporiumofwearableart.com.

Melody MacDuffee
Contact Melody via e-mail at writersink@msn.com.

Mel McCabe
Contact Mel in care of Kalmbach Books.

Anne Mitchell
Contact Anne via e-mail at anne@annemitchell.net, or visit her Web site, annemitchell.net.

Claudia Navarette
Contact Claudia in care of The Bead Shop at (650) 327-0900, or visit the Web site, beadshop.com.

Mary Libby Neiman
Mary Libby is the author of *Bead Knitting* and *Bead Crochet Basics*, published by Design Originals. Contact her via e-mail at marylibby@onsurface.com, or visit her Web site, onsurface.com.

Rachel Nelson-Smith
Contact Rachel via e-mail at contact@msrachel.com, or visit her Web site, msrachel.com.

Debbie Nishihara
Contact Debbie in care of *Bead&Button* magazine.

Hatsumi Oshitani
Contact Hatsumi via e-mail at beadingbees@yahoo.com, or visit her Web site, homepage3.nifty.com/ Hachimitsu8/.

Kim Otterbein
Contact Kim in care of The Bead House, 11 Constitution St., Bristol, RI 02809, or via e-mail at kimodesign@msn.com.

Rebecca Peapples
Contact Rebecca via e-mail at rspeapples@aol.com.

Carol Perrenoud
Contact Carol via e-mail at carol@beadcats.com. Carol offers kits through her Web site, beadcats.com.

Cheryl Phelan
Cheryl is a contributing editor for *Bead&Button* magazine. Contact her in care of *Bead&Button*.

Elaine Pinckney
Contact Elaine via e-mail at ebeadchaser@bellsouth.net.

Noriko Romanko
Contact Noriko via e-mail at noriko.r@sbcglobal.net. Noriko offers kits on her Web site, tobead.com.

Nancy Sathre-Vogel
Contact Nancy via e-mail at sathren@gmail.com, or visit her Web site, picturetrail.com/nancysv.

Angela Sawyer
Contact Angela via e-mail at angiesawyer@comcast.net.

Maryann Scandiffio-Humes
Contact Maryann via e-mail at info@buymair.com. Maryann's jewelry and accessories can be viewed on her Web site, buymair.com.

Karmen Schmidt
Contact Karmen via e-mail at schmidt1@ccwebster.net, or visit her Web site, pigandpanda.com.

Irina Serbina
Contact Irina via e-mail at irina@macrameboutique.com, or visit her Web site, macrameboutique.com.

Alice St. Germain
Contact Alice via e-mail at beadlady@comcast.net, or visit her Web site, succulentglass.com.

Deborah Staehle
Contact Deborah in care of Beads Plus in Stockton, California, at (209) 956-1000 or via e-mail at bead_demon@hotmail.com.

Beth Stone
Contact Beth by phone at (248) 855-9358 or via e-mail at bnshdl@msn.com, or visit her Web site, bethstone.com.

Christine Strube
Christine offers kits for the Carmen Miranda necklace. For more information, contact Christine via e-mail at chstrube@earthlink.net.

Gita Maria Sturm
Contact Gita at PO Box 918, Gold Beach, OR 97444 or by phone at (541) 247-9647, or visit her Web site, gitamaria.com.

Helene Tsigistras
Contact Helene via e-mail at htsigistras@kalmbach.com.

Lisa Olson Tune
Contact Lisa via e-mail at tunebdbdbd@aol.com.

Deni Whaley
Contact Deni via e-mail at bluelilly@chartermi.net, or visit her Web site, picturetrail.com/deninolo.

Wendy Witchner
Visit Wendy's Web site, wendywitchner-jewelry.com.

Index